GROW
COOK
EAT

GROW
COOK
EAT

A Food Lover's Guide *to* Vegetable Gardening,
Including 50 Recipes, Plus Harvesting and Storage Tips

Willi Galloway

Photographs by **JIM HENKENS**

SASQUATCH BOOKS
SEATTLE

For my husband, Jon, with love

Printed in China
Published by Sasquatch Books
17 16 15 14 13 12   9 8 7 6 5 4

Cover design: Anna Goldstein
Cover photographs: Jim Henkens
Interior design and composition: Anna Goldstein
Interior photographs: Jim Henkens

Library of Congress Cataloging-in-Publication Data

Galloway, Willi.
 Grow cook eat : a food lover's guide to vegetable gardening, including 50 recipes, plus harvesting and storage tips / Willi Galloway; photographs by Jim Henkens. — 1st ed.
    p. cm.
 Includes index.
 ISBN 978-1-57061-731-7
1. Kitchen gardens. 2. Vegetable gardening. 3. Herb gardening. 4. Fruit. 5. Cookbooks. I. Title. II. Title: Food lover's guide to vegetable gardening.
 SB321.G25 2012
 635—dc23

                    2011030900

Sasquatch Books
1904 Third Avenue, Suite 710
Seattle, WA 98101
(206) 467-4300
www.sasquatchbooks.com
custserv@sasquatchbooks.com

Contents

Acknowledgments vii
Introduction ix

CHAPTER ONE: Gardening Fundamentals

Planning the Garden 3 • Building Good Soil 7 • Planting the Garden 11 • Season Extension 21 • Smart Watering Practices 24 • Fertilizing 26 • Preventing Pests and Diseases 27 • Dealing with Weeds 31

CHAPTER TWO: Herbs

Preserving Herbs 35 • BASIL 37 / Nona's Pesto 41 • CHERVIL 42 / Cheesy Eggs with Chervil 44 • CHIVES 45 / Steak Sandwiches with Gorgonzola Chive Sauce and Caramelized Onions 49 • CILANTRO/CORIANDER 50 / Green Coriander–Marinated Chicken 53 • DILL 55 / Dill Compound Butter 57 • FENNEL 58 / Fennel, Potato, and Apple Gratin 60 • MINT 61 / Lemon Verbena–Mint Tisane 63 • OREGANO AND MARJORAM 64 / Feta Marinated in Olive Oil with Mediterranean Herbs 67 • PARSLEY 68 / Thérèse Jarjura's Tabbouleh 71 • ROSEMARY 72 / Rosemary-Rubbed Leg of Lamb 74 • SAGE 75 / Sage-Infused Vinegar 78 • THYME 79 / Slow-Roasted Tomatoes with Thyme 82

CHAPTER THREE: Greens

Baby Greens 101 85 • ARUGULA 86 / Arugula Salad with Blue Cheese, Dates, and Hot Bacon Dressing 89 • ASIAN GREENS 91 / Crispy Pot Stickers with Garlicky Asian Greens 93 • BROCCOLI RABE 94 / Lemony Broccoli Rabe 97 • LETTUCE 99 / Perfect Caesar Salad 102 • MUSTARD GREENS 103 / Mustard Green Turnovers 105 • RADICCHIO 107 / Tangy Grilled Radicchio 109 • SPINACH 110 / Spinach Risotto 114 • SWISS CHARD 115 / Swiss Chard Quesadillas 118

CHAPTER FOUR: Legumes

EDAMAME 121 / Herbed Edamame Salad 125 • FAVA BEANS 127 / Grilled Fava Beans 131 • PEAS 133 / Pea Shoot Salad with Shaved Parmesan and Lemon Vinaigrette 137 • SNAP AND SHELL BEANS 138 / Spicy Roasted Snap Beans with Raita 142

CHAPTER FIVE: The Squash Family

Planting Cucurbits 101 145 • Hand-Pollinating Cucurbits 145 • CUCUMBERS 147 / Cucumber Wedges with Chile and Lime 151 • MELONS 153 / Mixed Melons in Lemon Verbena Syrup 156 • SUMMER SQUASH 157 / Shaved Summer Squash with Pecorino Romano 161 • WINTER SQUASH 163 / Butternut Squash Tacos with Spicy Black Beans 166

CHAPTER SIX: The Cabbage Family

BROCCOLI AND CAULIFLOWER 169 / Garlicky Roasted Broccoli 173 • BRUSSELS SPROUTS 174 / Roasted Brussels Sprouts with Capers 177 • CABBAGE 179 / Spicy Cabbage Slaw 182 • KALE 183 / Co-Op Kale Salad 186

CHAPTER SEVEN: Roots, Tubers, and Bulbs

BEETS 189 / Oven-Roasted Beets with Winter Citrus Vinaigrette 193 • CARROTS 195 / Honey-Roasted Carrots 198 • GARLIC 199 / Bucatini with Fresh English Peas and Garlic Scape Pesto 203 • LEEKS 205 / Silky Braised Leeks 207 • ONIONS 208 / Balsamic-Roasted Onions 211 • POTATOES 213 / Potato Leek Soup with Chive Crème Fraîche 217 • RADISHES 218 / Tartines with Gruyère and Radish Greens 222 • SHALLOTS 223 / Everyday Vinaigrette 225 • TURNIPS 226 / Cider-Glazed Baby Turnips 228

CHAPTER EIGHT: Warm-Season Vegetables

CORN 231 / The Patrick Family's Southern Creamed Corn 234 • EGGPLANT 235 / Eggplant with Lemon Tahini Dressing 238 • SWEET AND HOT PEPPERS 239 / Roasted Jalapeños Stuffed with Goat Cheese 243 • TOMATILLOS 245 / Guacamole with Charred Tomatillos and Chiles 248 • TOMATOES 249 / Lemony Pasta with Cherry Tomatoes 254

CHAPTER NINE: Fruit

BLUEBERRIES 257 / Yogurt Parfaits with Almond Granola and Blueberries 260 • RASPBERRIES 261 / Raspberry-Infused-Vodka Spritzers 265 • RHUBARB 266 / Rhubarb Chutney 269 • STRAWBERRIES 271 / Strawberry-Basil Ice Cream 275

Resources   277
Glossary   283
Index   285

Acknowledgments

First of all, I must thank Jim Henkens for being such an amazing collaborator. I am incredibly grateful that Jim contributed his time and considerable talent to this project. I feel so lucky that my words are partnered with his beautiful photos.

The roots of this book stretch back to my childhood in Wyoming—thanks to my mom for letting me eat strawberries in the garden, my dad for reading to me every night before bed, my Grammie for taking me foraging for wild asparagus, my Nona for teaching me to make pesto, Emily for crafting mud pies, and Jordan for being a seriously cool brother.

I started writing and editing at *Organic Gardening* magazine, and I am so thankful that I had the opportunity to work with amazing people and learn so much about beautiful, organic food at the same time. I'm indebted to John Grogan, both for providing me with guidance so many times in my career and for leading me down the path to my awesome agent, Joy Tutela. Joy knew I could write this book when I doubted it and is a tireless advocate for me. I am so happy to have her in my corner.

Thank you to the team at KUOW, especially Steve Scher, Katy Sewall, and Sage Van Wing, for giving me the opportunity to answer gardening questions on *Greendays*. I consider the people who listen to that program, and those who read my blog, DigginFood, to be my extended gardening community, and their questions and ideas greatly influenced the content of this book. My friends Mari Malcolm, Robin Haglund, Lorene Edwards Forkner, Erin Ryan, Leigh Stewart, and Ivette Soler all gave me great guidance while I was writing.

Special thanks to the Sasquatch Books team, especially to my editor, Susan Roxborough, who asked the question every writer wants to hear: "Have you ever thought about writing a book?" Rachelle Longé and Diane Sepanski are a dream editing team, and I love Anna Goldstein's simple, elegant design.

Some of the photos in this book were made in the beautiful gardens of Octavia Chambliss, Scott Marlow and Jenifer McIntyre, and my neighbor Bob, as well as at Local Roots Farm.

I had a killer recipe-testing team: San San Chow, Mark Warren, Amy Taricco, Kari Keys, Jesse Southworth, Lisa Wilson, and my mom, Becky Evans. Hugs and kisses for my Uncle Ace and Aunt Buffe for opening up their guest bedroom and kitchen to me on countless occasions, and to Maren Hayes, Sana Sakr, Justine Dell'Arringa, John Hurd, Justin Niedermeyer, David Perry, Kenneth Patrick, and Matthew Dillon for sharing their delicious recipes and cooking ideas with me. Katy and Jim Gilmore also kindly let me write for several days in their little cottage, The Buffalo.

Most important, thank you to my husband, Jon, for giving me space and time to write during the whirlwind, cheerfully building every garden project I dream up, and enthusiastically eating all the vegetables I grow, even the weird ones.

Introduction

"Without a kitchen garden—that plot of land on which one grows herbs, vegetables, and some fruit—it is not possible to produce decent and savory food for the dinner table."

—ANGELO PELLEGRINI

This book came about because of a radish.

I discovered that radishes made seedpods—and that I could eat them—entirely by accident. I simply forgot to harvest a few rows of the spicy little roots. They grew large and woody, their foliage stretching up toward the sky. I thought all was lost, but the radishes had a surprise in store. They rewarded my inattention with delicate pink flowers followed by pods that looked like fat raindrops perched atop slender stems.

The appearance of something so pretty and unexpected gave me pause. On impulse, I snapped off a pod and popped it into my mouth. Crunchy, spicy, nutty, and decidedly radishy, that pod changed my perspective on kitchen gardening. I looked around, suddenly aware of all sorts of roots, leaves, blossoms, and seeds I'd never before considered as food, and asked myself a simple question: What else can I eat?

Fava greens, fennel pollen, kale flower buds, green coriander seed, carrot tops, squash flowers, and the tender tips of pea vines are now staples in my kitchen. I've also given myself license to harvest vegetables during all their myriad stages of growth. I pull garlic shoots in early spring, when they are slight and tender as scallions, and grill them. I rinse baby turnip roots off with the hose and eat them raw right out in the garden. I wait anxiously for my mustard greens to form flower buds because I love the sweet-spicy flavor they add to a stir-fry. Sometimes these delicious extras, as I've come to think of them, are available at farmers' markets. But if you really want to experience the full range of food that edible plants offer, you need to garden. To grow food is to really know food. Not just in the sense of knowing where the vegetables on your plate come from, but how their appearance, flavor, and texture change as they grow.

The vegetables found in grocery stores are invariably sold at the stage that requires the least labor to harvest and the most convenience for packing, shipping, and display. The delicious tops of beets, turnips, and carrots are severed and discarded; strawberries are picked early and then artificially ripened; and tomatoes, though red, are too perfectly round and almost always hard.

Gardening gives you the chance to reacquaint yourself with food you thought you knew—like radishes. I plant their roly-poly seeds in a thick row and don't worry about the spacing, because I know I can thin out and eat their delicious sprouts in a grilled cheese sandwich later. I harvest the roots when they are not much bigger than a marble and again later when they reach the familiar grocery store size. I cook their greens just like spinach, use the flowers as a garnish, and eat the pods as a snack. The whole radish plant is eminently edible and delicious—something I never would have discovered if I hadn't grown my own.

I garden because I love food. Or, perhaps I love gardening because I grow food. Either way, I think there is almost nothing more satisfying than cooking with food that you nurtured from a tiny seed or seedling, and then serving it to others. It creates a tangible connection between the environment, the food that nourishes you, and the people sitting around your table. This book is an invitation to explore the amazing diversity of food that becomes available to you when you plant a plot of land with vegetables, herbs, and fruit, and to gain the confidence to experiment in the kitchen with the delicious raw goods your garden will provide.

But a garden should reflect its gardener. So think of the guides and advice in these pages as a recipe you can make your own—add a cup more here, a pinch less there—and have as much fun as possible. The most important thing I've learned is that in the garden and in the kitchen, mistakes can be the greatest gifts. You just have to have the courage to taste them.

A FEW NOTES...

1. In each guide you'll find a list of edible parts of the plant. These are the parts I eat. There are surely other parts that are perfectly fine to snack on. The reason why they may not be listed is that I have probably not yet tried them.

2. If you want to help take the guesswork out of when to plant, buy a soil thermometer. I find that soil temperature is the most reliable indicator of when to plant, no matter where you live, and I often offer planting advice based on it. The thermometers are easy to use, inexpensive, and available at any well-stocked nursery.

3. Serious pest and disease problems are rare in healthy, organic gardens, but occasionally issues do crop up. I note common pest and disease problems in each guide and offer recommendations for excellent resources that detail how to deal with them in the Resources section (page 277).

CHAPTER ONE

GARDENING FUNDAMENTALS

WHEN YOU GO OUTSIDE ON A SUMMER DAY, your garden should throb with activity. You'll find bumblebees rubbing their fuzzy bellies on the inside of squash flowers, ladybugs hunting for aphids, and swallowtail butterfly larvae munching on parsley. These insects are a vital part of your garden. They pollinate the flowers, kill pests, help decompose the contents of the compost pile, and sometimes eat your plants. In addition, the weeds sprouting in your beds tell a story about the soil. They can indicate if it is compacted, nitrogen depleted, or nutrient rich, and they are a natural, if not always desired, ground cover. Diseases sometimes strike, but they will give you the opportunity to consider why your plants were susceptible. Growing a healthy, organic garden certainly does not involve spraying pesticides and fungicides to deal with weeds, insect problems, and diseases. But it is important to understand that choosing to be an organic gardener is about more than not using chemicals.

Organic gardening is about becoming a *good* gardener. And I don't mean that in a virtuous, holier-than-thou kind of way. Good gardeners don't need the crutch of pesticides and chemical fertilizers because they have mastered a few fundamental gardening principles. In the following pages, you'll find the essentials for starting a garden and becoming a good gardener, and at the end of the book I share resources that you can turn to for more in-depth information on garden design, seed starting and saving, and pest and disease identification and control.

PLANNING THE GARDEN

Having a backyard is not a prerequisite for growing food. If you give vegetables, herbs, and fruit good soil, plenty of sunshine, and water, they will thrive in the narrow "hell strip" between sidewalks and streets, and in former front lawns, side yards, and containers.

Choosing a Site

Photosynthesis is the plant process that harnesses the energy of the sun to convert water and carbon dioxide into sugars. Vegetables, herbs, and fruit grow best in full sun, which means they need six to eight hours of bright, direct sunshine to photosynthesize optimally. A warm, sheltered spot that faces southwest is ideal. Vegetables require consistent water, so make sure you put your garden in a spot where a hose will reach. Building the garden on a level site, or installing level terraces on a slope, helps prevent the soil from eroding and makes irrigating easier.

Getting Rid of the Lawn

Lawns make great spots for vegetable gardens because they are usually close to the house, in full sun, and fairly level, and are often underutilized. You could use a sod cutter to strip off the lawn and then build raised beds over the bare soil. But this instant gratification method takes a lot of effort. *Sheet mulching*—making a layer cake of organic matter on top of a lawn or weedy growth—smothers the vegetation and creates nutrient-rich, deep soil with no digging or machine rental required.

1. Determine where you want to site your new garden bed. Delineate its perimeter with spray paint. I find garden beds to be most accessible when they are no more than 3 feet across; any wider and it becomes hard to reach the middle of the bed.

2. Set your lawn mower to its lowest setting and mow down any weeds or grass within the bed's perimeter. Spread a 2-inch layer of composted steer manure (available bagged at nurseries) directly over the closely cropped vegetation. Place a single layer of heavy, plain brown cardboard over the manure to smother the underlying plants and prevent weed seeds from germinating. Be sure to completely cover the bed by overlapping each piece of cardboard 6 to 8 inches. Saturate the cardboard with water to aid its decomposition.

3. Place a 1-foot-deep layer of grass clippings mixed with straw or shredded dry leaves (in a 1:3 ratio) over the cardboard. Thoroughly soak the grass/straw mixture with water. Then top it with 8 inches of a 1:1 mixture of compost and topsoil.

4. If you sheet-mulch in the fall, cover the bed with burlap bags (these are available for free from coffee shops and roasteries) to prevent the soil from eroding over the winter. By spring the mulch, cardboard, and underlying vegetation will have decomposed. If you sheet-mulch in the spring, you can sow seeds or plant seedlings right

into the topsoil layer. If your new bed borders a lawn, edge it three times a season with a sharp spade to prevent grass from colonizing the garden space.

NOTE: You can also sheet-mulch a large area in the fall, installing raised beds and pathways over the grass-free area the following spring. Or you can create an inground garden by building borderless raised beds (rake the soil into ½-foot-tall, level mounds) and then spreading wood chips or straw in the spaces between the beds to create pathways.

Raised Beds

A raised bed is simply a frame that elevates the soil level above the adjacent soil. Most are 1 to 2 feet tall, but they can be built higher to accommodate gardeners with physical limitations. Frame them with wood, stone, brick, terra-cotta roofing tiles, stacked recycled concrete, metal sheets, or cinder blocks. The soil in raised beds drains better and warms up faster in spring than adjacent soil. One note of caution: When purchasing topsoil for a raised bed, always inspect it before buying to make sure it does not contain hard clods, rocks, garbage, or a lot of sand. And don't be tempted to build raised beds over grass without sheet-mulching first—the grass will creep in from below, and you will have to fight it for years.

Pathways

Leave at least 30 inches of width for the main thoroughfare through your garden. Make pathways between garden beds 18 inches wide (more if you can spare it); any narrower and you'll end up stepping on your beds and compacting their soil as you move around the garden. I usually spread *play chips* (small uniform wood chips that pack down into a fairly level surface) over pathways, but straw, brick, stone, and crushed gravel all work well. Just stay away from pea gravel—the round stones refuse to stay put and will spray into the beds as you walk.

Vertical Garden Structures

Growing plants that normally scramble along the ground up onto a trellis is the easiest way to squeeze more food into a small garden. Plants grown on trellises also tend to have fewer problems with disease, and the structures create tall focal points.

WELDED WIRE MESH
One of my favorite materials for building trellises is welded wire mesh. It is manufactured to reinforce concrete and sold at hardware stores in rolls and flat panels. I prefer the flat panels because you do not have to try to bend them into shape. Beans, peas, summer and winter squash, cucumbers, and melons all climb readily up the wire mesh, which also works well as a support for ornamental flowering vines. Don't worry if the mesh rusts—it won't hurt your plants, plus it makes the trellis less conspicuous.

There are two simple types of trellis you can build using welded wire mesh: fence trellises and freestanding trellises.

A fence trellis can turn an average wooden fence into a productive growing space; just attach a simple, inexpensive panel of welded wire mesh to it. First, choose a panel size that will fit your fence without requiring a lot of cutting (on my 6-foot-tall cedar fence, I used 6-by-4-foot panels). Cut the panels with wire cutters to fit.

Be sure to install the trellis on a fence that faces west or south and gets at least six hours of direct sunlight each day. Have a helper hold the metal tightly against the posts. Use a staple gun with ½- to ¾-inch staples to secure the mesh to the fence. Begin stapling close to the top left corner and work your way around the panel clockwise, placing staples at regular intervals around the entire panel. If growing beans or peas up the fence, plant one seed at the bottom of each horizontal wire. Space cucumbers and melons about a foot apart and summer and winter squash about 1½ to 2 feet apart.

Welded wire mesh also works well as a freestanding trellis in the garden. I often run panels down the center of beds and train cucumbers up them, or place them at the back of raised beds and large containers. To make a freestanding trellis, simply drive a rebar or bamboo stake into the ground on each side of the panel and then attach it to the stakes with zip ties.

BAMBOO

Bamboo looks natural in the garden, is an inexpensive, renewable resource, and lasts several seasons if stored indoors for the winter. I use U-shaped bamboo stakes to make pretty supports for peppers, eggplants, and other upright vegetables (see page 240), and tall bamboo poles to build teepees for beans, peas, and climbing varieties of squash and melons. The teepees can also double as a playhouse for kids in the summer!

For the most structurally sound teepee, make the diameter of the circular base at least 3 feet, and use six to eight sturdy 1-inch-diameter bamboo poles that are 7 to 8 feet tall. Position the poles at even intervals around the base perimeter (don't forget to leave room for a doorway if the teepee will serve as a playhouse) and drive them at a slight slant 12 to 18 inches into the soil. Cinch the poles together at the top with a zip tie—not twine, which tends to stretch and sag. For additional climbing surfaces, string twine horizontally between the poles, every foot or so.

Essential Garden Tools

When shopping for tools, look for ones with carbon fiber or stainless steel blades or tines, steel-strapped or forged sockets, and unpainted shafts with a straight, even grain. These high-quality tools usually cost nominally more than cheap tools and will last for years if you clean them occasionally and store them indoors.

TROWEL

Look for a trowel that feels heavy for its size and has a sturdy handle; there is nothing worse than digging a hole and having your trowel's handle cave under the pressure. Use it to dig holes for seedlings and to transplant volunteers.

SHOVEL

The round, pointy, slightly curved blade of a shovel is designed to scoop up soil. Its long handle helps lever plants out of the soil when dividing or transplanting.

SQUARE BLADE SPADE

A spade's sharp flat blade cuts straight into the soil; use it to create a clean edge between garden beds and lawn.

GARDEN FORK

A garden fork has wide, tapered prongs and a fairly short shaft that is usually topped by a D-shaped handle. It is designed for digging, not tossing straw or turning compost (use a pitchfork for those activities). Use it to loosen soil and lift plants out of the ground.

BOW RAKE

This rake has a row of short, inflexible tines; use it to level beds and smooth out the soil's surface.

CULTIVATOR

This tool features 4- to 5-inch-long, clawlike tines. Use it to gently work compost or granular fertilizer into the soil, break up clods, and dislodge weeds. A handheld cultivator also comes in handy for working in tight spaces.

STIRRUP HOE

This hoe makes dealing with weeds a breeze (see Buy a Stirrup Hoe on page 31). The best stirrup hoes have replaceable blades.

HANDHELD CIRCLE HOE

This tool has a small, angled, circular blade that slices through the soil. Use it in spots that are too tight for the stirrup hoe.

BYPASS PRUNERS

Bypass pruners have two curved blades, one that is thin and sharp and another that is heavy and flat, which slide past each other like scissor blades. Use them to make clean cuts when pruning and harvesting.

NEEDLE-NOSE SCISSORS

These narrow, sharp scissors squeeze into small spaces and make it easy to clip off herbs and vegetables with precision.

HEAVY CANVAS TARP

In lieu of a wheelbarrow, I often use a heavy canvas tarp to tote weeds to the yard waste bin and collect garden debris for compost. I also spread it out and divide plants on it (this makes cleanup a snap), and fold it up and use it as a knee pad.

BUILDING GOOD SOIL

*"There can be no life without soil, and no soil
without life; they have evolved together."*

—CHARLES KELLOGG

Soil Basics

There is more to soil than meets the eye. At its most basic level, soil is a combination of mineral particles and organic matter. But upon closer examination, it reveals itself to be a complex world full of microorganisms, insects, worms, and even mammals that interact with your plants' roots. Good soil can provide all the nutrients, oxygen, and water the vegetables, herbs, and fruit growing in your garden need to thrive. The basic idea of building good soil is simple: your plants use the soil's resources as they grow, and your job is to replace them.

Spending time improving your soil is the single most important thing you can do to ensure that you have plants that not only grow well, but taste good too. Just adding fertilizer is akin to taking a vitamin for all your body's nutrient needs instead of eating healthy food. Likewise, the goal of building good soil is to add materials that, yes, increase nutrients but also improve the soil's structure, create habitat for beneficial microorganisms, and help the soil hold just the right amount of water.

SOIL TEXTURE

Soil is composed of mineral particles that vary in size, with silt being the smallest, clay in the middle, and sand the largest. How coarse or fine a particular soil is depends on its mixture of these particles. The ideal soil texture is called *loam*, which contains fairly equal measures of silt, sand, and clay.

ORGANIC MATTER

Organic matter is simply any formerly living material that is decomposing. It can find its way into the soil in the form of compost, manure, mulch, or plants that are turned under. Many of the nutrients found in soil, especially nitrogen, are bound up in organic matter, which serves as a food source for microorganisms. As the microorganisms decompose the organic matter, they release the nutrients into the soil in a form that plant roots can take up. Organic matter eventually breaks down into a final product called *humus*. This stable form of organic matter is what gives soil its earthy feel and smell. It is a key component of the soil's structure and helps it hold water and nutrients.

SOIL STRUCTURE

A soil's structure, which is sometimes called its *tilth*, is determined by the composition of its particles and how they aggregate, or stick together. Humus is the glue that binds the particles together. These aggregates are important because the gaps between them provide pockets, or "pore space," for air and water. Clay soils, or "heavy soils," are composed primarily of silt and clay particles, and have a fine texture and small pore spaces, which slow water down as it drains through. Sandy soil has a coarse texture and larger pore spaces, which allow water to flow through it quickly. Loamy soil has a mix of small and large pore spaces and acts like a sponge, allowing most water to infiltrate and drain through, but holding on to just enough for plants and soil microorganisms to use.

Organic matter helps improve the structure of both sandy and heavy soils. In sandy soils, it helps glue the big mineral particles together, which reduces the amount of pore space and helps it retain water. In heavy soils, organic matter binds the tiny silt particles into larger aggregates, which opens up more pore space and allows water to drain through better.

Getting a Soil Test

A *soil test* provides an overview of your soil's health and amendment recommendations for fine-tuning its pH, organic matter content, and levels of phosphorus, potassium, calcium, magnesium, and boron. Getting a soil test is definitely not a prerequisite to planting, but the more information you have about your soil, the better you can care for your plants. Soil pH is important because it affects the solubility of nutrients and their availability to plants, as well as the degree of microbial activity. Most garden plants prefer a pH range that hovers between 6.0 and 7.5. Nitrogen availability in the soil fluctuates during the year, so soil tests often leave out information on nitrogen levels. However, soils with between 5 and 8 percent organic matter typically have enough nitrogen available for plants.

It's a good idea to get a soil test whenever you start a new garden and every few years in established gardens. If you are gardening in a parking strip or around an old house, or simply don't know the history of your soil, have it tested for heavy metals too. Call your local cooperative extension for a lab referral; when you send your soil sample in to the lab, request organic amendment recommendations.

Basic Soil Care Plan

Over the course of the growing season, organic matter breaks down, and plants take nutrients out of the soil. It's up to you to replenish the organic matter and adjust the nutrient levels annually. Spreading compost and soil amendments over a bed and tilling or digging them into the soil seriously disrupts its structure and the community of microorganisms that support your plants. I use a no-till method of adding nutrients to the soil that I learned when I gardened at the Interbay P-Patch in Seattle. It creates loose, nutrient-rich, drought-tolerant soil with hardly any effort at all.

1. Get a soil test in late summer, if you like. In fall pull spent vegetable plants out of the garden. Separate out any plants that had pest or disease problems and place them in a yard waste bin or otherwise dispose of them. Use a machete to chop the healthy plants up into 2- to 3-inch chunks.

2. Mix this fresh green vegetable material in a 1:1 ratio with fallen leaves. Add water to the mixed mulch until it feels about as wet as a wrung-out sponge. The leaves

decompose best if they are shredded before being added to the green material; you can do this by running them over with a lawn mower fitted with a bag. Or place a string trimmer in a clean 55-gallon garbage can, fill the can half full with leaves, and then run the string trimmer (be sure to wear eye protection).

3.   Sprinkle the amendments recommended in the soil test over each bed and gently scratch them into the soil with a cultivator. Then spread a ½- to 1-foot layer of the mulch over each garden bed. Sprinkle about two shovelfuls of finished compost over the top.

4.   Cover the mulch with overlapping burlap coffee bags. If you can't find coffee bags, purchase rolls of untreated burlap at a nursery. Pin the burlap to the ground with U-shaped landscape fabric pins. Keep the mulch moist over the winter.

5.   By spring the mulch will have broken down into dark, crumbly compost. Earthworms multiply like crazy under the burlap and carry the compost down into the underlying soil as they tunnel. In spring pull off the burlap bags and plant right into the bed.

Making Compost

Composting is an efficient way to recycle all the bolted greens, spent sunflowers, and other plant material that comes out of your garden. When making compost you need a combination of "greens" (fresh material that contains a high percentage of nitrogen, like grass clippings) and "browns" (material with a high percentage of carbon, like fallen leaves or straw). I like to gather leaves in the fall and store them outdoors in wire bins so that I have plenty of browns on hand in the summer when the garden produces lots of green material. You can make a big pile of compost or keep things tidier by containing it within a bin. How fast your compost breaks down depends on the composition, size, and moisture level of the pile and how often you turn it.

HOT COMPOSTING

The microbes found in compost give off energy as they work, and if a compost pile is large enough, it will trap the heat, accelerating the decomposition process (thus the name *hot composting*). Hot composting can kill weed seeds, pest eggs, and diseases, but it's a good idea to leave plants with problems out of compost piles just in case.

1.   Gather enough material to create a compost pile that has a base at least 3 feet square and is 3 feet tall. As you build the pile, put in one pitchforkful of green material and three of brown. Mix them together before adding in another layer. Sprinkle water on the material as you go, aiming for the moisture level of a wet, wrung-out sponge.

Piles that are too wet or have too many greens smell bad, and piles that are too dry or have too many browns break down slowly.

2. Within about a week, the center of the pile should feel hot to the touch. This is your cue to turn the pile. The easiest way to do this is to place two compost bins right next to each other and transfer the pile from one compost bin to the other with a pitchfork. Turning the pile adds oxygen and transfers outside materials in. When you turn the pile, check the moisture level and add more water or dry browns if needed. The more often you turn the pile, the faster the material will break down (once a week is ideal).

3. The compost is "finished" when it no longer heats up and the material has broken down into dark, crumbly, earthy-smelling organic matter that looks nothing like the original ingredients. Use finished compost to top-dress the soil around plants (see page 27) or spread a thin layer over the soil before planting.

COLD COMPOSTING

If you mix a bunch of plant material in a pile and let it sit, it will eventually break down, usually within a year to a year and a half. This passive method is called *cold composting* because the pile does not heat up. I often compost this way because it is so easy. However, weed seeds, pest eggs, and diseases are not killed in cold compost piles, and material on top of the pile decomposes at a slower rate than the lower layers.

PLANTING THE GARDEN

When to Plant

Planting vegetables at the right time influences their flavor and how well they grow. When deciding what to plant when, consider your USDA Plant Hardiness Zone, first and last frost dates, soil temperature, and moisture. And ask around: the vendors at your local farmers' market and experienced gardeners offer great localized advice.

USDA PLANT HARDINESS ZONE MAP

The USDA maintains a map that divides the country into 10 zones based on the average lowest temperature in winter (*hardiness* refers to a plant's capacity to withstand cold temperatures). The warmest areas are in zone 10, where temperatures do not often dip below 30 degrees F, and the coldest areas are in zone 1, where temperatures hit –50 degrees in winter. Descriptions of *perennials*—herbaceous (nonwoody) plants that survive for two or more years—often note which hardiness zones they grow in; for instance, 'Profumata' musk strawberry is hardy in zones 5 to 10. The usefulness of the zones is limited because they do not take climate into consideration. For instance, both Seattle, Washington, and Austin, Texas, fall into zone 8b, but the palette of plants available to gardeners in those cities varies drastically due to differences in their soil types, annual precipitation, and summer temperatures. You can find the hardiness zone map online (see Regional Resources, page 277) or contact your local cooperative extension for information on your zone.

FIRST AND LAST FROST DATES

Frost forms when temperatures drop below freezing (32 degrees F) and water vapor turns to ice. Tender plants like tomatoes, cucumbers, and eggplant die when exposed to frost, while other vegetables like carrots and brussels sprouts can taste sweeter after a frost. Knowing when frosts typically stop in spring and start in fall can help you plan when to plant and harvest. The *last frost date* refers to the average date in spring when the likelihood that a light frost will occur is less than 50 percent. The *first frost date* refers to the average date in fall when the likelihood that a light frost will occur is more than 50 percent.

When planting out tender crops, it is always a good idea to either wait to plant for two weeks after the average last frost or protect the plants with a row cover or other season-extending device (see page 21). Check with your local Master Gardeners or cooperative extension to find out the first and last frost dates in your area. Or visit the federal government's National Climatic Data Center online (see Regional Resources, page 277) for a handy map of every county in the United States and a chart that lays out the dates in spring and fall when there is a 50, 20, or 10 percent chance that frost will occur.

The National Weather Service typically releases a frost advisory when temperatures are expected to fall between 32 and 35 degrees F and remain there for several hours. These temperatures will kill tender plants like basil and cucumbers. A freeze warning is released when temperatures are expected to fall below 30 degrees for several hours. Most vegetables need to be harvested or protected before a freeze.

SOIL TEMPERATURE

Timing plantings by first and last frost dates alone is not a great strategy because soil temperature also impacts how well plants will grow. For instance, in my cool Pacific Northwest climate, the last frost date is in early April. If I followed the general advice to plant tomatoes two weeks after the last frost date, our soil would still be in the 50s, and the plants, which prefer soil temperatures in the 60s, would languish. So I wait to plant until both the danger of frost passes *and* the soil warms (I often use plastic to help warm the soil earlier; see page 22). Knowing the summer soil temperature can also help you determine whether the soil needs to be cooled before you plant fall crops like spinach, which germinates poorly in soil hotter than 75 degrees F. Investing in an inexpensive soil thermometer makes it easy to determine if the soil is warm—or cool—enough for vegetables to thrive.

SOIL WORKABILITY TEST

Soil that is at the right temperature might not be ready to plant. Digging in soil that is very wet damages its structure and creates rock-hard clods that take a long time to break down. To test if a soil is workable, dig a 6-inch-deep hole. Grab a handful of soil and squeeze it in the palm of your hand. Poke the soil with the fingers of your other hand. Ideally, the soil should crumble easily. If it sticks together in a clump, it is too wet. If the soil won't form a ball, it is too dry and needs to be moistened slightly before planting. Never dig in frozen soil. Whenever you sow, aim for the soil to feel crumbly like brown sugar and have the moisture level of a damp, wrung-out sponge. Sowing and planting in soggy soil literally drowns seeds and seedlings because water infiltrates the pore spaces between the soil particles, squeezing out the oxygen. Parched soil hampers germination because the seed coat needs moisture to soften up and allow the seedling to escape.

MATURITY RATE

Seed packets and catalog variety descriptions often note *days to maturity*—for example, 'Genovese' basil: 68 days. This is the approximate number of days it takes for a variety to mature after it is sown or transplanted. The date is helpful for determining when to plant and harvest. For instance, 'Napoli' carrots, which mature in about 58 days, taste sweeter if harvested just after the last frost. If your last frost is typically October 1, then you would want to count backward on the calendar and make a note to sow the carrots in late July or early August.

Planting Seedlings 101

Seedlings *want* to grow, so all you need to do is make their transition from container to garden as stress-free as possible. Plan on transplanting in the late afternoon or evening, or on a cool, overcast day, so the baby plants do not bake in the sun for hours. To prevent transplant shock, I always fully hydrate the seedlings by watering them 24 hours prior to planting and again two hours before they go into the garden.

Dig a hole as deep as the seedling's container is tall and twice as wide. Squeeze the bottom of the container to loosen the roots. Place one hand at the base of the seedling and use your other to slide the pot off the root ball. Seedlings are often grown in potting mixes that are lightweight and dry out quickly. Before planting, tease the roots of the seedling apart and remove as much of the potting mix as possible. Don't skip this step, even though it seems invasive. The loose roots will settle in and extend out into the surrounding garden soil much more quickly than those surrounded by a plug of very different soil. The exceptions to this rule are seedlings of *cucurbits* (members of the squash family, including zucchini and summer squash, pumpkins, winter squash, melons, and cucumbers) and *brassicas* (members of the cabbage family, including broccoli, cauliflower, and kale). Disturb their roots as little as possible when transplanting.

Set the seedling into the hole and spread its roots out in the bottom. Make sure the base of the plant sits at the same depth in the garden as it was in its pot. Adjust the level if needed and then back-fill the planting hole with soil. Gently firm it around the plant's roots. Always water seedlings with a watering can for the first few days, because the strong stream from a hose can easily knock over young plants.

To give the newly planted seedlings a kick start after planting, spike 1 gallon of water with 1 tablespoon each of liquid kelp and liquid fish emulsion. Give this diluted fertilizer a good stir and then pour it over the seedlings, making sure to fully soak their root zone. Seedlings have small root systems, so it is important to keep the top 3 to 5 inches of soil damp until their roots establish and they begin actively growing.

SPACING SEEDLINGS

If you aren't sure how much distance to leave between seedlings, try this trick: Imagine how big the plant will be when mature. Draw a circle in the soil representing the diameter and plant the seedling in the center of the circle. Draw another circle next to the first, overlapping their edges slightly, and plant the second seedling. Continue down the row.

SEED STARTING

When growing plants from seedlings, you need to either purchase them or start them indoors under lights. Growing them from scratch allows you to ensure your plants are organic from start to finish and gives you access to a huge range of varieties that are not normally sold as seedlings. Plus, it's fun! If you want to start your own seedlings, I highly recommend Nancy Bubel's *The New Seed-Starters Handbook*. It offers excellent step-by-step advice and has helpful charts detailing the optimal soil temperature range for various seeds and when to start seeds indoors. I buy most of my seedlings because our little house just doesn't have the space for an extensive seed-starting operation. Hunt around for seedlings of unusual or heirloom varieties at farmers' markets, plant sales hosted by gardening groups, and specialty nurseries.

HARDENING SEEDLINGS OFF

It is important to gradually expose seedlings to outdoor conditions before planting them in the garden, a practice known as *hardening off*. Start hardening off seedlings a week before you plan on transplanting them. Set the seedlings outdoors in a sheltered, shaded spot for two hours each day before bringing them back indoors. Over the course of the next several days, gradually increase the plants' exposure to sunlight and wind. At the end of the week, leave them outdoors overnight (unless frost is predicted). Always harden off seedlings started indoors. If you purchase seedlings at a nursery or plant sale, ask if they were hardened off.

Direct-Sowing Basics

Direct-sowing means planting seeds right into the garden's soil. The size of a seed determines how deep it can be sown. Every seed contains a food supply that feeds it as it germinates—the larger the seed, the bigger the food supply and the deeper it may be sown. Follow the guidelines on the seed packet when determining how deep to sow.

DIRECT-SOWING LARGE SEEDS

When sowing large seeds, like peas or sunflowers, dig a *furrow*, a shallow trench in the soil, at the depth you'd like to sow the seed. Place the seeds in the furrow at their recommended spacing. Backfill the furrow with soil and gently firm it with the palm of your hand. (If your soil tends to form a crust that seeds struggle to break through, backfill with compost or potting mix instead of soil.) Water the seeds in, using a watering can, and make sure the water soaks in at least 2 to 3 inches. Larger seeds planted too shallowly often push themselves up out of the soil as they germinate, causing their roots to dry out and killing the seedlings.

DIRECT-SOWING SMALL SEEDS

Sowing small seeds, including lettuce, arugula, carrots, broccoli rabe, mustard greens, basil, and lettuce, can be kind of nerve racking because it is so easy to bury the teensy tiny seeds too deep, which results in spotty germination. The following steps will help prevent this problem:

1. Make sure the soil is smooth, level, crumbly, and damp so the seeds will stick to the soil. Sow the seeds as evenly as possible in a row, or *broadcast* them—which means to simply sprinkle them over an area rather than in rows. Either way, aim to space the seeds an inch apart, but if they end up thicker than that, don't worry, as you'll be thinning them out later.

2. Settle the seeds into the soil by watering them in with a gentle stream from a watering can. Do not use a hose! The force of the water will pick up the seeds and wash them into a clump.

3. I use potting soil instead of garden soil to cover small seeds because it is lightweight and weed-free, distributes evenly, and does not crust. Scoop up a handful and sift a light layer over the seeds, just barely covering them. Gently pat the top of the potting soil and then finish by watering the seeds in again with the watering can. Once seeds get wet, it is important for them to stay moist because they will not germinate if they dry out.

4. When the seedlings first sprout, you'll often see their *cotyledons* (also known as seed leaves). Food storage structures found within seeds, cotyledons are the first "leaves" that emerge after germination and provide the young seedling with energy as it grows. On many plants, including squash, the cotyledons unfurl aboveground, while on other plants, such as peas, they emerge underground. Cotyledons often look very different from the plant's true leaves, and they wither once their energy supplies are spent. *True leaves* are the leaves that appear after cotyledons.

THINNING SEEDLINGS

Thinning is the process of selectively removing plants that are growing close together so the remaining plants have enough room, water, and nutrients to mature. Directly sown crops are typically sown close together and then thinned at some point to prevent them from growing into a hopelessly entangled mess. This practice functions as an insurance policy (since not every seed you sow will sprout) and also allows you to harvest and eat vegetables at different stages in their growth.

Snip off unwanted plants at the soil line with needle-nose scissors, rather than pulling them, to prevent disturbing the roots of the seedlings you choose to keep. After this initial thinning, you can pull up plants if they need to be thinned again later. Don't toss the thinnings into your compost pile—instead, think of them as your first harvest, and eat them in salads and sandwiches.

Storing Leftover Seeds

Seeds are alive, which means you must take good care of extras if you want them to stay viable for more than one year. For best results, store seeds in paper packages, which do not trap moisture. Label the seeds with the year they were purchased. Protect them from the evils of fluctuating temperatures and humidity by placing the packets in a sealed container, such as a mason jar, and keeping the container in the freezer.

Sowing Recommendations

CROPS TO DIRECT-SOW

Some plants resent having their roots disturbed and are thus best suited to direct-sowing, while others germinate so quickly it doesn't really pay to sow them indoors under lights or buy seedlings. Direct-sowing also offers a number of advantages: seeds come in a bigger range of varieties than seedlings, are less expensive, and, if stored correctly, can last more than one season. Note: Directly sown plants take longer to mature than those planted out as seedlings. For instance, you can harvest a head of lettuce planted as a seedling in about a month, but you'll need to wait two months or so to harvest heads of lettuce directly sown into the garden. The following plants do well when directly sown:

Arugula	Cilantro	Mustard greens
Beans (snap and shell)	Corn	Radishes
Beets	Cosmos	Spinach
Broccoli rabe	Edamame	Turnips
Carrots	Fava beans	

CROPS TO PLANT AS SEEDLINGS

I plant most warm-season crops and slow-growing brassicas (members of the cabbage family) as seedlings because the little plants give me a huge head start on the season. For gardeners in areas where the soil warms up quickly in spring, it may make more sense to direct-sow squash, cucumbers, and melons because they really only transplant well if the seedlings have no more than one set of true leaves. The following plants do well when planted as seedlings:

Big brassicas (broccoli, brussels sprouts, cabbage, cauliflower)
Chives
Eggplant
Garlic
Ground cherries
Leeks
Mint
Peppers
Perennial herbs (lovage, oregano, rosemary, sage, savory, thyme)
Potatoes
Radicchio
Shallots
Strawberries
Tomatillos
Tomatoes

CROPS TO GROW FROM EITHER SEEDS OR STARTS

For plants that grow well from both seeds and starts—including Asian greens, lettuce, peas, and *annual* flowers (those that complete their entire life cycle in a single year)—I often plant out some of each on the same day. This ensures a staggered harvest, with the starts maturing before the directly sown plants. I also prefer to harvest directly sown greens at the baby stage and allow seedlings to mature into heads. Seedlings also give the flexibility to plant onions, leeks, lettuces, and other greens at exactly the right spacing (no thinning required!) and in pretty patterns—I'm especially fond of planting rows of lettuce with alternating green- and red-leafed varieties. I intermix annual flowers with my vegetables because they attract beneficial insects and pollinators, plus it is fun to have a supply of flowers for bouquets. I plant both seedlings and starts of the following vegetables, herbs, and annual flowers:

Asian greens (bok choy, tatsoi)
Basil
Chervil
Cilantro
Cosmos
Cucumbers
Dill
Fennel
Kale
Lettuce
Melons
Onions
Parsley
Peas (English, sugar snap, and snow)
Summer squash
Sunflowers
Sweet peas
Swiss chard
Winter squashes (including pumpkins)
Zinnias

SELF-SOWING

Many vegetables and herbs *self-sow*, which means they flower, set seed, and drop the seeds to the ground. The seeds then germinate when the conditions are right, either in fall or the following spring. Self-sown seedlings are called "volunteers," and they often sprout close together and in an inconvenient spot. You can thin the volunteers and let them continue growing where they sprouted, or transplant them to a place where you actually want them to grow. When the volunteers' first true leaves emerge, use a trowel to dig them up. Gently tease the individual plants apart, being careful to handle them by their leaves or roots, not their stems. Transplant the seedlings to a new spot, settling them in at the same depth at which they were growing before and leaving the recommended distance between them. Donate unwanted self-sown seedlings to friends or toss them into the compost pile. Do not allow fennel, lemon balm, shiso, or angelica to self-sow—they can be very aggressive. The following plants are tamer:

Anise hyssop
Arugula
Chervil
Cilantro
Dill
Leeks
Lettuce
Mustard greens
Nasturtiums
Swiss chard

Succession Planting

In late winter I sit down and plan what I want to plant in each of my garden beds throughout the season. This process is called *succession planting*, and the basic idea is to ensure a steady harvest by planting vegetables at regular intervals during the growing season, rather than just in spring. Creating the plan is a helpful exercise, even if you don't end up following it to the letter, because it makes you think about what varieties you want to grow, what their growth habits are, and how you can fit them all into your garden.

To help streamline the process, I've created lists of fast, midseason, and long-season crops below (crops that do not tolerate frost are marked with an asterisk). To make your succession-planting plan, simply make a sketch of each garden bed for spring, summer, and fall (see example, opposite page) or just write out the basic details. As you fill in each seasonal bed, refer to the lists, and mix and match crops that mature at different times. Note your estimated planting date and aim to have garden space open up in late spring (so you can plant frost-sensitive crops) and in late summer (for crops that will mature in fall). For example:

SPRING BED: Trellis down back of bed with 'Golden India' snow peas (March 23/direct-sow). In front of trellis, 'Lacinato' kale (March 23/seedlings); in front of kale, 'Forellenschluss' and 'Breen' romaine lettuces (March 23/seedlings).

SUMMER BED: Trellis down back of bed with 'Trombetta' summer squash (June 5/seedlings). In front of trellis, 'Lacinato' kale; in front of kale, 'Genovese' basil (June 5/seedlings and direct-sow).

FALL BED: Spinach in one half (September 15/direct-sow) and shallots in the other (October 1/sets).

FAST CROPS

These can be sown multiple times a season and take 30 to 55 days to mature:

Arugula	Bush beans*	Mustard greens
Asian greens (bok choy, tatsoi, etc.)	Chervil	Radishes
	Cilantro	Spinach
Broccoli rabe	Lettuce	Turnips

MIDSEASON CROPS

These can be planted two or three times a season and take 55 to 70 days to mature:

Basil*	Edamame*	Parsley
Beets	Fennel	Peas
Broccoli	Kale	Potatoes*
Carrots	Leeks	Radicchio
Dill	Onions	Swiss chard

LONG-SEASON CROPS

These can be planted once or twice a season and take 75 days or longer to mature:

Cabbage	Fava beans	Shallots
Cauliflower	Garlic	Tomatillos*
Corn*	Melons*	Tomatoes*
Cucumbers*	Peppers*	Summer and winter
Eggplants*	Pole beans*	squash*

Frost-sensitive crop

SAMPLE SUCCESSION PLANTING DIAGRAM

SPRING

'Golden India' snow peas on trellis *Direct-sow/March 23*	
'Lacinato' kale *Seedlings/March 23*	
'Breen' romaine *Seedlings/March 23*	**'Forellenschluss' lettuce** *Seedlings/March 23*

SUMMER

'Trombetta' summer squash on trellis *Seedlings/June 5*	
'Lacinato' kale	
'Genovese' basil *Seedlings and direct-sow/June 5*	

FALL

'Tyee' spinach *Direct-sow/ September 1 and 15*	**Shallots** *Sets/October 1*

SEASON EXTENSION

Season extension simply means manipulating air and soil temperatures to best suit the plants you want to grow. A greenhouse is perhaps the most well-known season-extending tool, but I rely on a variety of flexible, inexpensive materials to start my garden season earlier in spring and extend it well into fall.

Cloches

A *cloche* is a glass or plastic bell-shaped jar placed over individual plants to keep them warmer than the ambient air temperature and protect them from frost (see photo on opposite page). The lightweight plastic versions often have a vent on top, which is helpful in regulating the temperature inside the cloche, but they must be staked into place with U-shaped metal pins. Traditional glass cloches are more expensive, but they do not blow over, and they look absolutely lovely.

Hoop Houses

A *hoop house* is a frame that can be used to support a variety of season-extending materials (see page 23 for building instructions), including:

ROW COVERS

These spun polyester fabrics let air and moisture in while protecting plants from pests, fluctuating temperatures, variable weather, and frost. The covers offer varying degrees of protection based on their weight: use lightweight covers in summer to protect plants from pests, including insects, deer, and groundhogs, and the heavier "frost blankets" to protect them from severe weather and cold. Reemay and Agribon are two common brands.

CLEAR PLASTIC

Clear plastic creates a temporary greenhouse when draped over a hoop house frame. I prefer to use UV-resistant, perforated plastic, such as Gro-Therm, which raises the air temperature within the hoop house an average of 10 degrees. Because this plastic is ventilated, air still circulates underneath the cover, which reduces disease problems and prevents the plants from overheating on hot days. You can also use regular four- or six-ply plastic sheeting, available in the painting section of hardware stores, but it must be vented on hot, sunny days.

SHADE CLOTH

This is a loosely woven black cloth that blocks out a certain percentage of sunlight based on the tightness of the weave. Drape it over a hoop house in summer to lower the air temperature around cool-season crops like salad greens and cilantro.

GARDEN CLIPS

These plastic clips are designed to secure row cover fabric, ventilated plastic, and shade cloth to hoop house frames. You can also use extra-large binder clips.

ROW COVER CLAMPS

It's important to secure row covers, plastic, and shade cloth firmly to the ground to prevent pests from sneaking underneath and wind from whipping them off. You can weigh the material down with rocks or two-by-fours, or buy clamps that snap onto the covers and can then be staked into the ground, which makes it easier to check your crops.

Heating Up the Soil

Waiting for the soil to warm up enough to plant warm-season crops can be frustrating, especially in climates with long, cool springs. Stretching clear or black plastic over the soil a couple of weeks before planting can quickly raise its temperature. Black plastic heats the soil more slowly, but it also blocks light and prevents weeds. Clear plastic works like a greenhouse, heating soil up quickly, but it can be left in place for only a few weeks, because weeds will grow underneath it.

It's best to purchase rolls of UV-resistant plastic from a garden supply company, but you can also use plastic sheeting.

A word about using plastic in the garden: I do not like to use a lot of plastic in mine, for both environmental and aesthetic reasons. However, I do find that using plastic to heat up the soil and cover certain warm-season crops can dramatically increase yields. It also allows me to grow more food for a longer period, which reduces the amount of food I need to buy from the supermarket. I carefully store any plastic indoors over the winter and find I can reuse it for many years. If using plastic gives you pause, investing in glass cold frames (which are essentially miniature passive solar greenhouses) and cloches is a fine alternative.

To install the plastic ground covers, do the following:

1. Rake the bed as smooth and level as possible, the soil heats up fastest if the plastic is in direct contact with it.

2. You will need to anchor the plastic to the ground. Dig a trench around inground beds, and pull the soil away from the frames of raised beds. Lay the plastic over the planting area, tuck one edge into the trench, and then stretch the plastic tightly over the bed, burying the edges as you go, or use landscape fabric pins to tack the plastic into place.

3. After two weeks check on the soil temperature. If it has warmed up past 70 degrees F, you can go ahead and plant. You can leave black plastic in place all season if you like—it will keep the soil warm, radiate heat around your plants, and prevent weeds; follow the directions in the section on melons for planting into black plastic mulch (page 153). If you've used clear plastic, remove it, plant, and then mulch with straw or grass clippings immediately to help the soil retain its heat.

BUILDING A HOOP HOUSE

A hoop house is simply a tent frame constructed over a garden bed. This easy-to-build, inexpensive structure allows you to manipulate the growing season and protect plants from pests, depending on what material you place over its top. Drape it with ventilated plastic and it becomes a greenhouse; tent it with row cover fabric to create a physical barrier between your plants and hungry insect pests or protect plants from frost; or cover it with shade cloth to keep salad greens cool during the summer.

MATERIALS:

½- or ¾-inch-diameter flexible plastic tubing

Two 18- to 24-inch rebar or bamboo stakes for each length of tubing

Ventilated plastic, row cover fabric, or shade cloth (60 or 72 inches wide works best)

Three garden clips for each length of tubing (medium for ½-inch tubing; large for ¾-inch tubing)

1. Cut several pieces of plastic tubing into 5- to 6-foot lengths, or lengths that will allow the tubing to arch about a foot above your plants when they are mature.

2. You want the hoops to arch crosswise over the bed. Position the stakes in each corner of the bed and then directly across from each other at 3-foot intervals (in my 3-foot-wide, 6-foot-long beds, I have three hoops, one on each end and one in the middle). Pound the stakes into the ground, leaving 8 to 10 inches of each one exposed. Be sure to buy rebar or bamboo that is a *smaller* diameter than the tubing, otherwise the tubing won't fit over the stake (I learned this the hard way!).

3. To make each arch, slide the tubing over a stake, bow it crosswise over the bed, and slide the other end of the tubing over the stake on the opposite side of the bed.

4. Drape plastic, row cover fabric, or shade cloth over the arches. Cut the material to fit, making sure you leave extra that can be weighed down or staked into place.

5. Secure by clipping the fabric/plastic to the arched tubing using garden clips (manufactured expressly to clasp material to hoop house frames) or large binder clips. Use bricks to weigh down the plastic, or buy special row cover clamps that fasten to the row cover and then stake into the ground.

SMART WATERING PRACTICES

Watering is crucial to the quality of your vegetables. Too little water can cause premature bolting, bitterness, tip burn, and deformed fruit. Too much water reduces flavor. Inconsistent watering encourages blossom-end rot and cracking.

Vegetables tolerate drought to varying degrees, but all grow and taste best when the soil around their root zones stays consistently moist. Soil type, air temperature, cloud cover, wind, natural precipitation, and plant maturity all influence how often you will need to water.

Soil Moisture Test

Rather than watering on a schedule, I recommend that you frequently evaluate your soil's moisture and then water as needed. This process is quite simple: just stick your pointer finger into the soil. For plants with shallow root systems, like salad greens, you'll need to water when the soil dries down to the top of your first knuckle. For deeper-rooted plants like tomatoes, or those that tolerate drier soil, like raspberries, wait to water until the soil dries down to the top of your second knuckle. Seedlings need constant moisture in the top layer of soil as their root systems establish. Once the plants actively begin to grow new leaves, you can begin reducing how often you water. Sandy soils need irrigation more frequently than clay or loamy soils.

Water Early

Giving your garden a drink in the morning allows the water to percolate down into the soil before the day warms up and allows your plants' foliage to dry off quickly. Watering later in the day increases evaporation loss and wastes water. Unless plants are wilted, avoid irrigating in the evening, because their foliage will stay damp through the night, which promotes the development of fungal diseases.

Saturate the Roots

The goal when irrigating is to completely soak the plant's root zone. This practice encourages the plants to send their roots deep into the soil in search of water. Watering frequently but superficially (to a depth of only 2 or 3 inches) encourages plants to develop smaller root systems, which means they will suffer during hot, dry weather. Aim to soak the soil to a depth of 8 to 12 inches each time you water.

Hand Watering

I always irrigate newly sown seeds and transplanted seedlings with a gentle stream from a watering can for the first few days, but its limited capacity makes it impractical for watering mature plants or large areas. Using a wand attached to a hose is time consuming (it takes an average of 30 minutes to hand-water 100 square feet of garden space) and challenging because water charges out of the hose so fast that it often runs off instead of seeping in. If you must water by hand, turn the hose on a low rate that allows the water to soak in. Position the nozzle at the base of your plants and repeatedly soak the soil around them.

Build 6-inch-deep wells of soil around larger plants like tomatoes and fill them with water. Flood the furrows of plants like leeks and corn. Let the water soak in and then repeat three or four times. When you think you've watered deeply, wait 20 minutes and then dig a hole to see how far the water has percolated into the soil. If it is less than 8 inches, continue watering. When hand watering mature plants, I like to use a wand with a lever on the handle that turns the water on and off, because this makes it easy to control the flow rate. Avoid using overhead sprinklers, as they lose a lot of water to evaporation and soak the plants' foliage.

Irrigation Systems

The most efficient way to water is to set up *soaker hoses*—special hoses that seep water out along their entire length—or *drip irrigation*, which has emitters that deliver a slow trickle of water right to your plants' roots. Both systems save time because you do not need to be present to irrigate; conserve water by reducing evaporation and eliminating runoff; and reduce costs by wasting less water. Watering plants at their base also prevents disease by helping to keep foliage dry.

Soaker hoses distribute water most evenly on level ground and in lengths of 25 feet or less. Help the hoses lie flat by securing them to the soil with U-shaped landscape fabric pins. You can place mulch over soaker hoses, but they clog if buried under soil.

Buying a kit is the easiest way to set up a drip irrigation system. Run drip tape or drip tubing between rows of vegetables. Individual emitters work best for watering large plants like tomatoes. Soaker hoses and drip systems can be hooked up to a timer that automatically turns them on early in the morning; if you use a timer, make sure to test your soil's moisture levels once a week and adjust the irrigation frequency and duration as needed.

Insulate the Soil

Spreading a layer of mulch over the soil holds moisture in, moderates the soil's temperature, and prevents weed seeds from germinating. Straw and grass clippings from organically maintained lawns are my favorite mulch for vegetable gardens. Make sure you buy organic straw, not hay, which tends to contain lots of grain and weed seeds. Thoroughly water and then place a 3- to 4-inch-deep layer over the soil after planting seedlings or when directly sown plants have grown 6 to 8 inches tall. Always leave a small ring of bare soil around plants to prevent the mulch from smothering them. If mulching around plants that grow best in warm soil, such as eggplants, wait to apply the mulch until the soil heats up to 70 degrees.

FERTILIZING

Vegetables grow rapidly and need a steady nutrient supply. Fertilizer can help supplement your plants' nutrient needs while you work on building healthy soil, but it should never be used in place of adding organic matter. Organic fertilizers are derived from natural sources, including animal and plant by-products and mineral powders.

What Is NPK?

On fertilizer labels you will see a series of three numbers. These *NPK numbers* refer to the percentages of nitrogen (N), phosphorus (P), and potassium (K) in the fertilizer (based on total weight). Organic fertilizers often have very low percentages (like 5-2-2), while conventional chemical fertilizers have higher levels (like 20-20-20). Nitrogen, phosphorus, and potassium are considered *macronutrients* because relatively large quantities of them are essential to a plant's health and growth. Plants use nitrogen to develop dark-green, leafy growth; phosphorus for root development and fruit and seed production; and potassium for overall plant health. When fertilizing, always follow the label's application rates and dilution recommendations.

NUTRIENT DEFICIENCY SYMPTOMS

When a plant's nutrient needs are not being met, its foliage often offers a visual clue that something is amiss. Tomatoes and members of the cabbage family are especially good indicators for nutrient deficiencies because they tend to show problems before other plants. If you notice these signs, foliar-feed the plants with diluted liquid organic fertilizer (see page 27) and get a soil test.

NITROGEN: The plant's leaves begin to turn yellow, starting with the lower ones.

IRON: Leaves turn yellow, but the veins stay bright green. Iron deficiencies often occur in alkaline soil.

POTASSIUM: Older leaves become scorched-looking on their tips and margins.

PHOSPHORUS: Leaves develop a purple tinge. This deficiency is especially noticeable on seedlings and is more apt to occur in acidic or cold soils.

Foliar Feeding

Foliar feeding—spraying a liquid fertilizer onto plants' leaves rather than applying it to the soil—makes nutrients available immediately. The liquid fertilizer is absorbed through the leaf cuticle (the waxy outer layer on leaves and stems) and through the leaves' pores. Here's how to make and use the liquid organic fertilizer that I refer to in the growing guides:

1. Prepare 1 gallon each of diluted liquid fish emulsion and diluted liquid kelp, by following the dilution recommendations on the labels. I mix the fertilizers separately in gallon juice jugs that have been washed with soapy water and rinsed.

2. Fill a pump sprayer or a new, clean spray bottle—never reuse a sprayer or spray bottle that contained cleaning supplies or chemicals—with a 1:1 mix of the diluted fish emulsion and diluted liquid kelp.

3. It is best to foliar-feed in the morning because leaf pores are typically fully open when it is cool. This timing also allows the leaves to dry after the fertilizer application, which prevents disease problems. Make sure to spray both the undersides and tops of the leaves. The liquid fish emulsion provides your plants with a dose of nitrogen, and the kelp is packed with micronutrients. (Don't worry, the distinctly fishy smell goes away as soon as the fertilizer dries.)

Granular Organic Fertilizers

Granular organic fertilizers are dry fertilizers. Sprinkle them over an entire bed or into the bottom of a furrow before planting, and work them into the soil with a rake or a three-tine cultivator.

Top Dressing

You can also spread a 1- to 2-inch layer of compost on top of the soil around the plants. As you water, the nutrients from the compost will seep into the soil below.

PREVENTING PESTS AND DISEASES

The best way to reduce problems in your garden is to spend time growing the healthiest plants possible. Planting your garden in full sun, maintaining healthy soil, growing a diverse range of plants, and providing consistent water and a steady supply of nutrients helps your plants fend off pests and diseases more than spraying them with chemicals ever could. You also need to pay attention. Spotting problems before they get out of control gives you a chance to deal with them in a minimally invasive way. This doesn't need to be a chore. Grab a cup of tea in the morning and wander about the garden. Find some orange squash bug eggs lined up like soldiers on the underside of a pumpkin leaf? Smoosh them. Notice powdery mildew on a few Swiss chard leaves? Clip them off and toss them in the trash. These quick interventions work most of the time and give you a chance to evaluate why the problem is occurring and take steps to fix it.

If your plants develop a persistent or serious problem, refer to Resources (page 277). There you will find recommendations for online and print resources that can help you identify and deal with specific pest and disease problems organically.

Pests

Pests are a fact of life in gardens. Slugs snack on lettuce. Leaf miners tunnel through spinach. These things happen. But pests are just a small part of the larger ecosystem. Ladybugs will swoop in and eat the aphids off your peppers, and birds will snag fat imported cabbageworms off your broccoli. Rather than micromanaging every insect in your garden, try to encourage a balanced community of pests and predators.

ATTRACT MORE BENEFICIAL INSECTS

Insect pests are a food source for *beneficial insects* (also known as beneficials). Ladybugs, which feed on aphids, are a common beneficial. Most insect predators also feed on nectar and pollen at some stage in their life cycles. Planting flowers that produce lots of both gives these insects an incentive to visit your garden. Intermix flowers, vegetables, and herbs. Allow cilantro, dill, thyme, catmint, and fennel to flower. Sow a carpet of sweet alyssum under pepper plants, and plant pockets of zinnias, sunflowers, cosmos, bachelor's buttons, calendulas, nasturtiums, and marigolds all around the garden. Grow perennials, including herbs, strawberries, and raspberries, to give the beneficials a place to hunker down over the winter. If you spot an insect in your garden you've never seen before, figure out what it is before you even think about killing it.

EXCLUDE INSECT PESTS

Constructing a hoop house over plants (see page 23) and tenting it with a lightweight row cover or bird netting forms a barrier between your plants and the pests that want to eat them. Leave the cover on all season if the vegetables underneath do not require insect pollination (for example, broccoli, cauliflower, and peppers). For plants that need pollination, such as cucumbers and squash, you can either keep the cover in place and hand-pollinate their flowers (see page 145) or remove it when the plants begin to flower; at this point they are often large enough to tolerate some pest damage.

Bird netting is a plastic mesh that prevents birds from unearthing large seeds like peas and beans, plucking newly planted seedlings from the soil, or pecking at ripe fruit. In vegetable gardens, drape bird netting over hoop-house frames or prop it up above the plants with twiggy branches. Laying it directly over newly sown seeds or seedlings isn't particularly effective because the plants become entangled in the netting as they grow, and birds can pull seeds and plants through the holes. Place the netting over blueberries or raspberries before the fruit ripens and pin it to the ground so birds can't fly up underneath.

HANDPICK

Manually removing pests helps reduce their population. Pluck larvae, nymphs, and adult pests, including caterpillars and beetles, off the plants. Fill a jar with soapy water (use a biodegradable soap), drown the pests, and then toss them into your compost pile. Scout for eggs, which are often laid in clusters on the undersides of leaves, and squish them.

DON'T USE PESTICIDES

Broad-spectrum pesticides kill all the insects they come into contact with, including beneficial insects and *pollinators* (organisms, usually insects, that move pollen between plants, to different flowers on the same plant, or from one flower part to another). These pesticides, even organic ones made with pyrethrums and rotenone, do not make sense for you or your garden. Insect pests can develop a resistance to pesticides, and their populations often rebound faster after a pesticide application than those of beneficial insects, which

ALL IN THE FAMILY

Most edibles are known by their common names (e.g. tomato), but like all plants, vegetables, herbs, and fruit are classified by botanic type and have botanic names that reflect this (e.g. *Lycopersicon esculentum*). Understanding the basics of botanic classification, as well as a few other terms commonly used to describe plants, will help you understand the relationship between plants and how they were bred.

FAMILY: A taxonomy category that groups together plants with many botanical features in common. For instance, peas and beans both belong to the family Fabaceae. Plants that are in the same family are often susceptible to the same pests and diseases.

GENUS: A taxonomy category that is below family and above species and includes a group of related species. The first word in a botanical name refers to the genus. For instance, melons (*Cucumis melo*) and cucumbers (*Cucumis sativus*) belong to the same genus but are different species.

SPECIES: The basic subcategory in taxonomic classification, it falls below genus. The second word in a botanical name refers to the species. For instance, basil belongs to the genus *Ocimum*, and its species name within that genus is *basilicum*.

VARIETY: A natural variation in a plant species that results from adaptation, cross-pollination, or mutation. For instance, the species *Beta vulgaris* has two common varieties: beets (*Beta vulgaris* var. *esculenta*) and Swiss chard (*Beta vulgaris* var. *cicla*). The term "variety" is often used as a synonym for "cultivar."

CULTIVAR: A "cultivated variety" of a plant, meaning it was purposely bred to exhibit certain characteristics. Cultivar names are denoted with single quotation marks (e.g. 'Walla Walla' onion).

OPEN-POLLINATED: A term applied to seeds of varieties and cultivars that grow true to type, which means they will produce plants with the exact same characteristics as their parent plants (provided the seeds are not cross-pollinated).

HEIRLOOM: An open-pollinated variety of any plant that was bred prior to World War II or is at least 50 years old.

HYBRID: A cross between two different plant varieties or species. Seed from a hybrid does not come true to type, which means it may or may not have the same characteristics as the parent plant.

means using pesticides can make pest problems worse over time. And chemicals that contain carcinogens and neurotoxins have no place in your garden or on your food.

I recommend the use of only two organic pesticides: insecticidal soap and iron phosphate–based slug baits. Insecticidal soap suffocates small, soft-bodied insects like aphids by coating them in a soapy film. The product must come into contact with the pest in order to kill it. Spray insecticidal soap all over the plant, making sure to coat the undersides of the leaves. Repeat a couple of days later if necessary. Always use a soap spray formulated for use on plants; the dyes, fragrances, and other ingredients found in household soaps can kill plant foliage.

The most effective way to deal with slugs and snails is to spread an iron phosphate–based organic bait around the garden. When slugs ingest iron phosphate bait, they lose their appetite and die of starvation. The baits are safe to use around children and pets. You could also set out beer traps: Bury a clean, shallow plastic container, like a sour cream tub, in the garden near susceptible plants. Leave 1 inch of the container above the soil line (to prevent beneficial ground beetles from falling in) and fill it with beer. The slugs are attracted to yeasty smells, so they crawl in and drown. Empty the containers daily and refresh with new beer.

ROTATE CROPS

Plants that belong to the same family share common pests and diseases. Crop rotation is an organic gardening technique that groups plants from each family together and then rotates them into different garden beds each year, ideally on a three- to five-year cycle. The idea is to curb pests by denying them their favorite host plants.

Diseases

Diseases are often a symptom of an underlying problem. Tomatoes are more apt to develop a fungal disease when air circulation between and within the plants is poor. Clubroot is more of a problem for cabbage, kale, and other brassicas in acidic soils. Maintaining healthy soil and taking a few precautions when planning and maintaining your garden can go a long way toward preventing disease.

CHOOSE VARIETIES CAREFULLY

Some plant varieties are more susceptible to disease than others. If a disease commonly affects a certain type of plant in your garden, try planting a variety that naturally resists the problem. Most seed catalogs have symbols that indicate whether a variety resists certain common diseases.

KEEP PLANT FOLIAGE DRY

You can't escape fungal diseases—their spores travel in the air and on water, and live in the soil—but you can prevent them from taking hold on your plants. The spores need to land on a wet leaf, and they need the leaf to remain moist for several hours, in order to establish. Spacing plants farther apart and selectively thinning out dense foliage improves air circulation and helps foliage dry quickly. Always irrigate plants at their base, never use overhead sprinklers, and harvest when foliage is dry.

MULCH

Many disease-causing fungi overwinter in the soil and infect plants when a rainstorm or irrigation kicks soil up onto their leaves. Placing a layer of mulch around the base of plants provides a buffer between them and the soil and reduces the incidence of disease.

DEALING WITH WEEDS

Vegetables thrive in healthy garden soil. Unfortunately, so do weeds. These aggressive, adaptable, and resourceful plants compete with your vegetables and herbs for water, nutrients, and space. Weeds spread from seeds—which can survive for decades in the soil—and root fragments, so it is important to always pull them before they flower and to remove as much of their roots as possible. I don't like to spend a ton of time weeding, so I use the following strategies to maximize my weed control with minimal effort.

Buy a Stirrup Hoe

This hoe saves more time than all the other tools in the shed combined. It has a rocking stirrup-shaped blade that runs just under the soil line, slicing off weed seedlings' roots without unearthing new weed seeds or disturbing surrounding vegetables' roots. The hoe works with a push-pull movement: pull the hoe toward you to uproot little weeds and then push it away to bury them under the soil, where they quickly decompose. Don't use a tiller, especially when you prepare beds for spring planting. Tillers stir up the soil and bring buried weed seeds to the surface, where they can germinate.

Eliminate Bare Soil

You almost never see bare soil in nature. Leaf litter and moss cover the forest floor. Grass and broad-leaf plants carpet meadows. The simplest way to reduce weeds in your garden is to cover the soil, either with mulch or with plants that you actually want to grow. Space low-growing plants like lettuce, spinach, and other greens so they will just touch when mature. In these close quarters the plants crowd out weeds and shade the soil, which makes it hard for weed seeds to germinate. Try sowing small, quick-growing crops, including baby salad greens, radishes, and chervil, underneath larger plants like broccoli or tomatoes. The "understory" plants act

INDICATOR WEEDS

Weeds, like all plants, prefer certain soil conditions. The following weeds can provide clues to the state of your soil:

LAMBSQUARTERS, PURSLANE, QUEEN ANNE'S LACE, HENBIT, CHICKWEED: rich, cultivated soil

BINDWEED, QUACK GRASS, PLANTAIN, CREEPING BUTTERCUP: compacted soil

CLOVER, RED SORREL: nutrient-deficient soil

HORSETAIL, PLANTAIN, KNOTWEED, BENT GRASS: acidic soil

like a living mulch, and they will mature before the bigger plants shade them out. You can also simply spread a 3- to 4-inch layer of straw or grass mulch around plants to smother weeds. Use mulch that breaks down slowly, such as wood chips or hazelnut shells, in pathways between beds.

Weed Early and Often

Weeding for 15 minutes once a week prevents weeds from growing out of control and turning into a more time-consuming chore. Simply run a stirrup hoe or a handheld circle hoe back and forth between your plants weekly to kill weed seedlings. Hand-pull any larger weeds that escaped your earlier attention. Removing weeds when they are small makes it easier to pull out their entire root system and prevents them from flowering and dropping seeds. I send weeds away in my yard waste rather than placing them in my home compost pile.

EDIBLE WEEDS

Some common garden weeds are so tasty that they have made the jump from wild plants to cultivated crops.

'Catalogna Frastagliata' dandelion is an Italian variety. Harvest the tender, slightly frilled leaves at 10 to 12 inches for the best flavor.

Golden purslane grows more upright than common purslane, which forms a mat over the soil in summer. Its succulent leaves and stems have a lemony flavor. To harvest, pinch off 3- or 4-inch sections of stem to right above a set of leaves.

'Magenta Spreen' lambsquarters belongs to the spinach family and has delightful light-green leaves with a pink flame at their base. Both cultivated and weedy forms of lambsquarters have a mild, mineral flavor. They taste best if harvested when the plant is 6 to 8 inches tall.

CHAPTER TWO

HERBS

FRESH HERBS MAKE ALMOST ANYTHING TASTE BETTER. The flavor
of their fragrant little leaves and flowers adds subtlety and depth to
the simplest foods. Take carrots: delicious raw, they become down-
right addictive when roasted with honey butter and thyme. Tossing
a few slivers of Thai basil, a sprinkle of pungent garlic chive flowers, and some chopped cilantro into leftover Chinese food elevates
it to a real meal. And drinking tea brewed with fresh mint leaves is
my favorite way to end a long day.

Herbs also produce a delightful array of delicious extras,
including crunchy seeds, delicate, sweet-tasting flowers, and spices
like fennel pollen. These wonderfully multipurpose plants do not
deserve to be sequestered into their own little garden, especially
since they mix so well with vegetables and flowers. Tuck basil into
mixed containers, grow thyme alongside sunny footpaths, place
a pot of mint by the back door, or plant a carpet of oregano under
roses. Grow them wherever you have a sunny spot, because once
you start using fresh herbs in the kitchen, it's hard to stop.

PRESERVING HERBS

Herbs taste best when harvested moments before cooking, but growing your own also gives you the opportunity to preserve some for use during the winter and to give as gifts.

Drying Herbs

Gather small bunches of herbs (the group of stems should be about as fat as a cigar). Strip the leaves from the bottom quarter of the stems. Tie a piece of twine about 2 inches from the bottom of the bunch, cinching it down tightly. Hang the herbs upside down in a warm, dark, dust-free spot. When the leaves become dry and crumbly, strip them off their stems and pack them into labeled glass jars. These freshly dried herbs have tons of flavor compared to store-bought versions, especially when used within 8 to 12 months. Rosemary, sage, oregano, marjoram, thyme, winter savory, tarragon, chamomile, mint, lemon verbena, and bay all dry well. Don't bother drying basil, dill, parsley, cilantro, fennel, or chervil—their delicate essential oils evaporate quickly, leaving behind tasteless green flakes.

Freezing Herbs

Dill, cilantro, parsley, chives, fennel, and basil all freeze well. Place 2 cups of clean leaves (stems removed) in a blender or food processor bowl fitted with a chopping blade. Drizzle in ½ cup olive oil and process, adding an extra tablespoon or two of oil if needed to make a loose purée. Spoon the purée into the cells of an ice cube tray and freeze. Pop the solid cubes out of the tray, wrap each one individually in plastic, and then store them in an airtight container in the freezer. Freeze pesto the same way.

IDEAS FOR USING FROZEN HERBS

Drop frozen cubes of herbs into a pot of simmering soup 5 minutes before serving. Try dill, fennel, or basil in potato leek soup; cilantro in chili; and parsley, chives, or basil in vegetable stews. Defrost one or two cubes and whisk them into mayonnaise. Spread the herbed mayo on sandwiches or stir it into tuna, egg, or chicken salad. Make a quick, creamy dressing by whisking one defrosted cube each of dill, parsley, and chives together with ½ cup Greek yogurt, 1 finely minced garlic clove, and 1 tablespoon lemon juice; whisk in olive oil to taste and season with salt and pepper. Mix a cube of defrosted herbs into a basic lemon or white wine vinaigrette.

Basil

Basil should not be grown in moderation. Fill entire raised beds with sweet, spicy 'Genovese' basil for pesto. Plant ruffled purple varieties to use as a garnish, cinnamon basil to flavor scones, licorice-flavored Thai basil for stir-fries and spring rolls, and lime and lemon basils for cocktails. Intermingle its lush, fragrant, and colorful foliage with annuals and perennials, or create a mini edible hedge by planting little-leaf basil around the perimeter of a bed.

Planting

Basil stubbornly refuses to grow when planted too early. Wait until the soil heats up to at least 60 degrees F, all danger of frost has passed, and nighttime temperatures stay above 55 degrees. Choose a sheltered, hot spot in full sun. In climates with long, cool springs, cover the bed with plastic to warm the soil earlier (see page 22).

Basil may be grown from seeds, seedlings, or cuttings. For a staggered harvest, plant basil seedlings and direct-sow seeds on the same day and again three weeks later; follow the instructions for direct-sowing small seeds (see page 15). The seeds typically germinate within 7 to 10 days. Basil seedlings are often sold in a clump rather than as individual plants in cell packs, and they grow into a stunted, tangled mess if not separated. Gently remove the soil from around the seedlings' roots. Tease out the individual plants and plant them 8 inches apart. Little-leaf varieties (also known as bush basil) grow best when planted as seedlings, but the small plants look reedy on their own. Cluster the seedlings in clumps of three to five and space the clumps 6 inches apart to encourage the little plants to grow into a thick row.

Growing

With the exception of some bush basils, most varieties grow 1½ to 2 feet tall. Thin directly sown plants to 4 inches apart once they are large enough to handle and to 8 inches when they have four sets of leaves. Water stress reduces basil's flavor: irrigate when the soil dries down to the top of your first knuckle and mulch with 2 inches of grass clippings. Foliar-feed once a month and immediately following each large harvest.

All basil grows best when daytime temperatures reach the 80s and nighttime temperatures stay above 60 degrees. Frost quickly kills this tropical plant, but its flavor begins to suffer when nighttime temperatures dip below 50. Growing basil under a hoop house tented with vented plastic for all or part of the season dramatically increases yields and protects the plants' flavor (see page 23). In my cool Pacific Northwest garden, I get the best harvests when I put a hoop house over basil immediately after planting and leave it in place throughout the summer, but gardeners in warmer climates need to install one only if they would like to extend the harvest once temperatures grow chilly in fall.

Harvesting

The biggest mistake people make when growing basil is not harvesting it often enough. Basil leaves toughen and their oil content reduces with age, diluting their flavor. Regular,

proper harvesting encourages bushy growth and fresh flushes of foliage. Basil leaves grow in sets of two with the leaves positioned opposite each other. If you examine the point where the leaves meet the stem, you will see tiny leaves growing out of the junction. When harvesting, always pinch directly above these little leaves, as this signals them to grow into branches.

The following harvesting strategy will enable each plant to yield more than 20 cups of leaves: When the plant develops four sets of leaves, use your thumb and forefinger to pinch off the top two sets. Repeat this process with each pair of branches as they grow. Once the plant reaches 14 to 18 inches high, cut it down to just above the fourth-lowest set of leaves. Harvest smaller amounts as needed by pinching off the top set or two of leaves from each stem. Regular pinching also forestalls flowering, which causes the basil to stop producing new leaves and harshens the flavor of existing ones. If the white or purple flowers end up forming, cut off the whole stem and use the tasty flowers in the kitchen.

Storing

Refrigeration ruins basil—the leaves lose their signature spicy-sweet flavor when exposed to temperatures below 50 degrees and turn black at temperatures below 45 degrees. Immediately after harvest, place the stems in a short, stout jar of water and keep them out of direct sunlight. Change the water every other day. If left in the water long enough, the stems will grow roots. Once they have a nice bundle of roots, you can plant these cuttings in small pots and then transfer them into the garden after a few weeks. (You can also propagate mint, lemon balm, and shiso this way.) Basil also freezes well (see page 35).

Cooking Ideas

Shower a pizza with tiny 'Fino Verde' leaves. Use large-leaf basils such as 'Mammoth' as the outside layer for wraps and spring rolls. Muddle basil with soda water or sparkling grape juice and serve over ice. Garnish drinks with flower stalks, or pull the flowers off and scatter them over a cheese omelet as it cooks. Purée 1 cup extra-virgin olive oil with 1 packed cup basil leaves. Brush the basil oil on pizza crust or sandwich bread, drizzle it over fresh mozzarella and tomatoes, or toss it with pasta and roasted vegetables.

Delicious Varieties

'Genovese'. 68 days. *The* classic Italian basil, 'Genovese' has an intoxicating sweet-spicy taste and aroma. Perfect for pesto. For extra-large sweet basil leaves, grow 'Napolitano'. Open-pollinated.

'Fino Verde'. 63 days. A little-leaf variety with excellent flavor and pale-green foliage. 'Pistou' and 'Spicy Bush' are also tasty petite basils. Open-pollinated.

'Red Rubin'. 76 days. 'Red Rubin' produces purple leaves with a spicy basil flavor and maintains its deep color in hot climates. I also like 'Siam Queen', a purple-and-green Thai variety with a pronounced anise undertone. Open-pollinated.

BASIL

Ocimum basilicum

PLANT FAMILY: Lamiaceae

EDIBLE PARTS: Leaves, flowers

POTENTIAL PROBLEMS: Slugs, aphids, Japanese beetles, fusarium wilt, gray mold

Nona's Pesto

3 plump garlic cloves, peeled

½ cup pine nuts

4 cups packed fresh basil leaves

½ cup packed finely grated Parmesan (about 1 ounce)

½ cup extra-virgin olive oil

Sea salt

My grandmother Inez was born in a western Wyoming coal-mining town to immigrants from northern Italy. Italian was her first language, and she learned to cook on a wood-burning stove. This heirloom recipe comes straight from her kitchen. I make it all summer long and freeze several batches for the winter. Use the proportions in this recipe as a baseline and experiment by substituting different greens and herbs (such as parsley, cilantro, arugula, and fava or radish greens) and using different nuts, especially walnuts, and sunflower or toasted squash seeds.

. . . .

Pulse the garlic and pine nuts in a food processor until finely chopped. Add the basil and Parmesan and process into a smooth paste. Scrape down the sides of the bowl. With the blade running, slowly drizzle in the olive oil. Process until the oil is thoroughly incorporated and the pesto is smooth. Taste and add salt if desired.

To keep refrigerated pesto from turning black, lay plastic wrap coated with olive oil directly over it, and seal the container with a lid. It will keep for at least a week refrigerated and several months frozen. Bring it to room temperature and stir thoroughly before using. When using frozen pesto in pasta, thaw it and stir in 1 tablespoon pasta water before tossing with cooked pasta—this helps distribute pesto evenly.

Chervil

Chervil's flavor falls somewhere between tarragon and parsley, and it sprouts in spring just in time to season peas and new potatoes. Pretty white flowers follow the flush of ferny leaves and provide an early source of nectar to pollinators. The plants completely dry up and disappear during the heat of summer, but they self-sow readily, and a new crop emerges in autumn all on its own. Chervil is one of the most overlooked and underutilized herbs, but it is absolutely worth growing. I sow it anywhere I notice a bare spot, and it is a staple in my kitchen because its mild anise flavor adds a bright, unexpected dimension to salads, vinaigrettes, roasted vegetables, soups, and egg dishes.

Planting

Chervil's well-behaved, low-growth habit makes it an excellent candidate for undersowing larger plants like broccoli. When sown under taller plants, fast-growing chervil covers the ground and acts as a living mulch, plus it adapts to a variety of soil conditions. It performs best when planted in partial shade in warm climates. Long days and warm weather encourage chervil to bolt, so begin sowing it in late winter or early spring, as soon as the soil becomes workable and warms up to 45 degrees F. Chervil's small seeds need exposure to light to germinate. Sow the seeds 1 inch apart in all directions and water them in with a stream from a watering can. This helps settle the seeds into the soil without completely burying them. Cover them with a very fine scrim of potting soil before watering them in again.

Expect chervil to germinate in 10 to 14 days. Plant four successive crops two weeks apart to ensure a steady supply. Chervil also grows well from seedlings. Like basil, the seedlings are often sold as a clump in a small container. Be sure to separate the individual plants (see page 13) before planting them 6 inches apart. Sow fall crops or plant seedlings beginning about four weeks before the first frost. Chervil often grows through the winter down to USDA zone 7.

Growing

Weeds quickly overwhelm dainty chervil. Scuffle a stirrup hoe around the plants once a week to keep down weeds. Thin the seedlings to 6 inches apart when they grow large enough to handle. Water whenever the soil dries down to the top of your first knuckle. Foliar-feed with diluted liquid organic fertilizer three weeks after the chervil germinates. When chervil bolts, it produces a seed stalk that grows up to 2 feet tall; allow plants to flower and drop seed to the ground before pulling them from the garden.

Harvesting

Begin harvesting the lacy green leaves when the stems reach about 3 inches tall. Harvest from the outside in, using scissors to cut back the stems as close to the plant's base as possible. Aim to harvest before the plant bolts or develops overmature, mauve-colored leaves. Cut the flowers just as they open to use as a garnish or salad addition.

Storing

Store this very perishable herb as you would arugula (see page 87). Keep it in the refrigerator crisper drawer for three to five days.

Cooking Ideas

Chervil's delicate flavor gets lost when cooked, so finely chop the leaves and sprinkle them over food just before serving. Chervil is a classic ingredient of fines herbes, a traditional French mix of finely chopped chervil, parsley, tarragon, and chives that is used to flavor everything from roasted chicken to grilled fish. Mash potatoes with parsnips or celery root, butter, milk, chervil, a bit of horseradish, and freshly ground pepper. Roast whole carrots and wedges of red onion in olive oil and garnish with chervil. Make a compound butter with chervil and garlic (see page 57 for technique) and slice it into thin coins to float on soup or melt over vegetables. Mix chervil into sour cream and swirl into soups and stews. Make a tuna salad with lemon zest, chopped chervil, capers, and a bit of garlic mayonnaise. Add whole chervil leaves to salad mixes. Whisk chopped chervil into white wine vinaigrettes.

Delicious Varieties

'Brussels Winter'. 60 days. This cultivar produces mounds of finely lobed leaves. Slow to bolt and quite cold tolerant. Open-pollinated.

|||||||||||||||||||||||||||||||||||||||||| **CHERVIL** ||||||||||||||||||||||||||||||||||||||||||

Anthriscus cerefolium

PLANT FAMILY: Apiaceae (Umbelliferae)

EDIBLE PARTS: Leaves, flowers

POTENTIAL PROBLEMS: Chervil rarely suffers problems with pests or disease.

||||||||||||||||||||||||||||||||||||||||||||||||||||||||||||||||||||||||||||||||||||||||||||||||||||||||||||

Cheesy Eggs with Chervil

8 large eggs

¼ cup crème fraîche or sour cream

½ cup finely grated Parmesan (about 1 ounce)

2 tablespoons butter

2 teaspoons finely minced chervil (or a mix of finely minced chervil, parsley, and thyme)

Salt

Freshly ground pepper

Butter, crème fraîche, and cheese all make eggs taste delicious, but for the best flavor and color, try to track down eggs from pasture-raised or backyard hens for this recipe. Prevent the scrambled eggs from sticking—and ensure a soft, creamy texture—by cooking them in a well-seasoned cast-iron skillet over low heat. Don't be tempted to cook the eggs on medium or medium-high heat. I like to serve them on thick slices of toasted bread.

Crack the eggs into a large mixing bowl and whisk until the yolks and whites are well combined. Thoroughly whisk in the crème fraîche and Parmesan.

Heat a large cast-iron or nonstick skillet over medium-low heat. Add the butter and swirl it around the pan as it melts, coating the sides. When the butter begins to foam, pour in the egg mixture. Immediately begin stirring the eggs with a spoon or spatula, scraping the pan's edges.

When the spoon begins to leave a trail in the pan, about 1 minute, remove the pan from the heat and continue stirring vigorously for about 30 seconds. (This helps prevent the eggs from sticking and encourages big curds to develop.) Place the pan back over the heat and continue stirring, lifting the eggs from the bottom and folding them over as they thicken. Continue cooking until the eggs develop a soft, pillowy texture and are moist but not raw, about 2 minutes. Fold the chervil into the eggs. Remove from the heat and season to taste with salt and pepper. Serve immediately.

Chives

Spotting chive shoots pushing through the soil in early spring always cheers me up. The slender, grassy-green leaves emerge when the soil begins to warm, signaling the beginning of the spring planting season. I grow regular chives (*Allium schoenoprasum*), which produce adorable purple pom-pom flowers and hollow leaves with a mild onion flavor, and flat-leafed garlic chives (*Allium tuberosum*), for their pronounced garlic flavor and spicy white flowers.

Planting

Choose a site in full sun or light shade with well-drained, damp soil. Grow chives from nursery-grown seedlings or divisions made from established clumps. Plant these members of the onion family in spring when the soil becomes dry enough to work. Space them 8 to 10 inches apart. Chives look particularly pretty when planted en masse as a border or under tall roses with perennials such as catmint or geranium.

Growing

Both chives and garlic chives grow to about 1 foot tall and die back after frost. Keep the plants healthy by top-dressing around them with 2 inches of compost in spring and fall. Note: Grass is difficult to distinguish from chive leaves and nearly impossible to remove once it invades a chive clump. Hand-pull grass and other weeds regularly and mulch with a 2-inch layer of grass clippings to prevent their invasion. Water whenever the soil dries down to the bottom of your second knuckle. Both types of chives benefit from dividing every three years, or when leaf production slows. In early fall, cut all the foliage back to 2 inches and dig up the chive clump. Tease the plant apart into smaller sections and remove any intertwined grass or weeds. Replant clumps of 10 chive bulbs and 6-inch sections of garlic chive rhizome, which often has bulbs attached.

In Asia, blanched garlic chives (which have been denied light while growing) are quite popular. To blanch garlic chives, shear a clump down to 1 inch and place a black plastic pot over it. The new growth that emerges over the next two to three weeks will be pale yellow and exceptionally tender. After harvesting the blanched leaves, allow the chives to regrow with full sun exposure.

Harvesting

The leaves, buds, and flowers of both chives and garlic chives are all edible. Begin harvesting leaves in spring when they reach 6 inches tall. Frequent harvesting encourages the plant to send up new shoots, which have a more tender texture and subtler flavor than older leaves. Grasp a small section from the outside of the clump with one hand and cut it off at ground level. For large harvests, or to revive clumps when they flop over in midsummer,

tie a piece of twine around all the leaves before shearing the whole clump down to 2 inches with a sharp pair of scissors. Pour 1 cup of diluted liquid organic fertilizer over the clump after shearing it back. A second crop of tender leaves will appear within a few weeks. Always cut off the flowers of both types at the bud stage or just after they open to prevent rampant self-sowing.

Storing

Store chives and their blossoms as you would arugula (see page 87) for up to one week in your refrigerator crisper drawer. Freeze chives as directed on page 35.

Cooking Ideas

Thinly slice chives and garlic chives or use scissors to snip the leaves into small pieces. Mix the chives into creamy dressings, mayonnaise, butter, or scrambled eggs. Use flower buds whole in stir-fries, or pull the individual florets of the flowers apart and use in egg and potato dishes, dressings, and salads. Infuse vinegar with chive blossoms—it results in a delicious-tasting vinegar with a pale pink color (see page 78 for the technique).

||||||||||||||||||| CHIVES AND GARLIC CHIVES |||||||||||||||||||

Allium schoenoprasum and *Allium tuberosum*

PLANT FAMILY: Alliaceae (Liliaceae)

EDIBLE PARTS: Leaves, flowers

POTENTIAL PROBLEMS: Chives rarely suffer problems with pests or disease.

Steak Sandwiches with Gorgonzola Chive Sauce and Caramelized Onions

2 tablespoons butter, divided

1 large onion, thinly sliced

Salt

1 scant tablespoon flour

½ cup half-and-half

2 tablespoons white wine

⅓ cup crumbled Gorgonzola (about 2 ounces)

½ cup finely snipped chives

1 tablespoon vegetable or canola oil

Four 6-ounce hanger steaks (or other preferred cut), sliced into 2-inch-wide strips

Freshly ground pepper

4 French rolls

My friends Jesse and Kari use their weekly trip to the farmers' market as a jumping-off point for creating inventive, delicious dishes. They kindly shared their recipe for a decadent blue cheese–chive sauce with me. The tangy, creamy sauce pairs perfectly with sweet caramelized onions and savory steak.

. . . .

Melt 1 tablespoon of the butter over medium-high heat in a heavy-bottomed cast-iron skillet. Add the onions, sprinkle with salt, and toss to coat. After about 1 minute, when the onions begin to sweat, reduce the heat to medium-low. Partially cover the skillet and let the onions cook, stirring occasionally, until very soft and caramel colored, about 40 minutes.

Meanwhile, melt the remaining butter in a small saucepan over low heat. Whisk in the flour; stir frequently for 1 minute. Add the half-and-half and wine. Continue stirring until the sauce just begins to thicken, 1½ to 2 minutes. Stir in the Gorgonzola. When the cheese fully melts, add the chives and cook, stirring frequently, until the sauce coats the back of a spoon, 30 seconds to 1 minute. (If the sauce becomes too thick, add a small amount of half-and-half or wine to thin.) Keep the sauce warm over low heat, stirring occasionally.

When the onions are done, remove from the heat and set aside. Wipe the skillet, return it to the stove, and heat the oil over medium-high heat. Generously season the steak with salt and pepper. Place the meat in the skillet, turning when nicely browned. When the slices are browned on both sides and pink in the middle, about 8 minutes, remove from the heat and slice crosswise into ½-inch pieces.

Cut the rolls lengthwise three-quarters through, making sure to leave a "hinge" (this prevents the sandwich filling from slipping out). Scoop out some bread from the top half of the roll to make room for more filling. For each sandwich, layer steak onto the roll, top with a quarter of the caramelized onions, and drizzle with Gorgonzola sauce.

Cilantro/Coriander

Cilantro divides people into two camps: those who like its distinctive taste and those who do not. Whichever group you fall into, this bright-green herb is worth growing for its seeds, which are the spice coriander. The coriander seeds form after the cilantro sends up its pretty white flowers, which provide an early source of nectar for pollinators and beneficial insects. You can harvest the seeds when they are fresh and green or dry and brown—either way they have a bright, citrusy flavor that tastes nothing like the leaves.

Planting

Cilantro grows about 10 to 12 inches tall, but the coriander seed stalks can reach 3 feet high. Choose a site in full sun that will accommodate the height of the plant as it grows. Scratch granular organic fertilizer into the soil before sowing (follow the label's recommended application rate). Direct-sow anytime after the soil reaches 50 degrees F and is workable. Sow the round seeds ½ inch deep and 2 inches apart. Keep the soil consistently moist until seedlings appear, which can take almost a month.

Cilantro belongs in salsa but often bolts before tomatoes and peppers ripen. Ensure a consistent supply of leaves by making successive sowings every two weeks through early fall. To delay bolting during the summer months, grow cilantro in a spot that stays damp and gets afternoon shade, such as underneath tomato plants. Skip starting seeds indoors or buying cilantro seedlings, because they tend to bolt prematurely.

Growing

Thin cilantro to 4 inches when the seedlings develop their first set of true leaves. Water whenever the soil dries down to the top of your first knuckle and mulch with 2 inches of grass clippings. Foliar-feed every three weeks until the plants go to seed; after a large harvest of leaves, pour ½ cup of diluted liquid organic fertilizer around each plant. Long days, heat, and dry soil trigger cilantro to bolt. When this happens, the center of the plant stretches skyward, and the round, lobed leaves become feathery. The stalks are topped with umbrella-shaped clusters of white flowers. I often plant cilantro near my cucumbers, melons, and squash and allow it to flower, as the blossoms attract pollinators that then also visit the cucurbits.

Harvesting

Begin harvesting individual stems when the plant reaches 4 inches. Cut them off where they connect with the plant's main stalk. Or, when the plant grows more than 8 inches tall, grasp all the leaves in one hand and cut them off 2 inches from the soil line—new growth will soon emerge from the center of the plant. Stop harvesting leaves when the plant bolts, because the feathery foliage develops an unappetizing soapy flavor.

Clip off cilantro flowers just after they open. Allow some flowers to remain, because after they fade a most delicious treat forms: citrusy green coriander seeds (see photo on page 33). To harvest, clip the seed head just after it forms, when the seeds are green and shiny, and pull off the individual seeds. For the more mellow, mature coriander seeds, wait to cut the seed heads until three-quarters of the seeds turn light brown; then hang the seed heads upside down in a paper bag until the seeds drop to the bottom. One plant yields a few tablespoons of seeds. Allow some mature coriander seeds to drop to the ground and self-sow. These seeds will germinate all on their own in the fall or the following spring. Self-sown seedlings transplant well if dug up and replanted when they have one or two sets of true leaves.

Storing

Store cilantro as you would arugula (see page 87). Wash and spin it dry just before use. Store fresh green coriander seeds in a small, lidded container in the refrigerator for two weeks or in the freezer for one year. Keep dry, ripe seeds in a lidded glass jar in a cool, dry place; use within one year.

Cooking Ideas

Muddle 2 ounces of gin with cucumber, cilantro, and a chopped hot chile; strain and serve with soda water over ice. Substitute cilantro for basil and toasted squash seeds for pine nuts in pesto recipes. Add cilantro in place of parsley in a chimichurri sauce and drizzle it over steak sandwiches, rice, or eggs. Mix minced red onion, diced avocado and tomato, fresh corn kernels, cilantro, and lime juice and serve with tacos. Use whole flowers as a garnish, or pull them apart and sprinkle over salads. Crush green coriander seeds with the flat edge of a knife and add to marinades, poultry brines, and salad dressings. My friend David Perry stuffs five or six green coriander seed heads into a fifth of vodka and allows them to infuse for six weeks. The coriander-flavored liquor makes excellent vodka-tonics. Add ½ teaspoon of ground mature coriander seeds to recipes that call for cumin, as the flavors complement each other.

Delicious Varieties

'Calypso'. 50 days. Very slow to bolt, even in hot weather, making it an excellent choice for leaf production and in climates with warm summers. Open-pollinated.

'Delfino'. 50 days. Features very pretty, feathery bluish-green dill-like leaves that have a pronounced cilantro flavor. Fairly heat-tolerant. 'Confetti' has similar leaves, but with a milder taste.

CILANTRO/CORIANDER

Coriandrum sativum

PLANT FAMILY: Apiaceae (Umbelliferae)

EDIBLE PARTS: Leaves, flowers, green and ripe seeds

POTENTIAL PROBLEMS: Powdery mildew

Green Coriander–Marinated Chicken

Four 8-ounce boneless, skinless chicken breasts

3 tablespoons green coriander seeds

1 garlic clove, minced

1 hot chile, such as serrano, seeded and minced

1 teaspoon lemon zest

2 tablespoons white wine vinegar

¼ cup extra-virgin olive oil

This chicken is full of citrusy flavor, thanks to the addition of green coriander seeds to its marinade. Either fresh or frozen green coriander will work well in this recipe. Toss together a simple salad as the chicken broils (or grills), and serve it with wedges of warm pita bread on the side.

Rinse the chicken breasts under cool water; pat dry with a paper towel.

Crush the coriander seeds with the back of a knife and place in a resealable plastic bag, along with the garlic, chile, lemon zest, vinegar, and oil. Seal the bag and shake until the marinade is well combined.

Open the bag, slide in the chicken breasts, seal the bag again, and shake until the chicken is well coated. Marinate for 1 hour at room temperature, shaking and turning the bag occasionally.

Preheat the broiler and position an oven rack 4 inches beneath it. Line a rimmed baking sheet with aluminum foil. Remove the chicken breasts from the marinade and place them smooth side down on the baking sheet. Broil until lightly browned, about 4 minutes. Flip the chicken over and broil until lightly browned and cooked through, another 3 to 4 minutes (thicker breasts may take 5 to 6 minutes). Remove the chicken from the oven and allow to rest for 5 minutes before serving.

Dill

I grow dill for its finely textured leaves, flavorful seeds, and bright-yellow flowers, all of which play a role in flavoring dill pickles. This versatile herb looks cheerful when planted behind zinnias, short orange cosmos, and annual coreopsis. The flowers disguise the herb's lanky stems and, along with the dill's blossoms, attract parasitic wasps and other pollinators to the garden.

Planting

Long days and warm weather trigger dill to flower and set seed. To ensure a balance of both seeds and leaves (which are also called dill weed), begin direct-sowing in early spring as soon as the soil can be worked and after nighttime temperatures stay above 30 degrees F. Keep sowing a small amount every three weeks through early fall, as dill handles light frost. Sow the seeds 2 inches apart and ¼ inch deep in a site with full sun and well-drained soil. Keep the soil moist until the seedlings appear, usually within 7 to 14 days. Dill seedlings grow best when set out small (two sets of leaves or about 3 inches tall) and tend to be less tolerant of drought than plants grown from seed. Sow dill in bare spots to fill in perennial borders or between rows of lettuce. Grow the short variety 'Fernleaf' in front of pea and pole bean trellises.

Growing

Dill grows 1½ to 3 feet tall, and statuesque varieties, such as 'Mammoth', may need to be staked in windy areas. Irrigate the plants when the soil dries down to the top of your first knuckle. When the seedlings are a few inches tall, thin them to clusters of two or three plants, spacing the clusters 4 inches apart. Place a 3-inch layer of mulch around the plants to conserve soil moisture and reduce competition from weeds. Foliar-feed with diluted liquid organic fertilizer every three weeks. In late summer, allow a couple of flowers to set seed and self-sow for an early crop of dill the following spring.

Harvesting

Dill leaves may be harvested at any time: simply cut back a stem to the main stalk. For pickling, cut flowers when three-quarters of the head turns fully yellow, along with 3 inches of stem and any attendant leaves. Add the flowers to the canning jars along with the vegetables and brine. Harvest the seeds just as they begin to turn brown; use the same technique as for coriander (see page 51). One plant yields ⅔ cup seeds or more.

Storing

Store fresh dill leaves in a perforated plastic bag zipped three-quarters of the way shut. Refrigerate in the crisper drawer for one week. Wash and spin the leaves dry right before use, or freeze them (see page 35). Dill flowers stay fresh for a couple of days when kept in a jar of water placed out of direct sunlight. Store the seeds in a glass jar in a cool, dry place for up to one year.

Cooking Ideas

Mix a bit of chopped dill with some sour cream; place a dollop of this mixture on a good cracker along with a sliver of smoked salmon for a simple appetizer. Sauté spring vegetables, including peas, asparagus, and radishes, in a bit of olive oil until tender and top with chopped dill and a squeeze of fresh lemon juice. Make a salad with cooked lentils and rice, and flavor it with olive oil, crumbled sheep's milk feta, toasted pine nuts, lemon zest, and finely chopped dill and spearmint. Add a few teaspoons of dill seeds to your favorite dinner roll dough.

Delicious Varieties

'Bouquet'. 40 to 55 days. A perfect choice for pickling, this variety produces large flowers and seed heads earlier in the season. Grows to 3 feet tall. Open-pollinated.

'Dukat'. 40 to 55 days. This bolt-resistant variety grows 2 feet tall and yields loads of leaves before flowering. Open-pollinated. Grow the petite variety 'Fernleaf', which tops out at 1½ feet, in containers.

|||||||||||||||||||||||||||||||||||||||||||| **DILL** ||||||||||||||||||||||||||||||||

Anethum graveolens

PLANT FAMILY: Apiaceae (Umbelliferae)

EDIBLE PARTS: Leaves, flowers, seeds

POTENTIAL PROBLEMS: Aphids

||||||||||||||||||||||||||||||||||||||||||||||||||||||||||||||||||||||||||||||||||||||||||||||||||||

Dill Compound Butter

¼ pound (1 stick) unsalted butter, at room temperature

2 tablespoons finely chopped dill

2 tablespoons finely chopped flat-leaf parsley

1 tablespoon finely snipped chives

½ teaspoon lemon zest

1 teaspoon finely chopped shallot

Pinch of salt

A compound butter is simply softened butter that has been mixed with herbs, herb blossoms, spices, mustard, citrus zest, anchovies, or other flavorings. You can make sweet versions (think cinnamon, vanilla bean, and honey) or a savory version like this one, which tastes delicious melted over grilled fish or boiled new potatoes. Adding herbs to compound butter and freezing it is an especially wonderful way to preserve their flavor for the winter.

Place all the ingredients in the bowl of a stand mixer fitted with a paddle attachment, or use a hand mixer. Blend until the herbs are evenly distributed throughout the butter.

Tear off a 12-inch piece of waxed paper. Scrape the dill butter out of the bowl onto the middle of the paper. Fold one edge of the paper over the butter and roll the butter into a log shape. Wrap in the waxed paper and chill until firm, about 2 hours. Then wrap the log tightly in plastic wrap. It will keep, refrigerated, for a week, and frozen for 6 months or more.

Fennel

Fennel is a delightfully multipurpose edible: various parts of the plant are used as a vegetable, an herb, and a spice, and it tastes at home in both savory and sweet dishes. I grow two types: bronze fennel (*Foeniculum vulgare* var. *vulgare* 'Rubrum') and Florence fennel (*Foeniculum vulgare* var. *azoricum*). Bronze fennel grows to nearly 6 feet tall and produces canary-yellow flowers and loads of leaves, pollen, and seeds. Florence fennel produces a tender, bulbous white base topped with a fountain of green, ferny foliage. I like to plant Florence fennel in neat rows in front of a trellis of sweet peas in spring, and I use bronze fennel to add height and texture in vegetable beds and flower borders.

Planting

Florence fennel grows best in the sweet spot on either side of summer when daytime temperatures hover in the 60s and 70s; grow it as an annual. Bronze fennel survives the winter in USDA zones 7 and higher and may be grown as an annual in colder zones. Scratch alfalfa meal into the soil prior to planting (follow the label's recommended application rate). Sow Florence fennel seeds or set out seedlings after the last spring frost when the soil reaches 50 degrees F and again every other week for four to six weeks. Resume sowing eight to ten weeks before the first fall frost in zones 7 and warmer. Sow or plant bronze fennel once in spring. Expect the seeds to germinate within three weeks; plant seedlings when growing it as an annual.

Sow the seeds of both fennel types in rows ½ inch deep and 1 inch apart in a spot with full sun and moist, loose, well-drained soil. Fennel seedlings are often sold as a clump in a small pot. Separate the seedlings before planting, as you would with basil (see page 37). Set seedlings out when they have just two sets of leaves: any larger and Florence fennel plants tend to bolt before developing a bulb. Space Florence fennel seedlings 10 inches apart and bronze fennel 16 to 18 inches apart.

Growing

Florence fennel bolts with the slightest provocation. Root disturbance, crowding, drought, and heat all encourage the plant to stretch its center toward the sky, creating a woody stalk that ruins the succulent bulbous base. To prevent this, grow heat-resistant varieties and thin the plants to 10 inches apart when they grow to 2 inches tall; thin bronze fennel to 16 inches apart. When the "bulb" (which is really thickened leaf bases, not a true bulb) grows to the size of a large egg, mound soil up around it to blanch the stalks and keep them tender. Mulch with 2 inches of grass clippings, and water whenever the soil dries down to the top of your first knuckle. Hand-pull weeds regularly and foliar-feed every three weeks.

Harvesting

Snip off the anise-flavored leaves as needed once the plant develops a fairly full top. Harvest Florence fennel bulbs when they grow to 4 to 6 inches across, or sooner if you suspect the plant may bolt; either pull up the plant or slide a sharp knife just under the soil line and sever the bulb from its roots. Cut fennel flowers off the plant just after they open.

Citron-colored fennel pollen has a sweet, extraordinarily mild anise flavor and is a wonderfully rare spice. Bronze fennel tends to make more pollen and seeds than Florence fennel. To harvest the pollen, pick 20 to 30 flower heads just after they open. Hang them upside down in a large paper bag in a warm, dry spot for two weeks. Shake the bag daily to release the pollen from the drying flowers. For fennel seeds, allow the seed heads to remain on the plant until they turn a uniform tan color and the stalk begins to yellow. Then harvest in the same manner as coriander (see page 51).

NOTE: Fennel can be weedy or invasive in some climates; do not allow the plants to set seed in these areas. Harvesting all the flowers for fennel pollen fully utilizes the plant and prevents it from self-sowing and becoming a problem.

Storing

Store fennel leaves and flowers as you would arugula (see page 87). Store fennel pollen and seeds in separate lidded glass jars in a cool, dark place; use within one year.

Cooking Ideas

Layer lemon slices and fennel fronds over fish fillets and grill or bake. Place ½ cup leaves in a pitcher of water; chill in the refrigerator overnight and strain before drinking. Pull apart the flower heads' individual florets and sprinkle them over the top of salads and vegetable dishes. Sprinkle fennel pollen over buttered pasta. Rub fennel pollen on chicken and pork before roasting, or dust it over fromage blanc and serve with crackers. Substitute fennel bulbs for celery in recipes. Add fennel seeds to sausage recipes, or sprinkle them over the top of scones or bread before baking.

Delicious Varieties

'Perfection'. 80 to 85 days. Produces very large bulbs that stay tender at 6 and even 8 inches across. Grows up to 2 feet tall and produces abundant fronds. Bolt resistance makes it good for both spring and fall plantings. Open-pollinated.

ⅢⅢⅢ FLORENCE FENNEL AND BRONZE FENNEL ⅢⅢⅢ

Foeniculum vulgare var. *azoricum* and *Foeniculum vulgare* var. *vulgare* 'Rubrum'

PLANT FAMILY: Apiaceae (Umbelliferae)

EDIBLE PARTS: Bulbous fleshy stems, leaves, flowers, pollen, seeds

POTENTIAL PROBLEMS: Aphids

Fennel, Potato, and Apple Gratin

FOR BREAD CRUMB TOPPING:

3 tablespoons butter, melted

¾ cup panko (Japanese bread crumbs)

FOR GRATIN:

1 medium fennel bulb (about 1 pound)

2 tablespoons butter

½ large yellow onion (about 8 ounces), thinly sliced

1 large Granny Smith apple (about 12 ounces), peeled, cored, quartered, and very thinly sliced

1 large russet potato (about 1 pound), peeled and very thinly sliced

1½ cups grated Gruyère (about 6 ounces)

1 cup heavy cream

1 teaspoon minced thyme

¼ teaspoon freshly ground pepper

True comfort food, this rich gratin is the perfect dish for warming up a cool fall evening. The apples and fennel provide just a hint of sweetness. Serve it with a roast chicken and braised Swiss chard.

Preheat the oven to 375 degrees F.

To make the bread crumb topping, pour the butter over the panko, stir to coat, and set aside.

To make the gratin, remove the leaf stalks and roots from the fennel. Slice the bulb in half lengthwise and cut out the core. With a knife or mandoline, slice the bulb thinly crosswise. Melt the butter over medium heat in a large heatproof skillet, preferably cast-iron. Add the fennel and onion and sauté until tender, about 10 minutes.

In a large mixing bowl, combine the cooked fennel and onion, apple, potato, Gruyère, cream, thyme, and pepper.

Pour the vegetables back into skillet (or into a greased 6- to 8-cup baking dish) and pack them down. Sprinkle the panko mixture evenly over the top. Cover with aluminum foil and bake for 30 minutes. Remove the foil and continue baking until the potatoes are tender and the panko is toasted, about 15 minutes more.

Mint

I plant spearmint (*Mentha spicata*) near my back door so I can run my hand past its fragrant leaves when I walk by. This mint belongs on the list of essential culinary herbs because its intensely aromatic leaves taste equally good in sweet and savory dishes. But beware: planting spearmint opens the door to wanting to grow and cook with orange, bergamot, grapefruit, and apple mints, and, of course, peppermint.

Planting

Mint grows lustily—spreading from a network of rhizomes. Always plant mint in a container, unless you want it to thoroughly fill in an area and crowd out other plants. I grow it in the ground but contain its roots within a submerged pot. To do so, use a 5-gallon plastic or terra-cotta container. Cut out two squares of nylon window screening slightly larger than the pot's mouth. Overlap the squares in the bottom of the pot, completely covering the drainage holes. Fill the pot to within 2 inches of the rim with a mix of one part compost to five parts garden soil. Plant the mint in the center of the pot. Bury the pot in the garden, leaving 1 inch of its rim above the soil line. Place woody mulch or compost around the pot to disguise it. Mint grows in sun or part shade and may be set out in the garden anytime during spring or summer, but it performs best when planted early, as soon as the soil warms up to about 55 degrees F. Mint can be grown from seedlings purchased at a nursery, divisions, or cuttings (see page 37).

Growing

Top-dress around the plants with 2 inches of compost in early spring, and water whenever the soil dries down to your first knuckle. Monitor mint throughout the summer and clip off any rhizomes that try to sneak over the edge of the pot. Mint ends up looking a bit rangy and spindly if left unpruned: keep the plants bushy and neat by cutting them back by half in early summer when they form flower buds and again in late summer. Cut the stems off at the soil line in fall before the first frost. After any of these maintenance prunings, you can dry the leaves for later use.

Container plants, both above- and inground, need dividing after one or two growing seasons, because they become quite root bound. In spring, just as the mint begins to emerge, run a sharp knife around the edge of the pot to loosen the root ball. Pull out the mint and divide it into quarters, making sure to untangle the roots of each division. Before refreshing the pot with new soil and compost and replanting the divisions, double-check that the screening is still in place in the bottom of the pot and in good shape.

Harvesting

Wait to make a large harvest until the mint forms flower buds, because the aromatic oil concentration in the leaves is highest at this stage of growth. The stems can be quite tough, so use sharp scissors and make the cut right above a set of leaves. Cut back no more than two-thirds of each stem at one time. Otherwise, cut off the top two or three sets of leaves of a stem as needed. Cut mint flowers just as they open and use them as a garnish.

Storing

Store fresh mint leaves in a partially closed plastic bag in the refrigerator for 7 to 10 days. Dry or freeze the leaves (see page 35).

Cooking Ideas

Fresh mint makes summer cocktail season infinitely better: think mojitos, mint juleps, and mai tais. Crush fresh orange mint leaves and stir them into lemonade. Grill zucchini and top with crumbled feta and chopped spearmint. Infuse milk with peppermint and use it to make ice cream. Use fresh or dry mint to flavor tabbouleh (see recipe on page 71) and other whole-grain salads. Make a dip for crudités by mixing Greek yogurt, minced garlic, chopped cucumber, olive oil, and a bit of minced mint, parsley, and chives.

Delicious Varieties

Orange mint (*Mentha aquatica* 'Citrata'). A lovely lower-growing mint with citrus undertones. Also known as bergamot mint. Hardy to zone 4.

Peppermint (*Mentha × piperita*). For a classic candy-cane taste, you can't beat peppermint. Pretty dark-green leaves and blackish stems. Grows up to 3 feet tall.

Spearmint (*Mentha spicata*). With wrinkled, light-green leaves and an upright habit, this is the mint to plant if you have room for only one type.

||||||||||||||||||||||||||||||||||||||||||||| **MINT** |||||||||||||||||||||||||||||||||||||||||||||

Mentha spp.
PLANT FAMILY: Lamiaceae
EDIBLE PARTS: Leaves, flowers
POTENTIAL PROBLEMS: Verticillium wilt

|||||||||||||||||||||||||||||||||||||||||||||||||||||||||||||||||||||||||||||||||||||||||||||||||||||||||

Lemon Verbena–Mint Tisane

2 tablespoons fresh mint leaves per cup of water

1 tablespoon fresh lemon verbena leaves per cup of water

Water (1 to 2 cups per person)

Several years ago I had the opportunity to tour the production garden at The Herbfarm, a five-star restaurant located in Woodinville, Washington. At the end of the visit, the head farmer turned our group into the field and instructed us to pick herbs for our own custom *tisane*: boiling water infused with the flavor from herbs. I chose a mix of different mints and lemon verbena, and this delicious blend has been a favorite ever since. Lemon verbena's bright, citrusy flavor pairs particularly well with orange mint and spearmint. All mints work as a wonderful natural digestive aid, and I often drink this blend—or a plain peppermint tisane—after dinner or to relieve an upset tummy.

Place the mint and lemon verbena in a teapot. Bring a kettle of fresh, cold water to a boil. Pour the boiling water over the herbs and allow them to steep for 8 minutes. Strain the tea through a fine-mesh sieve before serving.

HERBAL TISANES

Both fresh and dried herbs make excellent tisanes. When hosting a brunch, take a cue from The Herbfarm and let your guests loose in the garden to harvest and create their own custom blend (use 2 to 3 tablespoons fresh herbs per cup of water). Harvest and dry herbs throughout the summer and then make packets of homegrown herbal tea to give as gifts during the winter (use 1 tablespoon dried herbs per 2 cups of water). Here are a few of my favorite herbal tea blends, all of which taste delicious when brewed with fresh or dried herbs and sweetened with honey or agave syrup:

Anise hyssop

Chamomile blossoms, lavender, and rose petals

Chocolate mint and dried orange peel

Plain mint (try peppermint, apple mint, and orange mint)

Rosemary and slices of fresh lemon

Spearmint and chamomile blossoms

Oregano and Marjoram

Oregano and marjoram are cousins—both of these essential culinary herbs belong to the large genus *Origanum*. Many plants in this group have little or no culinary value, and nurseries commonly mislabel oreganos and marjorams and sell ornamental types with the culinary ones. Before I purchase a new plant, I always nibble on a leaf to make sure its flavor suits my palate. While the flavors of edible marjorams and oreganos differ, they all share a woodsy tone that complements roasted meat, tomatoes, peppers, and cheese.

Planting

Grow oregano and marjoram from nursery starts or from divisions of established plants, as plants grown from seed produce variable results. *Origanum* plants grow best when planted in full sun and in soil that drains quickly. Plant anytime after the last spring frost, spacing the plants 6 to 10 inches apart in the garden. In USDA zones 7 and cooler, plant *Origanum* plants in a terra-cotta container that can be brought indoors for the winter. Choose a container size that is double the diameter of the plant's root ball and has drainage holes. Plant marjoram and Italian oregano as a carpet under roses or espaliered fruit trees or in a border with drought-tolerant herbs and perennials such as santolina, rudbeckia, and ornamental salvias.

Growing

After planting, pinch back the top inch of each stem to increase branching. All oreganos and marjorams grow best in dry, extremely well-draining soil; once established in the garden, *Origanum* plants require little supplemental water. Keep the soil moist until the plants double in size; after that you can wait to irrigate until the soil dries down to the base of your second knuckle. Place a 1-inch layer of gravel mulch around the plants' base to encourage good drainage and prevent fungal disease problems. Care for potted plants as you would rosemary (see page 72). Foliar-feed container plants every other week and garden plants once a month.

Origanum plants grow rapidly in hot weather and look rather disheveled if left unpruned. In late spring, cut out any dead stems and prune each plant back by a third, aiming for a gently rounded shape; repeat in summer when flower buds form. Cut the plant back to 6 inches above the ground in fall. Either dry the harvest of leaves that results from this maintenance pruning or compost them.

Divide potted and inground plants annually to prevent them from dying out in the middle. Dig up the plants and use a sharp knife to cut out any dead or especially woody growth. Divide the plant into 4-inch-wide, healthy sections and then replant. Like thyme, *Origanum* plants can also be propagated by layering (see page 79).

Harvesting

Use scissors to clip off 3- to 6-inch-long sections of individual stems as needed. Cut the plant back by a third to a half just after the flower buds form in summer; dry the leaves. When harvesting or performing maintenance pruning, always pinch or cut right above a set of leaves. *Origanum* flowers are best used as a garnish.

Storing

Store fresh oregano and marjoram as you would rosemary (see page 73). Dry the leaves for winter use (see page 35).

Cooking Ideas

Mince marjoram, add to toasted bread crumbs, and sprinkle them over buttered spaghetti. Slide slices of lemon and sprigs of oregano or marjoram under the skin of a chicken before roasting. Sauté halved cherry tomatoes, garlic, and a few teaspoons of oregano or marjoram until soft; serve over grilled fish. Roast sweet or semihot peppers, such as 'Beaver Dam', and marinate in oil, red wine vinegar, and marjoram; serve with warm chèvre and baguette slices.

Delicious Varieties

Italian oregano, or hardy marjoram (*O. × majoricum*). This tender herb survives winters down to USDA zone 7. It features large, soft leaves with a mild woodsy flavor and is often mislabeled as sweet marjoram.

Oregano (*O. vulgare*). The most popular type of *O. vulgare* is Greek oregano (*O. vulgare* subsp. *hirtum*), which is hardy to USDA zone 6 and lends an intense, spicy flavor to food. Plants labeled as oregano can range in flavor from mild to harsh, and some cultivars, including the popular golden oregano 'Aureum', have little culinary value.

Sweet marjoram (*O. majorana*). Sweet marjoram has soft, gray-green leaves and a mild sweet-spicy aroma. This tender perennial grows best as an annual in most parts of the United States, as it is only hardy down to USDA zone 9.

|||||||||||||||||||| **OREGANO AND MARJORAM** ||||||||||||||||||

Origanum spp.

PLANT FAMILY: Lamiaceae

EDIBLE PARTS: Leaves, flowers

POTENTIAL PROBLEMS: Oregano and marjoram rarely suffer problems.

Feta Marinated in Olive Oil with Mediterranean Herbs

MAKES ABOUT 1½ CUPS

10 to 15 fresh herb sprigs

½ pound sheep's milk feta in brine

Red pepper flakes

Freshly ground pepper

½ to ¾ cup extra-virgin olive oil

Feta marinated in herbs and a good-quality olive oil makes for a very simple but seriously delicious appetizer. Highlight a single herb's flavor, such as basil, or mix and match thyme, rosemary, and marjoram or oregano. Serve with bread and crackers, and be sure to include a spoon so you can drizzle extra olive oil over the cheese.

· ·

Wash the herbs, shake off excess water, and trim into 4-inch-long sprigs. Roll the sprigs back and forth between your palms to crush the herbs and release their essential oils.

Drain the feta and cut into ½-inch cubes. Select a medium container that is deeper than it is wide and place a layer of feta on the bottom. Sprinkle with red pepper flakes and a good grind of black pepper, and then cover with 4 to 6 herb sprigs. Repeat until the container is full.

Pour the olive oil over the feta until all but the top layer is completely submerged (the amount of oil needed depends on the container's size and shape).

Set the container aside and let the cheese marinate at room temperature for at least 2 hours, stirring it occasionally. Refrigerate any leftovers and eat within 3 days; allow the cheese to come to room temperature before serving. Use any remaining seasoned olive oil as a dip for bread or to dress a salad or roasted vegetables.

Parsley

Both the curly and the flat-leaf (also known as "Italian") types of parsley look superb planted as an edging around vegetable beds, where they help define borders and provide a visual foil to larger leafy vegetables. Growing big swaths of this nutritious herb makes sense for the kitchen too, because its lush, deep-green leaves enliven the flavor of so many vinaigrettes, salads, sauces, and soups.

Planting

Choose a spot in full sun with moist, well-drained soil. Starting with seedlings results in a faster crop; plant them 10 inches apart and water in with diluted liquid organic fertilizer. Like basil, parsley seedlings are often sold in a clump in a small pot, so be sure to tease apart the individual plants before planting (see page 13). Parsley seeds germinate notoriously slowly and inconsistently. To speed things along, sow the seeds ¼ inch deep and 2 inches apart as soon as the soil reaches 50 degrees F and can be worked in spring. Place a strip of burlap over the seeds and secure it with U-shaped pins in each corner (see page 9). Water the seeds in and keep the burlap moist, which in turn keeps the underlying seeds and soil damp. Check under the burlap each day. As soon as you see green growth, which can take as long as a month, pull back the burlap and expose the little seedlings to sunlight. Make three sowings three weeks apart for a continued harvest.

Growing

Thin the seedlings to 10 inches apart when they reach 2 inches tall. Scuffle the soil around the plants with a stirrup hoe to prevent competition from weeds. Water when the soil dries down to the bottom of your second knuckle. Foliar-feed every three weeks. The chubby black, yellow, and green larvae of black swallowtail butterflies feed on parsley, so it never hurts to sow a few extra plants for them to snack on.

Parsley is a *biennial* (a plant that takes two growing seasons to complete its life cycle). Biennials typically establish their root system and foliage in the first year, surviving the winter to produce flowers and set seed in the second. (Swiss chard and carrots are other common biennials.) Parsley occasionally bolts in its first year if exposed to temperatures below 40 degrees for several weeks. Its beautiful, nectar-rich flowers lure beneficial insects, but the leaves from bolted plants taste harsh. Pull the plants after flowering and compost them.

Harvesting

Wait to begin harvesting until the plant is 6 inches tall and has several stems. Cut individual stems off close to the plant's base, harvesting from the outside in. Or grasp the leaves from an entire plant in one hand and cut all the stems down to 2 inches above the soil line—new leaves will quickly regrow.

Storing

Store parsley in a perforated plastic bag in the refrigerator crisper drawer for up to two weeks. Wash and spin dry right before use. Parsley also freezes well (see page 35). Store parsley root as you would carrots (see page 196).

Cooking Ideas

Blend together 2 cups chopped parsley, one serrano chile, a clove of garlic, and ½ cup olive oil; stir into prepared hummus. Mix a few tablespoons of chopped parsley together with minced garlic, chopped kalamata olives, red pepper flakes, and olive oil; serve as a garnish on potato leek soup. Add whole parsley leaves to salad. Mix together shredded chicken, crumbled Gorgonzola, chopped walnuts, minced parsley, and just enough mayonnaise to bind everything together; stuff the chicken salad into a ciabatta bun drizzled with balsamic vinaigrette. Roast parsley root and mash with potatoes, butter, and caramelized onions or shallots. Purée roasted parsley root with butter, a bit of heavy cream, and chervil; serve with a steak.

PARSLEY ROOT

Hamburg parsley (*Petroselinum crispum* var. *tuberosum*) produces an edible white taproot that resembles a parsnip and has strongly flavored leaves. Sow the seeds for parsley root in late spring and early summer in the same manner as regular parsley; thin to 6 inches apart. Give this root crop the same care you would carrots (see page 195). Harvest when the top of the root is 1½ to 2 inches in diameter.

Delicious Varieties

'Giant Italian'. 85 days. An Italian parsley with exceptional flavor; grows to 2 feet. Use the smaller 'Titan' for edging borders. Open-pollinated.

'Petra'. 85 days. Forms adorable 1-foot mounds. Finely chop the extremely curly, dark-green leaves before using, because they have an unpleasant, rough texture whole. Open-pollinated.

PARSLEY

Petroselinum crispum

PLANT FAMILY: Apiaceae (Umbelliferae)

EDIBLE PARTS: Leaves, root (of Hamburg type)

POTENTIAL PROBLEMS: Aphids, flea beetles

Thérèse Jarjura's Tabbouleh

SERVES 4 AS AN APPETIZER OR SIDE DISH

½ cup coarse bulgur

⅓ cup freshly squeezed lemon juice, including pulp (from 3 small lemons)

3 medium slicing tomatoes, cut into small cubes, with their juice

1½ packed cups finely chopped fresh flat-leaf parsley

6 to 8 spearmint leaves, finely chopped, or 1 teaspoon dried

2 scallions, white and green parts finely chopped (about ½ cup)

½ teaspoon sea salt

¼ teaspoon freshly ground black pepper

⅓ cup extra-virgin olive oil

¼ cup cold water

Sana Sakr taught me how to make this authentic Lebanese recipe. Sana's late aunt, Thérèse, who lived in Zgharta, North Lebanon, grew an entire bed of parsley in her backyard to use in her famous tabbouleh, which, unlike many recipes found in the United States, calls for very little bulgur wheat and ample amounts of parsley. Thérèse often scooped spoonfuls of this light, lemony salad into romaine lettuce leaves and served them like little boats to her family. For the best texture, use a coarser bulgur, such as #2 grind, which is available online and in specialty food stores.

. . . .

Place the bulgur in a large bowl. Pour the lemon juice, including any pulp, over the bulgur. Set aside for about 10 minutes.

Combine the remaining ingredients in a medium bowl, then stir into the bulgur. Set aside for 2 hours, or until the bulgur has softened to your preference. Taste and adjust seasonings, adding more salt, pepper, lemon juice, or olive oil as desired. Serve at room temperature. The tabbouleh keeps, refrigerated, for 2 to 3 days.

Rosemary

When sunlight hits rosemary on a warm day, the plant's waxy, needlelike leaves release a delicate woodsy scent into the surrounding air. Resinous and strong, rosemary lends itself to flavoring meats and cheese, though its flavor also complements citrus drinks and desserts if used in moderation.

Planting

Even though this Mediterranean plant is a perennial in its native climate, it is often grown as an annual. Upright rosemary varieties reliably survive the winter only down to USDA zone 8, while prostrate versions are even less cold tolerant. Grow rosemary from nursery starts, planting them out in a spot with full sun anytime after the last spring frost. Space the plants 2 feet apart. Rosemary grows best in a raised bed because it prefers loose soil that drains quickly. In zones 7 and cooler, plant rosemary in a container with a diameter that is double the size of the plant's root ball and has drainage holes. Grow prostrate types at the edge of containers and retaining walls. Plant upright varieties with drought-tolerant salvias and penstemons in sunny, dry perennial borders.

Growing

Soggy soil causes rosemary's leaf tips to brown and encourages disease. When growing it in a pot, choose a terra-cotta container, as this porous material allows the soil to dry quickly between waterings. Set the container on pot feet, rather than in a saucer, so the water drains out freely. Let the soil dry just slightly between waterings, irrigating container-grown plants only if you think they will wilt during the heat of the day. In the garden, water when the soil dries down to the top of your second knuckle.

Spread a 1-inch layer of sand or fine gravel around the base of both inground and container plants. These mulches radiate heat, keeping the surface area dry and warm while still helping to retain moisture in the soil below. Foliar-feed container plants every other week and garden plants once a month. Prune the fast-growing plants back frequently to prevent them from outgrowing their allotted space.

In colder climates, bring rosemary inside in fall after the first light frost. However, lack of light, low humidity, and overwatering often kill indoor rosemary. Keep the plant in a bright, south-facing window and allow the soil to dry between waterings. Increase humidity around the plant by setting its pot on a metal or plastic tray filled with flat stones. Pour water into the tray, making sure that the water level stays below the pot's base; add more water as it evaporates. Foliar-feed once the plant begins to actively grow in spring.

Harvesting

Use scissors to snip off 3- to 6-inch sections of stem as needed, cutting right above a set of leaves. Take care to consider the overall shape of the plant as you harvest. Cut back the entire plant by a third in midsummer. Dry this harvest for later use. Stop harvesting fresh leaves one month before the first hard fall frost. Pick off the flowers and use them as a garnish.

Storing

Store fresh rosemary in a sealed plastic bag in the refrigerator for up to two weeks. Strip the leaves off the stem and rinse them just before use. Rosemary also dries well (see page 35).

Cooking Ideas

Strip the leaves off and use the woody branches as barbecue skewers—the wood infuses food with rosemary flavor. Muddle rosemary in lemonade. Wrap figs or dates in thin slices of pancetta; bake at 375 degrees F until the pancetta crisps. Remove from the oven, drizzle with honey, and top with a sprinkle of finely chopped rosemary.

Delicious Varieties

'Arp'. This upright, cold-hardy variety grows to 5 feet tall in warm climates and overwinters down to zone 6 if planted in a protected, warm spot with very well draining soil.

'Blue Boy'. Perfect for growing in pots, this diminutive prostrate variety grows to only 1½ feet tall and features small leaves and pretty lavender-blue flowers.

|||||||||||||||||||||||||||||||||||||| **ROSEMARY** ||||||||||||||||||||||||||||||||||||||

Rosmarinus officinalis

PLANT FAMILY: Lamiaceae

EDIBLE PARTS: Leaves, flowers

POTENTIAL PROBLEMS: Mealybugs, twospotted spider mites, thrips

||||||||||||||||||||||||||||||||||||||||||||||||||||||||||||||||||||||||||||||||||||||

Rosemary-Rubbed Leg of Lamb

One 6-pound bone-in leg of lamb, at room temperature

1½ cups chopped rosemary

½ cup chopped garlic (10 to 12 cloves)

10 anchovy fillets, rinsed and chopped

1 tablespoon red pepper flakes

Salt

Freshly ground pepper

Canola or vegetable oil, for brushing grill

Justin Niedermeyer, who founded the Seattle restaurant Spinasse, made this amazing leg of lamb to celebrate the summer solstice. When rubbed with rosemary, garlic, and anchovies and then grilled over wood charcoal, the lamb takes on an incredible smoky flavor. Serve with roasted potatoes and plenty of good bread to sop up the meat juices.

Using a paring knife, score the lamb leg all over in a grid pattern, spacing slits about 2 inches apart.

Combine the rosemary, garlic, and anchovies on a cutting board and mince together with a sharp knife until they form a chunky paste. Alternatively, place the ingredients in a food processor and pulse until a chunky paste forms. Stir in the red pepper flakes.

Season the lamb with salt and pepper, then rub with the rosemary paste, working the seasoning into the slits. Brush the grill with oil and bring to medium heat (you should be able to hold your hand about 6 inches above the grate for 5 seconds). Place the lamb directly on the grill, bone side up. Cover the grill and cook the lamb, turning occasionally, until an instant-read thermometer inserted into thickest part of the leg registers 125 degrees F (for medium-rare), about 30 minutes, though cooking time varies widely based on the grill used.

Sage

Culinary sages belong to the large genus *Salvia*, which claims close to a thousand species, including pineapple sage (*Salvia elegans*), a spectacular plant with brilliant red flowers that attract hummingbirds. The sage most commonly used in the kitchen, however, is garden sage (*Salvia officinalis*). My favorite garden sage variety, 'Berggarten', produces long, silvery-green, oval leaves and grows into a large, softly mounded clump. This exceptional plant, as well as the variegated varieties 'Golden' and 'Tricolor', looks brilliant when planted in ornamental borders, where its cool-colored foliage provides a calm contrast to bright perennial flowers.

Planting

Grow garden sage from nursery starts. Plant anytime after the last frost, though sage establishes best when planted as early in the season as possible. Choose a spot in full sun with well-drained soil. Space the plants 1½ to 2 feet apart. 'Berggarten' survives winters down to USDA zone 4, but 'Purple', 'Tricolor', and 'Golden' are hardy only to zone 7; in cooler climates, plant these varieties in pots and bring them indoors for the winter.

Growing

Sage tolerates periods of drought once established, but the plants thrive in just barely moist soil. Irrigate when the soil dries down to the base of your second knuckle. Sage becomes leggy and woody and dies back in the middle if not pruned properly each year. When new growth emerges in early spring, cut back each stem on mature plants by a third, making the cut right above a set of leaves. The plant looks a bit sparse after pruning, but the young growth soon fills in. Compost the prunings; the overwintered leaves tend to be leathery. Foliar-feed when new growth appears in spring and again around the summer solstice. Grow and overwinter sage in containers as you would rosemary (see page 72). Short-lived garden sage often dies after just three or four years, so plan on replacing it occasionally.

Harvesting

In the first year, pinch off pairs of leaves judiciously throughout summer. About two months before the first frost, cut the tips of each stem back 3 inches and

dry this large harvest for winter use. Harvest mature plants at six- to eight-week intervals beginning in late spring, cutting back 3 to 5 inches from each stem or pinching the tips back as needed. Use sharp scissors or pruners, and always cut just above a set of leaves; avoid cutting into woody growth. Culinary sages rarely send up their spikes of purple, pink, or white flowers, but when they do, it's a treat—the edible, slightly spicy flowers have a floral flavor with woodsy undertones. Snip off the flower stalks just after the blossoms open.

Storing

Store fresh sage and sage blossoms in a perforated plastic bag in the refrigerator for up to one week. Wash the stems and pinch off the leaves just before use. Sage also dries well (see page 35).

Cooking Ideas

Fry large sage leaves in olive oil until crisp. Slice cornbread into wedges and place a fried leaf on top of each one; crumble the leaves over roasted butternut squash; or toss pasta with the oil, leaves, and Parmesan. Add a tablespoon of minced sage to a big batch of garlic mashed potatoes. Stuff slivers of garlic, whole sage leaves, and sage and thyme blossoms under the skin of Cornish hens before roasting. Infuse vodka with sage leaves for cocktails.

Delicious Varieties

'Berggarten'. This fabulous German variety has a very mild flavor. It grows into a 3-foot-wide mound in the space of one growing season, and its velvety, silvery leaves fry exceptionally well.

'Golden'. This sage's variegated chartreuse and dark-green leaves glow when planted at the edge of borders. Grows in a 2-foot-wide mounded clump.

SAGE

Salvia officinalis

PLANT FAMILY: Lamiaceae

EDIBLE PARTS: Leaves, flowers

POTENTIAL PROBLEMS: Powdery mildew

Sage-Infused Vinegar

MAKES 2 CUPS

1 cup loosely packed fresh sage leaves

2 cups white wine vinegar

Herbs gradually release their aromatic oils when immersed in vinegar, infusing it with a delicate flavor. The vinegar can then be used to make vinaigrettes or mayonnaise. This particular recipe calls for sage, but rosemary, thyme, tarragon, oregano, chive blossoms, and dill all add their own special dimension to vinegars. Simply use 1 loosely packed cup of fresh herbs for every 2 cups of vinegar. Tall, narrow jars with a neck and plastic lids work best for storage, as they help keep the herbs from floating to the top, and metal lids corrode over time. Plastic lids are available wherever canning supplies are sold.

Choose a glass canning jar large enough to hold the vinegar and herbs. Wash the jar thoroughly in hot, soapy water; rinse; and immerse completely in boiling water for 10 minutes. Use tongs to remove the jar from the water. Place the sterilized jar upside down on a clean dish towel to dry.

Meanwhile, wash the sage and blot with paper towels until the leaves are completely dry. Pack the sage into the bottom of the sterilized jar. Pour the vinegar into a stainless-steel or enameled pan and heat over medium-low until it just simmers. Pour the hot vinegar over the sage, making sure the leaves are completely immersed. Place a plastic lid over the jar mouth. Place the jar in a sunny, warm spot and allow the vinegar to infuse for 2 to 4 weeks. If the leaves float to the top of the vinegar, pack them back down with a clean metal spoon.

When the vinegar reaches the desired flavor, pour it through a fine-mesh sieve into clean glass bottles that have been sterilized as described above. If desired, add a fresh, clean sage sprig to each bottle before sealing with a plastic cap. Refrigerate the vinegar and use within 6 months.

Thyme

More than 300 different species of thyme exist, but two particular types play an important role in the kitchen: shrubby *Thymus vulgaris* (known as English, French, or common thyme) and fragrant *Thymus × citriodorus* (lemon thyme). Thyme's distinct taste lends itself particularly well to chicken and egg dishes. I always grow a few plants right outside my back door because I use it so often as a flavoring in vinaigrettes.

Planting

Thyme grows best from nursery starts. Always choose plants with a pleasant aroma and taste, and avoid thymes with fuzzy, unappetizing leaves. This Mediterranean herb prefers sandy, fairly dry soil and full sun. Thyme grows in normal kitchen-garden soil, but it often peters out after a few seasons, especially when the soil stays consistently moist year-round. Improve the plant's health and longevity by planting it in a terra-cotta container, or grow it in a raised bed and mulch around the plants with 1 inch of sand or fine gravel (see page 72). Thyme may be planted anytime after the last frost, but it develops a larger root system—and overwinters better—if planted earlier in the season. Space the plants 1 to 1½ feet apart. Grow thyme in containers as you would rosemary (page 72).

Growing

English thyme grows into a blowsy 1-foot-tall plant whose leaf size and shape depends on the cultivar planted, while lemon thyme forms a low 8- to 12-inch mound. In their first year, keep the soil moist until the plants double in size; after that, you can wait to irrigate until the soil dries down to the base of your second knuckle. Foliar-feed when new growth appears in spring and again around the summer solstice. Care for container-grown thyme as you would rosemary (see page 72). Thyme's stems turn woody as they age and become more susceptible to winter damage. Keep the stems lush and pliable by pruning them back by a third in spring after the last frost. All thyme plants produce pretty spikes of flowers that attract loads of pollinators, especially honeybees. After it flowers, gather the thyme together in one hand and cut off the spent blossoms, making your cut just into the leaves below.

Divide lemon thyme growing in the garden every other year and container-grown plants annually. Dig up the plant, shake away the excess soil from the roots, and use a sharp knife to divide the plant into smaller pieces. Cut out and compost any woody or dead sections and then replant small, 3- to 4-inch-wide divisions. Shrubbier English thyme does not always divide well. Instead, try *layering*—a propagation technique that encourages a stem to root while it remains attached to the mother plant. In early summer, take a low-growing stem and secure it to the soil with a ∪-shaped landscape pin. Cover the pinned area with damp soil. Keep it moist. Sever the stem from the mother plant once a robust bundle of roots has developed. Transplant it into a small pot and allow the roots to establish for eight weeks before planting it in the garden. Stems of thyme and other woody herbs that come into contact with damp soil often layer themselves naturally, and this technique also works well for propagating rosemary, sage, oregano, winter savory, and catmint.

Harvesting

Use scissors to snip off 3- to 6-inch sections of stem as needed. Cut right above a set of leaves to encourage branching. If you'd like to harvest a large crop to dry, cut back the plant by half in early summer just before it blooms, because the leaves have the highest aromatic oil content at that point. Cut flowers just as they begin to open. Stop harvesting leaves one month before the first hard fall frost.

Storing

Store fresh thyme in a perforated plastic bag in the refrigerator for up to two weeks and blossoms for five to seven days. Wash and strip the leaves from the stem just before use. Dry thyme for winter use (see page 35).

Cooking Ideas

Add thyme to scrambled eggs or cheese omelets. Whisk lemon thyme into lemon vinaigrette. Add caraway thyme to potato leek soup. Stuff trout with slices of lemon and thyme blossoms before grilling. Bake rounds of goat cheese until puffed and golden; top with a generous drizzle of honey and a sprinkle of thyme.

Delicious Varieties

'Argenteus' silver thyme. A *Thymus vulgaris* cultivar with silvery-green leaves and a full-bodied flavor.

'Aureus' golden lemon thyme. These pretty golden leaves are ringed with dark green and have an intense lemon flavor. Add them whole to salads and vinaigrettes.

Caraway thyme (*Thymus herba-barona*). This caraway-flavored variety is one of the only culinary creeping thymes. Plant it between stepping stones in pathways.

|||||||||||||||||||||||||||||||||||||||||||||| **THYME** ||||||||||||||||||||||||||||||||||||||||||||||

Thymus spp.

PLANT FAMILY: Lamiaceae

EDIBLE PARTS: Leaves, flowers

POTENTIAL PROBLEMS: Thyme has no serious pest or disease problems.

||||||||||||||||||||||||||||||||||||||||||||||||||||||||||||||||||||||||||||||||||||||||||||||||||||||||

Slow-Roasted Tomatoes with Thyme

MAKES ABOUT 2 CUPS

15 to 20 dense-fleshed tomatoes

3 tablespoons extra-virgin olive oil, plus more for drizzling

2 teaspoons minced fresh thyme leaves

Sea salt

Freshly ground pepper

Slow-roasted tomatoes are incredibly versatile: you can include them in a meze platter, toss them with pasta, cut them into chunks and add them to whole-grain salads, layer them on sandwiches, place them on top of toast, or eat them straight from the pan. They also freeze quite well and are such a winter treat. Be sure to use tomatoes with dense, drier flesh, such as the paste tomatoes 'Principe Borghese' and 'Striped Roman' or small slicing tomatoes such as 'Jaune Flamme'.

Preheat the oven to 225 degrees F.

Slice the tomatoes in half lengthwise and arrange them in rows, cut side up, on a rimmed baking sheet. Drizzle the olive oil on top. With your hands, rub the oil all over the tomatoes, making sure they are completely coated. Sprinkle the thyme over the tomatoes and season to taste with salt and pepper.

Place the baking sheet in the oven and let the tomatoes slowly reduce. Check on them about once every hour. If they start to dry out, drizzle more olive oil on top. They are done when they become very soft, edges are wrinkled, and the middle is jamlike in consistency; depending on tomato size and juiciness, this will take 4 to 6 hours.

CHAPTER THREE

GREENS

GROWING A BIG MIX OF GREENS means that putting a healthy meal on the table is never more than 30 minutes away. Bring the basket of a salad spinner—one of the world's best inventions—right out into the garden and fill it with whatever strikes your fancy. Pinch individual baby spinach, lettuce, and Swiss chard leaves, plus a bit of chervil, parsley, and nasturtium blossoms, for a salad. Cut a big bunch of pungent mustard greens and nutty kale for a stir-fry. Or if cooking just isn't in the cards one evening, add a veneer of wholesomeness to a frozen pizza by tossing big handfuls of arugula on top of it just before it comes out of the oven.

No rule dictates that greens must be grown in rows. Try sowing a carpet of baby greens, including lettuce, spinach, and arugula, under taller plants such as broccoli or tomatoes. The small plants act as a living mulch for the larger ones, and this underplanting strategy uses garden space efficiently. When harvested young, greens taste mild and succulent and make undeniably good salads. Just don't follow the unfortunate trend of eating only immature greens. Allowing greens to fully develop gives you the opportunity to experience the full range of their flavor and texture—and the chance to harvest the delicious flower buds, blossoms, and seedpods that come only to those who wait.

BABY GREENS 101

Baby greens are simply any salad greens, including lettuce, mustard, kale, arugula, and chard, that are grown in a thick row and harvested when their leaves are small and tender. I grow baby greens in vintage wooden packing crates on my patio and in the garden wherever I can squeeze them in. Broadcast the seeds over the soil in the container, aiming to space them ½ inch apart in all directions (follow the instructions for direct-sowing small seeds on page 15). In the garden, plan on sowing the seed in 8- to 12-inch-wide bands and in rows 6 to 8 inches apart. Do not thin the seedlings—you want them to grow into a thick strip of greens. Harvest baby greens when they reach about 4 inches tall (about three to four weeks after sowing). Grasp a group of plants in one hand and use scissors or a sharp knife to cut the plants off 1 inch above the soil line. Pour diluted liquid organic fertilizer over the row after harvesting (1 cup of fertilizer per 3 feet of row or per container).

This type of growing is often called "cut-and-come-again" because the greens quickly regrow, and you can harvest two or more crops from a single sowing. To create salads with a medley of greens, either grow a *mesclun mix*—which contains a blend of several different greens in one seed packet—or sow rows of individual varieties and mix and match them after harvest. An 8-inch-wide, 3-foot-long row of baby greens produces enough salad for two people for one week (assuming a salad is consumed every day).

Inexpensive Seedlings

Baby greens can also serve as an inexpensive, homegrown source of seedlings. When the little greens develop two or three leaves, use a trowel to dig up a clump of them. Tease the individual seedlings apart and transplant them into rows, making sure to replant them at the same depth at which they were growing before. This strategy works particularly well when you want to harvest greens at both the baby and mature stages. You can also use this technique to transplant volunteer seedlings from self-sown crops.

Edible Flowers

The number of pollinators buzzing around the flower of an edible plant offers the best indication of how good the flower will taste. Pollinators are attracted to flowers with loads of pollen and nectar, which both add a hint of sweetness and floral undertones to the blossom's flavor. I favor flowers that taste like a delicate version of their parent plant, including herb flowers, nasturtiums, and the cheery blossoms of plants in the brassica (cabbage) family.

Arugula

Arugula adds a welcome nutty, spicy flavor to the salad bowl. Garden arugula (*Eruca sativa*) has tender, lobed leaves with a spicy taste that increases with maturity. This popular salad green bolts quickly during long days with hot weather and produces delicate white flowers. Slow-growing wild arugula (*Diplotaxis tenuifolia* or *D. muralis*) produces cute yellow flowers and narrow, deeply serrated, fleshy leaves with more pronounced stems and a pungent flavor. This green bolts slowly, even in hot weather, and tolerates cold better than garden arugula, making it an excellent choice for sowing during the summer and fall.

Planting

Skip buying arugula starts or sowing the seeds indoors, as transplanted seedlings tend to bolt prematurely. Choose a spot with full sun or light shade. Direct-sow tiny arugula seeds in the garden in spring as soon as the soil is workable and reaches 50 degrees F. Rake the bed smooth and level, and follow the guidelines for direct-sowing small seeds (see page 15) or for growing baby greens (see page 85). Expect seedlings to appear within 7 to 10 days. Sow a crop every two weeks throughout early fall for a consistent supply of leaves.

Growing

Garden arugula (see photo on page 83) grows to about 10 inches tall and wild arugula to about half that height. If you plan on growing the plants to their mature size, thin them to 4 inches apart in all directions as soon as the seedlings grow big enough to handle. Water whenever the soil dries down to the top of your first knuckle. Pour diluted liquid organic fertilizer over the plants after the first harvest (use 1 cup of fertilizer per 3 feet of row). Flea beetles love to feast on arugula, chewing tiny round holes in the leaves, especially in late spring and early summer. The damage rarely kills fast-growing arugula—it is more a cosmetic issue—but you can protect the plants by growing them under a hoop house tented with a light row cover fabric. Always allow a few plants to go to seed. The self-sown seeds will germinate in fall or the following spring; the seedlings transplant well if dug up and moved just after their first true leaves emerge.

Harvesting

Begin harvesting garden arugula four weeks after sowing and wild arugula two weeks later. Harvest baby greens as described on page 85; you can expect two or three cut-and-come-again harvests before the plants bolt. Harvest individual leaves from the outside in, pinching the leaves off as close to their base as possible.

Garden arugula bolts within 40 to 50 days of sowing, sending up a stalk with flower buds followed by crisp, peppery pods. Use its purple-veined white flowers as a garnish, and pinch off the young pods just after they form. Cut the bolted plants down to the ground and strip off the big, spicy, mature leaves before composting the stalk. The older leaves are too pungent and tough for salads, but cooking brings out their robust, nutty flavor. Wild arugula bolts slowly, but the leaves turn fibrous with age—so harvest them at 4 to 5 inches for the best flavor and texture. The plant's little yellow flowers make a fine garnish, but the pods are too tough to eat.

Storing

Poke a few holes in a zippered plastic bag and place a dry paper towel inside it. Fill the bag loosely with dry arugula leaves and zip it three-quarters of the way shut. Store this very perishable green in the refrigerator crisper drawer for three to five days. Wash the leaves and spin them dry just before use. Store the pods in the same way; use the flowers immediately.

Cooking Ideas

Sauté garlic in a little bit of olive oil, add some chopped mature arugula leaves, and cook until wilted; toss with pasta, chopped tomatoes, and sliced oil-cured black olives. Substitute baby arugula for basil in pesto. Scatter arugula over pizza. Serve roasted beets over a bed of arugula; garnish with toasted walnuts. Eat the raw seedpods with carrot sticks as a snack or add a handful to a stir-fry. Scatter arugula blossoms over a salad before serving.

Delicious Varieties

'Astro'. 38 days. This garden arugula has a mild flavor and is bolt resistant. Produces large, pale-green leaves with rounded lobes. Tastes best raw when harvested at the baby stage, 4 inches or smaller. Open-pollinated.

'Sylvetta'. 35 days. A wild arugula with a lovely peppery flavor. Long-lasting in heat and tolerant of heavy frost. Open-pollinated.

||||||||||||||||||||||||||||||||||| **ARUGULA** |||||||||||||||||||||||||||||||||||

Eruca sativa, Diplotaxis muralis, D. tenuifolia

PLANT FAMILY: Brassicaceae

EDIBLE PARTS: Leaves, flowers, young seedpods

POTENTIAL PROBLEMS: Flea beetles

Arugula Salad with Blue Cheese, Dates, and Hot Bacon Dressing

5 Medjool dates

4 cups loosely packed baby arugula

⅓ cup crumbled blue cheese (about 2 ounces)

4 strips bacon

2 tablespoons white wine vinegar

2 tablespoons water

1 tablespoon packed light brown sugar

Coarsely ground black pepper

Arugula blossoms, for garnish (optional)

This salad is a riff on one of my favorite appetizers: dates stuffed with blue cheese and wrapped with bacon. Arugula's spicy leaves provide the perfect counterbalance to the creamy cheese, savory bacon, and sweet dates.

. . . .

Halve and pit the dates and slice each in half again. Place the arugula in a large salad bowl and top with the dates and blue cheese.

Cook the bacon in a heavy skillet over medium heat, turning occasionally, until crisp, 6 to 8 minutes. Remove the skillet from the heat and transfer the bacon to paper-towel-lined plate. Reserve ¼ cup of the bacon grease.

Whisk the reserved bacon grease, vinegar, water, and brown sugar together in the skillet. Place the skillet back over medium heat and whisk the dressing constantly until it boils. Taste and add more vinegar if desired. Pour the hot dressing over the arugula. Crumble the bacon into the salad and toss well. Season to taste with pepper and garnish with arugula blossoms before serving.

Asian Greens

Two of my favorite seed companies, Kitazawa Seed Company and Evergreen Seeds, specialize in Asian vegetable varieties, and both offer an astonishing range of unusual greens. You'll find the green, spoon-shaped leaves of tatsoi and misome, succulent bok choy, loose Korean cabbage, and upright Chinese cabbage, among many others. These leafy vegetables offer an invitation to experiment with different Pacific Rim cuisines, but they can also be used in any recipe that calls for greens.

Planting

The Asian greens discussed here all belong to the brassica (cabbage) family and grow best in early spring, fall, and winter. Begin sowing or planting seedlings in spring as soon as the soil can be worked and nears 50 degrees F. Choose a spot in full sun and sow or transplant seedlings every other week for six to eight weeks. Resume sowing and planting six weeks before the first frost for fall and winter harvests. Scratch alfalfa meal into the soil before sowing or planting to give the plants a nitrogen boost (follow the label's recommended application rate).

Growing Asian greens from seedlings gives you the opportunity to plant them in pretty patterns, in symmetrical grids, or in a row like fence pickets. When direct-sowing, rake the bed smooth and level and follow the instructions for direct-sowing small seeds (see page 15). Space seeds 2 inches apart and rows 10 to 12 inches apart. Seedlings typically appear within a week after sowing. Thin directly sown seedlings and plant transplants at the following distances: baby bok choy, tatsoi, yu choy, and misome, 3 to 4 inches; loose heads of cabbage, 8 inches; upright heads of cabbage, 10 inches.

Growing

Foliar-feed Asian greens with diluted liquid organic fertilizer three weeks after transplanting and directly sown crops when they develop three sets of true leaves. Water whenever the soil dries down to the top of your first knuckle. Do not mulch, as damp grass clippings and straw attract slugs, which love to feed on the greens' succulent foliage. Construct a hoop house over the bed and tent it with a row cover immediately to protect the plants from imported cabbageworms and flea beetles.

Harvesting

Many of the smaller Asian greens, including bok choy, tatsoi, loose-leaf cabbages, mustards, and spinachlike greens, are ready for harvest about 4 to 6 weeks after planting. Harvest Chinese cabbage heads when they feel tight and firm, 50 to 70 days after planting. To harvest cabbage, bok choy, and whole tatsoi and loose-leaf plants, slide a knife just under the soil line and sever the plant from its roots. Harvest the individual leaves of plants from the outside in, cutting them off at the plant's base with a sharp knife. All of the plants begin to loosen and lengthen when they bolt, so try to harvest before this point. If the plants do send up a flower stalk, just harvest the tender buds as you would with mustard rabe (see page 103) or eat the tasty blossoms.

Storing

Store Asian greens in a perforated plastic bag in the refrigerator crisper drawer as you would arugula (see page 87). Use them within a week. Store the flowers as you would mustard green blossoms (see page 104).

Cooking Ideas

Make kimchi—a spicy pickled cabbage dish from Korea—with loose-leaf or upright cabbages. Chop bok choy lengthwise or pull tatsoi heads apart, and add to soups, or stir-fry with chopped ginger and garlic. Use leafy, loose greens in any recipe that calls for mustard greens or spinach.

Delicious Varieties

Green bok choy. 40 days. Vase-shaped plants with pale-green, juicy bases and dark-green, tender leaves. Heat tolerant.

Tatsoi. 20 days (baby stage), 40 to 50 days (mature). Forms flat rosettes of dark-green, spoon-shaped leaves that have a very mild mustard flavor. Pick young and eat raw in salads or allow to mature for cooking. Pick while the greens are glossy, as they turn dull right before bolting.

ASIAN GREENS

Brassica spp.

PLANT FAMILY: Brassicaceae

EDIBLE PARTS: Leaves, flower buds, flowers

POTENTIAL PROBLEMS: Imported cabbageworms, cabbage loopers, cabbage maggots, flea beetles, slugs, snails

Crispy Pot Stickers with Garlicky Asian Greens

SERVES 2

2 cups vegetable or chicken broth

12 heads baby bok choy or 1 head mature bok choy (or 4 or 5 cups chopped mixed greens)

2 teaspoons olive oil

2 large garlic cloves, minced

⅓ cup finely chopped, mildly spicy red peppers

3 teaspoons vegetable oil

One 16-ounce package frozen pot stickers

Pot stickers get their name for a reason—they stick terribly if you try to cook them in a regular frying pan. I've found that cooking them over medium heat using a nonstick skillet (or a very well seasoned cast-iron skillet) coated with a few teaspoons of oil results in crispy, well-browned dumplings.

. . . .

In a small saucepan over medium heat, bring the broth to a simmer, then reduce the heat to low. Cut the bok choy into quarters lengthwise and rinse in cold water.

Heat the olive oil in a cast-iron or nonstick skillet over medium heat. When the oil shimmers, add the garlic and cook until fragrant, about 30 seconds. Add the peppers and cook until they begin to soften. Add the bok choy (with water still clinging to the leaves) and cook until the tops wilt and turn bright green and the white bases pierce easily with a fork, 3 to 5 minutes. Divide the vegetables between two deep soup bowls.

Wipe the skillet, then heat the vegetable oil over medium heat. Place the frozen pot stickers in the skillet, flat side down, and cook, turning occasionally, until evenly browned, about 8 minutes total. Divide the pot stickers between the bowls and pour 1 cup broth into each. Serve immediately.

Broccoli Rabe

Broccoli rabe (sometimes spelled "raab"), also known as rapini, jumps out of the ground in spring and is ready for harvest in just over a month. This substantial, cold-tolerant green produces tender flower stalks topped with small, broccoli-like buds. More closely related to turnips than to broccoli, it has deep green leaves that taste slightly bitter, while the buds are sweet, with undertones of mustard.

Planting

Broccoli rabe grows so well from seed that starting seedlings indoors or purchasing starts is unnecessary. Begin sowing this cool-season crop in very early spring, as soon as the soil reaches 45 degrees and becomes workable. Scratch alfalfa meal into the soil before sowing to give the plants a nitrogen boost (follow the label's recommended application rate). I grow broccoli rabe in beds reserved for warm-season crops because it finishes before tomatoes, peppers, and cucumbers are ready to plant. Either sow the seeds in rows spaced 8 inches apart or broadcast seeds in 2-foot-wide sections of a raised bed, gradually filling the bed as you make successive sowings. Follow the instructions for direct-sowing small seeds (see page 15). The seeds germinate within 7 to 10 days. For a consistent supply, sow a small crop once a week until daytime temperatures consistently hit the high 60s. Resume sowing in late summer through mid-fall.

Growing

Broccoli rabe grows 8 to 10 inches tall and produces flower buds in under two months. In that short time, a variety of insect pests still manage to find it, including flea beetles, imported cabbageworms, and leaf miners. Place a hoop house tented with a row cover fabric over the bed immediately after sowing to protect the plants from pests. The insulating layer also allows you to start sowing earlier in spring and grow into winter, as this brassica survives subfreezing temperatures.

Thin plants to 4 inches apart in all directions when they grow big enough to handle. Water whenever the soil dries down to the top of your first knuckle, and foliar-feed three weeks after germination. Allow a couple of plants to fully flower; the nectar-rich blossoms provide a food source for beneficial insects.

Harvesting

Aim to harvest after the flower buds form but while they still remain tightly closed and are about the size of a half-dollar. Use scissors to cut the whole plant off at the soil line. Broccoli rabe's harvest window is short. If you wait too long, the stalk grows tough and fibrous, and the buds become loose and then open to reveal clusters of small yellow flowers. If this happens, simply cut the plants off at the soil line, strip the leaves off the tough stalks, and snip off the flowers. Cook the leaves as you would mustard greens and eat the flowers—they have a slightly sweet flavor and taste delicious in both salads and stir-fries.

Storing

Bundle three or four plants together. Store broccoli rabe in the refrigerator crisper drawer as you would arugula (see page 87) for five to seven days. Wash and spin it dry just before use; trim off the lower stems and leaves if they feel tough. The opened flower buds are quite perishable; store them as you would mustard blossoms (see page 104).

Cooking Ideas

Blanch broccoli rabe in boiling water prior to preparing it for a recipe (see directions in Lemony Broccoli Rabe on page 97). For a simple side dish, mix sautéed broccoli rabe with toasted pine nuts and currants, or top it with crisped pancetta. Overcooked broccoli rabe turns a drab olive green, so always remove it from the pan when it looks bright green.

Delicious Varieties

'Cima di Rapa'. 60 days. This delicious Italian variety tops out at about 1 foot. The buds are sweet with a hint of mustard flavor. Open-pollinated.

BROCCOLI RABE

Brassica rapa

PLANT FAMILY: Brassicaceae

EDIBLE PARTS: Leaves, flower buds, flowers

POTENTIAL PROBLEMS: Imported cabbageworms, cabbage loopers, cabbage maggots, flea beetles, leaf miners

Lemony Broccoli Rabe

1 large bunch broccoli rabe, tough stem ends trimmed

2 tablespoons olive oil

2 large garlic cloves, minced

2 teaspoons lemon zest (from 1 small lemon)

1 tablespoon freshly squeezed lemon juice

¼ teaspoon red pepper flakes

Salt

Blanching broccoli rabe in boiling water for a couple of minutes knocks down its bitter flavor a few notches. Serve this recipe on its own as a side dish, or chop the rabe and mix it with 8 ounces of cooked penne, Parmesan, and buttered, toasted bread crumbs for a main dish.

. . . .

Bring a large pot of salted water to a boil. Working in batches, add the broccoli rabe to the boiling water and cook until the stems are just barely tender, about 2 minutes. Transfer with a slotted spoon to a colander and rinse with cool water. Place on a clean dish towel and blot dry. If tossing with pasta, roughly chop the broccoli rabe.

Heat the oil in a large, wide skillet over medium-high heat. Add the garlic and cook until fragrant, about 30 seconds. Add the broccoli rabe and sauté until tender but still bright green, about 2 minutes. Stir in the lemon zest, cook for 30 seconds, then remove from the heat. Sprinkle the broccoli rabe with the lemon juice, red pepper flakes, and salt to taste. Serve immediately.

Lettuce

Thomas Jefferson grew nearly twenty varieties of lettuce in his kitchen garden at Monticello. It is easy to understand why, since this queen of the salad greens comes in so many delicious forms. Leaf lettuces form a loose head with ruffled, oak-leaf-shaped, or rounded leaves. Butterheads (also called Boston and Bibb lettuce) have slightly rumpled leaves that round over each other to form a tender core. Iceberg lettuces produce globe-shaped, crunchy heads surrounded by a whorl of tender, loose leaves. Romaines grow upright with tender, pale leaves at their heart, while the leaves of heat-tolerant Batavians, or summer crisps, grow in a loose halo around a crunchy central head.

Planting

Lettuce grows best in moist, crumbly, completely weed-free soil. (See page 31 for instructions on preparing the soil.) Choose a spot in full sun, and direct-sow seeds or plant seedlings as soon as the soil becomes workable in spring and reaches 50 degrees F. Rake the bed smooth and level and follow the directions for direct-sowing small seeds (see page 15). For head lettuce, sow seeds 2 inches apart in single rows that are 10 to 12 inches apart. Sow baby greens as described on page 85. Water the seeds in with a watering can and keep the seedbed moist. Expect the lettuce to sprout within five to seven days. When transplanting seedlings or thinning directly sown lettuce, leave 8 inches between Batavian, romaine, and crisphead lettuce seedlings, and 6 inches between leaf and butterhead seedlings. Water seedlings in with diluted liquid organic fertilizer.

For a staggered harvest, plant seedlings and sow seed on the same day, every other week; the seedlings will mature before the directly sown crop. Lettuce bolts quickly when temperatures hit the 70s or higher. Either take a break from growing lettuce in the summer, or try growing it in a spot that stays damp and gets afternoon shade, such as underneath tomato plants. For summer crops, plant seedlings of heat-tolerant Batavians, green romaines, or iceberg types, or grow lettuce as a baby green, because you can usually harvest at least once before the plants bolt. In late summer, begin sowing or planting seedlings of cold-tolerant varieties, like 'Rouge d'Hiver', once a week, stopping about 3 weeks before the first frost. Lettuce survives temperatures down to the low 20s.

Growing

Lettuce develops a bitter flavor and bolts prematurely when the soil dries out. Carefully monitor your soil and water whenever it dries down to the top of your first knuckle. I don't mulch around lettuce because it attracts slugs and also finds its way into the heads, which makes cleaning a pain. Instead, I aim to space lettuce so the plants just touch when mature—this helps keep down weeds, and the plants shade their own soil. Foliar-feed with diluted liquid organic fertilizer every other week. Set out beer traps or spread an organic slug bait around the plants to prevent slug damage. In fall, right before the average first

frost, construct a hoop house tented with a heavy row cover to extend the lettuce season.

Harvesting

Harvest lettuce anytime after the leaves grow to 3 inches. Use a sharp knife to cut individual leaves off near the plant's base, harvesting from the outside in. When harvesting a whole head, do not just pull it out of the ground. This sprays grit into the surrounding plants that must then be carefully rinsed out later. Instead, take a sharp knife and slide it just below the head, severing it from its roots. Pick off any dirty leaves around the bottom. Harvest baby greens as described on page 85.

Storing

Poke a few holes in a zippered plastic bag and place a dry paper towel inside it. Place a single head of lettuce in each bag, or fill it loosely with dry baby lettuce leaves. Zip the bag three-quarters of the way shut and store in the refrigerator crisper drawer for up to one week. Wash the leaves in cold water and spin them dry just before use.

Cooking Ideas

Pull apart the leaves of a butterhead and place a heaping tablespoon of egg or chicken salad in the cupped portion of the leaf. Arrange six or eight leaves on a plate and serve. Roll up cheese and sliced turkey or ham in a large lettuce leaf. Cut wedges of iceberg lettuce and top with homemade Roquefort dressing, fried capers, crumbled bacon, and sliced scallions. Mix baby lettuces with small, spicy nasturtium leaves and flowers.

Delicious Varieties

'Australian Yellow Leaf'. 50 days. This tender leaf lettuce has ruffled, chartreuse leaves, which provide an exceptional counterpoint to darker green plants in the garden. Heirloom.

'Forellenschluss'. 55 days. My all-time favorite lettuce. This romaine features lovely green-and-red-speckled leaves that are crunchy at their bases and tender on top. Tasty harvested as both baby greens or a mature head. Heirloom.

'Red Iceberg'. 50 days. Iceberg lettuces have a bad reputation for being tasteless, but this variety develops gorgeous, tightly packed heads surrounded by a swirl of red-and-green-tinged leaves, which are full of flavor and have a satisfying crunch, especially in sandwiches. Tolerates heat and cold well. Heirloom.

'Tom Thumb'. 34 days. This adorable, tiny butterhead lettuce grows just 5 inches across. Very tender leaves are perfect for salad. Pull apart each single-serving head and arrange the leaves on a plate. Resists bolting. Open-pollinated.

LETTUCE

Lactuca sativa

PLANT FAMILY: Asteraceae

EDIBLE PARTS: Leaves

POTENTIAL PROBLEMS: Slugs, snails, downy mildew

Perfect Caesar Salad

¼ cup olive oil

3 garlic cloves, crushed

1 teaspoon dry mustard

1 ounce anchovy paste

3 tablespoons freshly squeezed lemon juice (from about 2 small lemons)

3 tablespoons red wine vinegar

2 heads romaine lettuce, leaves separated, washed, and spun dry

1 cup finely grated Romano or Parmesan (about 2 ounces)

The dressing for this Caesar salad is the *best*: a light vinaigrette with plenty of lemon and salty undertones from just the right amount of anchovy. Top it with buttery homemade croutons, grilled chicken, or salmon if you like.

In a medium bowl, combine the oil, garlic, dry mustard, and anchovy paste. Whisk in the lemon juice and vinegar and set aside.

Stack 5 lettuce leaves together and slice very thinly crosswise; repeat until all the lettuce is cut. Place the lettuce in a large salad bowl, fluff up with your fingers, and lightly dress: the lettuce should glisten with dressing, not be weighted down by it. Sprinkle the Romano over the top and toss to combine.

Divide the salad among 6 plates. If adding croutons, grilled chicken, or fish, arrange them on the salad and drizzle a few extra teaspoons of dressing over the top before serving.

Mustard Greens

One nibble of a mustard green leaf reveals this cool-season vegetable's flavor to be peppery, pungent, and undeniably mustardy. These intensely flavored greens are delicious, but they are just a precursor to the plant's real treat—the small flower buds that form as the growing season turns long and warm. The buds, sometimes called mustard rabe, taste like sweet broccoli with a dash of spice thrown in and are almost impossible to find anywhere but in a garden.

Planting

Mustard greens germinate and grow so quickly that purchasing seedlings or starting them indoors is entirely unnecessary—though it can be awfully hard to resist pretty mustard seedlings in spring. Choose a spot in full sun. Begin sowing as soon as the soil reaches 45 degrees F and becomes workable in spring. Rake the bed smooth and level and follow the instructions for direct-sowing small seeds (page 15). Grow mustard for baby greens (see page 85). If you plan on harvesting it at a larger size, sow it in rows spaced a foot apart or in small clumps in bare spots in the garden. Make three successive sowings two weeks apart. For fall crops, resume sowing every other week as soon as daytime temperatures stay in the low 70s and continue until one month before the first frost. Watch for seedlings to appear one to two weeks after sowing.

Growing

For mature plants, dig up clumps of baby greens when they have two true leaves and transplant the seedlings into rows. Or use needle-nose scissors to thin out unwanted seedlings. Either way, make the final spacing between plants 8 to 10 inches in all directions. Irrigate whenever the soil dries down to the top of your first knuckle. Foliar-feed two weeks after the mustard germinates and again two weeks later. After harvesting baby greens, pour diluted liquid organic fertilizer over the plants (1 cup for every 3 feet of row). When the plants send up their tall, slightly contorted flower stalks, allow some to flower and set seed. The flowers, which attract hordes of pollinators, conveniently open just as cucumbers and squash begin to flower. If allowed to self-sow, volunteer seedlings will germinate in fall or the following spring, and they transplant well if dug up and replanted just as their true leaves emerge.

Harvesting

Mustard greens become increasingly spicy as they mature. Baby greens mature in 3 to 4 weeks and can be harvested as described on page 85. Harvest larger greens for cooking once the plants get 8 to 10 leaves. Cut the leaves off close to the base and harvest from the outside in. Snip off the delicious flower buds, along with 4 inches of stem, while they are still tightly closed. Larger mustards, like 'Osaka Purple', tend to have the biggest buds. Allow some flowers to open because the edible yellow blossoms have just a hint of spice and a delightful floral flavor; cut the flower head when three-quarters of the flowers open.

Storing

Store both baby and mature greens and flower buds in a perforated plastic bag as you would arugula (see page 87) for up to five days. Wash the leaves just before serving. Spin dry if using in a salad; for a stir-fry, add the mustard to the pan with water still clinging to its leaves. Place the cut flowers in a jar of water and use within two days.

Cooking Ideas

In a large skillet, sauté a tablespoon each of chopped garlic and fresh ginger in 2 tablespoons of olive oil over medium heat. Add 6 cups of chopped greens, stir to combine, and cook, covered, until tender and wilted; squeeze fresh lemon juice over the greens before serving. Substitute mustard for bok choy when making pot stickers (see recipe on page 93). Sauté the flower buds with garlic and toss with a bit of soy sauce just before serving: use mustard rabe in any recipe that calls for broccoli rabe. I like to snack on the flowers out in the garden, but they also taste delicious added to a stir-fry at the last moment or scattered over a salad.

Delicious Varieties

'Green Wave'. 50 days. This bolt-resistant mustard grows to nearly 2 feet tall and produces mild, deeply ruffled leaves and tons of flower buds. The curly leaves retain a pleasant texture when steamed and taste delicious even when harvested at 10 to 12 inches long. Alternate with rows of onions for a great textural display in the garden. 'Osaka Purple' is another lovely larger-leafed mustard. Open-pollinated.

'Ruby Streaks'. 20 days (baby stage), 40 days (mature). This cold-tolerant mustard produces burgundy leaves with bright chartreuse veins. The deeply serrated leaves look delicate but pack a big mustard taste with just a hint of wasabi. Also try 'Golden Streaks', which has citron-colored leaves. Open-pollinated.

|||||||||||||||||||||||||||| **MUSTARD GREENS** ||||||||||||||||||||||||||||

Brassica juncea

PLANT FAMILY: Brassicaceae

EDIBLE PARTS: Leaves, flower buds, flowers

POTENTIAL PROBLEMS: Flea beetles, slugs, snails

|||||||||||||||||||||||||||||||||||||||||||||||||||||||||||||||||||||||||||||||||||||||

Mustard Green Turnovers

1 bunch (about 1 pound or 4 packed cups) mustard greens, stems removed, leaves finely chopped

1 tablespoon olive oil

1 cup chopped onion

1 garlic clove, minced

¼ teaspoon salt

5 oil-cured black olives, pitted and finely chopped

8 slow-roasted tomato halves, finely chopped

¼ cup crumbled feta (about 1 ounce)

2 sheets frozen puff pastry, defrosted according to package directions

1 egg, lightly beaten

I got the idea for stuffing greens into a pastry pocket from Deborah Madison's classic cookbook *Vegetarian Cooking for Everyone*. I think my version makes the perfect snack: tuck one of these savory turnovers into your pocket before taking off on a hike. If you don't have slow-roasted tomatoes on hand (see recipe on page 82), look for them at a well-stocked olive bar or substitute sun-dried tomatoes. You can also skip stuffing the greens into turnovers and serve them as a side dish instead.

Preheat the oven to 400 degrees F. Place the mustard greens in colander, rinse with cool water, and set aside.

Heat the oil in a large skillet over medium heat. Add the onions and cook until they turn soft and translucent, about 3 minutes. Add the garlic and salt and cook until the garlic is softened, about 1 minute. Add the greens, with water still clinging to their leaves; cook until they wilt and turn tender and most of the pan juices evaporate, about 5 minutes. Transfer the greens to a colander and press to extract any extra liquid. Place them in a large mixing bowl and stir in the olives, tomatoes, and feta. You should have about 1½ cups filling.

Unfold the puff pastry on a lightly floured surface. Depending on pastry size, cut each sheet into four 4-inch squares or four 5-inch squares. Divide the filling among 8 pastry squares, leaving a 1-inch border. Fold each square into a triangle, enclosing the filling, and seal the pastry by firmly pressing fork tines along the open edges. Use a sharp knife to make two ½-inch-long vents in the top of each turnover. Place the turnovers on parchment-paper-lined baking sheet and brush their tops with beaten egg. Bake until golden brown, 25 to 30 minutes. Serve hot or at room temperature.

Radicchio

Radicchio's lineage stretches back to the hills of Italy, where this bitter green, known as *radicchio rosso*, enjoys enormous popularity. The two main types of radicchio, elongated Treviso varieties and rounded Chioggia varieties, are both named for Northern Italian towns. I often choose heirloom varieties over newer ones, but not with radicchio. Most radicchio heirlooms require a long growing season, and their thick, bitter leaves must be cut off in late summer to induce the tender, rouge-colored heads to form in fall. New varieties, including the hybrids 'Indigo' and 'Fiero', offer the distinct advantage of heading up without the need for cutting.

Planting

Radicchio prefers temperatures from 55 degrees to 75 degrees F, though the plants tolerate temperatures into the high 80s as long as they receive a steady supply of water. Young seedlings bolt before forming a head if exposed to nighttime temperatures below 50 degrees for several days.

Due to these considerations, I usually skip planting radicchio in spring, because the plants often bolt as the days lengthen and warm, and the heads that do form have a less vibrant color and a more bitter flavor than those that mature in fall. For fall and winter crops, plant seedlings 60 days before the first frost, as they head up more reliably than directly sown plants. Choose small seedlings with just two or three true leaves, space the plants 8 inches apart, and transplant them into a sunny spot in the garden. Soak the soil around each seedling with diluted liquid organic fertilizer after planting. If you do plant a spring crop, set seedlings out at the same time you plant lettuce.

Growing

Radicchio grows about 12 inches tall, and the head is surrounded by a halo of loose outer leaves. The plant tolerates dry soil, but watering regularly reduces bitterness and *tip burn*: a problem where the interior leaves develop brown tips. The plants sit just above the soil line, and their bases are prone to rotting when they come in contact with damp soil or mulch. Prevent this by allowing the soil surface to dry between waterings and irrigating only when the soil dries down to the top of your first knuckle. Trim off lower leaves if they begin to rot. Foliar-feed every three weeks. Scuffle a stirrup hoe between the heads once a week to prevent weeds. In fall, after the first light frost, position a hoop house tented with a heavy row cover over radicchio to extend the harvest season into winter.

Harvesting

Harvest about two months after transplanting, when the heads feel firm and round, like a well-filled volleyball. Harvest as you would a head of lettuce (see page 100). Overmature heads often erupt in the middle with a pointed mound of leaves.

Storing

Remove any loose outer leaves and then place the dry heads in a perforated plastic bag. Store in the refrigerator crisper drawer. Radicchio maintains its appearance for up to one month, but tastes best if used within two weeks. Cut heads in half from the crown through the stem for grilling or roasting, leaving the core intact. For salads, cut out the core and separate the individual leaves in the head.

Cooking Ideas

Radicchio gives you the opportunity to make creamy dressings, like honey mustard or Roquefort, because the green's substantial leaves hold up under the dressing's weight. When making a salad with radicchio, experiment by mixing in chopped apple or pear, dried fruit and berries, toasted nuts, blue or goat cheese, and a mix of mild lettuces and spicy arugula or mustard greens. Sauté thinly sliced radicchio and fennel in olive oil over medium heat until very tender. Sprinkle with balsamic dressing and serve over soft, buttery polenta with Parmesan. Toss a few handfuls of slivered radicchio into brothy soups 5 minutes before serving. Separate the leaves of a small round head and place a few teaspoons of blue cheese or a small mound of chicken salad in the base of each leaf.

Delicious Varieties

'Fiero'. 65 days. Treviso-style radicchios grow upright (similar to romaine lettuce). This variety produces slightly bitter, deep-burgundy-colored leaves. The elongated heads hold together well when cut into quarters and grilled. Hybrid.

'Indigo'. 65 days. Gorgeous palm-sized Chioggia variety with snowy white ribs and burgundy-blushed leaves that reliably color up, even in warmer weather. Its heat and cold tolerance make it an excellent choice for both spring and fall crops, and this variety resists tip burn and bottom rot. Substitute the small, mild, cup-shaped leaves for Belgian endive in recipes. Hybrid. 'Palla Rossa Special' is a newer, open-pollinated variety that reliably produces heads.

RADICCHIO

Cichorium intybus

PLANT FAMILY: Asteraceae

EDIBLE PARTS: Leaves

POTENTIAL PROBLEMS: Radicchio does not suffer from serious pest or disease problems.

Tangy Grilled Radicchio

SERVES 4

2 large or 3 small radicchio heads

1 tablespoon rice vinegar

Zest and juice of 1 small lime

2 tablespoons honey

1 teaspoon finely minced garlic

1 teaspoon peeled and finely minced fresh ginger

2 teaspoons soy sauce

3 tablespoons vegetable oil

1 teaspoon sesame oil

Salt

Freshly ground pepper

Marinating radicchio in this savory-sweet marinade and then grilling it helps mellow out the green's bitter flavor. Serve the pretty wedges with grilled halibut or salmon.

Quarter the radicchio lengthwise, leaving the core intact. In a medium bowl, whisk together the vinegar, lime zest and juice, honey, garlic, ginger, soy sauce, and vegetable and sesame oils. Pour into a shallow dish large enough to accommodate everything. Add the radicchio and turn several times to coat. Cover and refrigerate overnight.

Bring a grill to medium-high heat. Remove the radicchio from the marinade and place directly on the grill, discarding the marinade. Cook, turning the radicchio occasionally, until it just begins to wilt and is charred in spots, about 6 minutes total. Sprinkle with salt and pepper. Serve warm.

Spinach

Spinach tastes so *green*—it is succulent and slightly sweet, its mineral undertones attesting to the fact that ample amounts of calcium, iron, and vitamins A, C, and E are locked into its leaves. Spinach varieties are divided into three basic types: savoy, smooth or flat-leaf, and semisavoy. The crumpled foliage of savoy and semisavoy spinaches lend themselves well to cooking, because they retain more texture than smooth or flat-leaf varieties, which blend well in salad mixes, especially when harvested at the baby stage.

Planting

Direct-sow in spring as soon as the soil can be worked and reaches 45 degrees F. Choose a spot in full sun or light shade. Sow the seeds 1 inch apart and ¼ inch deep in rows spaced 8 inches apart; expect germination within seven to ten days. Start sowing cold-tolerant varieties, such as the smooth-leaf 'Olympia', and switch to a heat-tolerant variety, such as the semisavoy 'Space', as spring progresses. Sow a small crop every other week for a consistent supply, stopping one month before temperatures typically hit 70 degrees in your area. Resume sowing in late summer for fall and overwintered crops.

Spinach germinates poorly in soil with temperatures above 75 degrees F. Improve germination rates in late summer by shading the soil. About seven weeks before the first frost, water the planting bed well and then cover it with 4 inches of straw. One week later, simply pull back the straw to form a row and sow a cold-tolerant variety, such as the heirloom savoy 'Bloomsdale Long Standing'. This strategy gives the plants time to establish robust root systems and top growth before frost hits.

Growing

Thin out every other plant when the seedlings grow large enough to handle. Continue thinning over the next few weeks until the remaining plants are spaced 4 inches apart. Spread an organic slug bait to prevent slug and snail damage. Warm weather and lengthening days cause spinach to bolt. The leaves become arrow-shaped and develop a bitter flavor just before the plant sends up its seed stalk. As soon as you notice this change, pinch off all the remaining rounded leaves and then pull and compost the plants. Prevent bolting by mulching around the plants with a 2-inch layer of grass clippings or straw, as this helps keep the soil moist and cool. Water whenever the soil dries down to the base of your first knuckle, and foliar-feed the plants every two weeks.

To overwinter spinach planted in late summer or early fall, pile a loose, 10-inch layer of straw over plants after the first few frosts. For extra protection, build a hoop house over the bed and tent it with a heavy row cover. The plants stop growing over the winter. In early spring, pull back the mulch and tuck it under and around the plants when they begin to grow.

Harvesting

Harvest from the outside in and pick leaves either at the baby stage (3 inches long) or when mature (4 to 5 inches long). Pinch the leaves off as close to the base of the plant as possible. To harvest an entire plant, gather all the leaves together and cut them off with scissors right above where small leaves emerge from the crown (typically about 1 inch above the soil line); new leaves will develop within a few days.

Storing

Pack dry leaves into a perforated plastic bag lined with a paper towel (see page 100). Keep spinach in the refrigerator crisper drawer for no more than five days. Pinch off any tough or fibrous stems, then wash and spin the leaves dry just before using.

Cooking Ideas

Plan on steaming or stir-frying 3 packed cups of fresh leaves per person, because spinach wilts down dramatically when cooked. Flat-leaf varieties are easier to clean than savoy types, making them the best choice for salads, especially when harvested young. Toss baby spinach with crisped bacon, toasted pecans, chopped dried figs, blue cheese, and a balsamic vinaigrette. Stir two large handfuls of spinach leaves into miso soup just before serving. Squeeze fresh lemon juice over steamed spinach and drizzle with brown butter. Make a nest of steamed spinach on a plate and fill it with cooked lentils or wild rice.

SUMMER SPINACH

To keep a regular supply of spinachlike greens on the table through summer, grow Malabar spinach (*Basella rubra*) or New Zealand spinach (*Tetragonia tetragonioides*), which thrive in hot, humid weather. Malabar spinach is a climbing tropical plant with ruby-colored stems and large emerald leaves. New Zealand spinach grows into a bushy plant with pointy leaves. To harvest either green, just pinch off the tips plus one or two sets of lower leaves.

Delicious Varieties

'Bordeaux'. 40 days. Burgundy-colored stems and veins and long, slightly pointed, smooth leaves make this European-bred spinach one of the prettiest salad greens. Bolts quickly in heat, so harvest at the baby stage. Hybrid.

'Tyee'. 45 days. Hands down the best variety for late-spring plantings. This heat-tolerant spinach continues producing succulent leaves even when temperatures rise into the 70s. The dark-green, semisavoy leaves also resist downy mildew and tolerate frost admirably. Hybrid. 'Bloomsdale Long Standing' is an excellent slow-bolting heirloom alternative with very tender savoy leaves.

|||||||||||||||||||||||||||||||||||||||| **SPINACH** |||||||||||||||||||||||||||||||||

Spinacea oleracea

PLANT FAMILY: Chenopodiaceae

EDIBLE PARTS: Leaves

POTENTIAL PROBLEMS: Leaf miners, downy mildew

||||||||||||||||||||||||||||||||||||||||||||||||||||||||||||||||||||||||||||||||||||||||||||||||||||||||||||||||

Spinach Risotto

4 tablespoons (½ stick) butter, divided

⅓ cup minced onion

5½ cups chicken broth

1½ cups arborio rice

½ cup dry white wine

3 firmly packed cups (about 5 ounces) baby spinach leaves, stems removed

⅓ cup (about 1 ounce) Parmesan, plus more for serving

1 lemon, quartered and seeded

½ cup pine nuts, toasted

Following a three-week trip to Sicily several years ago, my friend Maren returned home and settled upon the task of perfecting risotto. After preparing countless batches for her lucky husband, Mike, she succeeded in developing this light, lemony version. It is the perfect way to celebrate the first spring harvest of spinach!

. . . .

In a large heavy-bottomed pot, melt 3 tablespoons of the butter over medium heat. Add the onions and sauté for 3 minutes; do not let them brown. Meanwhile, bring the chicken broth to a simmer in a medium saucepan and then reduce the heat to low.

Add the rice to the onions and stir to coat it with butter. Cook, stirring constantly, until the rice begins to look translucent, about 2 minutes. Pour in the wine and stir until it is completely absorbed, about 2 minutes.

Start adding the chicken broth to the rice one ladleful at a time (about ½ cup per addition). Stir until each addition is absorbed before adding another. Continue adding broth until none remains, about 15 minutes.

When the last broth addition is partially absorbed, mix in the spinach leaves, remaining butter, and Parmesan. When the broth is fully absorbed and the rice is tender and creamy, remove the pot from the heat and set aside for a few minutes to allow the rice to fully plump up. Divide the risotto among 4 wide, shallow bowls. Squeeze a wedge of lemon over each serving and sprinkle with the pine nuts and Parmesan.

Swiss Chard

Vintage gardening books sometimes refer to Swiss chard as "perpetual spinach" or "leaf beet." Both names suit this adaptable, easy-to-grow green, which belongs to the spinach family and is so closely related to beets that they share the same species. Chard produces a generous and steady supply of broad, rumpled leaves, even during summer when other greens fizzle out in the heat.

Planting

Begin sowing as soon as the soil is workable and warms to about 50 degrees F. I typically sow seeds or plant seedlings twice in spring, two weeks apart, and again around the summer solstice for a fall and winter crop. Sow chard thickly, as you would for baby greens (see page 85), if you plan on exclusively harvesting small leaves for salads. Otherwise, direct-sow Swiss chard seeds ½ inch deep and 1 inch apart, with rows 12 to 18 inches apart. Water newly sown seeds with a gentle stream of water and keep them consistently moist. Expect the seeds to germinate in 5 to 7 days. Help the seeds germinate in hot weather by placing a burlap bag over the bed a week prior to sowing and pinning it into place with U-shaped landscape fabric pins; this will shade and cool the soil. Soak the seeds in water the night before planting. Remove the burlap and sow the seeds. Chard seedlings are often sold as a clump in a small pot. Separate them before planting, as you would with basil (see page 37). Space the seedlings 5 inches apart, gradually thinning them to 10 inches apart. Grow chard in a spot in full sun or light afternoon shade. I often plant it as a border in front of trellised squash or cucumbers.

Growing

Like beet seeds, Swiss chard seeds tend to produce a cluster of seedlings because the "seeds" are actually a fruit that contains three to five seeds. Don't thin out baby green crops. If you want mature plants, thin directly sown seedlings when they develop two true leaves. Dig up each cluster of seedlings and tease out the individual plants. Replant the seedlings 5 inches apart. Once they develop six to eight stalks, use a sharp knife to cut off every other plant at the soil line, for a final spacing of 8 to 10 inches. You can also thin chard by snipping off unwanted plants at the soil line with needle-nose scissors. Water whenever the soil dries down to the base of your first knuckle, and foliar-feed once a month. Chard easily overwinters, even in cold climates, if the soil is insulated with a thick layer of mulch and the plants are protected by a hoop house tended with row cover material. Just expect the biennial plants to bolt in their second year.

Harvesting

Chard leaves become leathery and the colorful stalks turn tough and stringy as they age. Harvest frequently, from the outer leaves in, to encourage the plant to develop new leaves.

Use a sharp knife to cut off each stalk at its base. Harvest when the whole leaf, including the stalk, is 12 to 14 inches long. Harvest sooner for more tender leaves; larger leaves tend to be tougher. Cut chard grown for baby greens as described on page 85.

Storing

Store both baby and mature Swiss chard leaves in a perforated plastic bag as you would arugula (see page 87). Baby greens keep for one week and larger greens for two weeks in the refrigerator crisper drawer. Wash the leaves just before serving. Spin dry if using in a salad; for stir-fries, add the chard to the pan with water still clinging to its leaves.

Cooking Ideas

Chard is naturally high in sodium, so always taste dishes made with chard before adding salt. When sautéing chard, chop the stems and add them to the pan first. When they become tender, add the leaves. Toss hot gnocchi or pasta with ribbons of steamed chard leaves, melted butter, and a generous handful of grated cheese. Stuff large, mature chard leaves with leftover risotto or cooked rice, along with grated cheese or crumbled sausage (see the cabbage cooking ideas on page 180 for instructions on how to prepare the leaves for stuffing). Seattle-based chef Matthew Dillon first introduced me to pickled Swiss chard stems. Simply cut the colorful stems in half lengthwise and then into matchsticks. Pack the stems tightly into a quart canning jar. Prepare your favorite pickling brine; while it is hot, pour it over the chard stems, making sure to submerge them. Seal the jar and refrigerate for at least one week.

Delicious Varieties

'Bright Lights'. 40 days (baby greens), 60 days (mature greens). A mix of vibrant gold, magenta, red, white, and orange stems support shiny, bronzy-green leaves that make excellent wrappers. Open-pollinated.

'Erbette'. 35 days (baby greens), 55 days (mature greens). An elegant chard with an upright habit; slender, pale-green stems; and exceptionally tender, mild-flavored leaves that taste more like spinach. Open-pollinated.

|||||||||||||||||||||||||||||||||||| **SWISS CHARD** ||||||||||||||||||||||||||||||||||||

Beta vulgaris var. *cicla*

PLANT FAMILY: Chenopodiaceae

EDIBLE PARTS: Leaves, stems

POTENTIAL PROBLEMS: Leaf miners, powdery and downy mildew

||||||||||||||||||||||||||||||||||||||||||||||||||||||||||||||||||||||||||||||||||||||||||||||

Swiss Chard Quesadillas

SERVES 4

1 large bunch Swiss chard (12 leaves)

1 tablespoon olive oil

1 cup finely chopped onion

¼ cup sour cream

4 medium flour tortillas

¼ cup cilantro, chopped

1 cup grated pepper jack cheese (about 4 ounces)

1 cup crumbled Cotija cheese (about 4 ounces)

1 teaspoon ground coriander, divided

1 teaspoon ground cumin, divided

½ teaspoon smoked paprika, divided

Hot sauce, such as Tapatío (optional)

1 lime, cut into wedges

Vegetable oil

Taped to my fridge, I keep a list of easy-to-make, healthy dishes that require only pantry staples and garden produce. Whenever I feel tired and tempted to go out, I glance at the list, and it reminds me that there are plenty of reasons—such as these crowd-pleasing quesadillas—to stay home and cook.

Wash, but do not dry, the chard leaves. Cut off the stems and slice them ¼ inch thick; cut the leaves into ½-inch ribbons. Set aside.

Heat the oil in a large skillet over medium heat. Add the onions and cook until they are soft and translucent, about 3 minutes. Add the chard stems and cook, stirring often, until they are tender but retain a slight bite, 6 to 8 minutes. Add the chard leaves and cook, stirring frequently, until they wilt and become quite tender, 3 to 5 minutes.

For each quesadilla, spread 1 tablespoon sour cream on a tortilla. Top with 1 tablespoon cilantro, ¼ cup pepper jack, one-quarter of the chard mixture, and ¼ cup Cotija. Sprinkle with ¼ teaspoon coriander, ¼ teaspoon cumin, ⅛ teaspoon paprika, and a dash of hot sauce. Squeeze lime juice over the top. Fold the tortilla in half to enclose the filling. Brush a large skillet with vegetable oil and place over medium heat. Place the quesadilla in the pan and cook, turning once, until the tortilla is golden on both sides and the cheese is melted, about 4 minutes total. Repeat with the remaining quesadillas.

CHAPTER FOUR

LEGUMES

PART OF THE FUN OF GROWING vegetables in the legume family, which includes peas, favas, edamame, and beans, is peeling open their pods and revealing the green seeds snuggled together inside. These seeds taste deliciously sweet when eaten off the vine, and the pods of many legumes are often quite tasty too, as long as you harvest them at just the right time. Some legumes climb, twining their way up trellises in a race toward the sky. Others stay closer to the ground, their weighty pods dangling just above the earth. But all legumes perform a bit of magic as they grow.

When the roots of these plants extend down into the soil, they form a symbiotic relationship with rhizobial bacteria. The tiny beneficial microorganisms form nodes on the legumes' roots and convert nitrogen in the air—which plants cannot access—and fix it into the soil in a form that the legumes and other plants can use. In return, the legumes provide the bacteria with essential carbohydrates and minerals. When the legumes finish growing, the nitrogen deposit lingers in the soil, just waiting to be taken up. With a little planning, you can use this to your advantage by planting legumes before crops that need a lot of nitrogen (like tomatoes, corn, or squash) or after them to replenish the soil.

Edamame

Savory and delicious, soybeans have a pleasantly toothsome texture and nutty flavor and are extraordinarily high in protein. Frozen edamame beans and pods are commonly available in grocery stores, but fresh beans are difficult to find outside specialty Asian markets, which is all the more reason to grow your own.

Planting

Grow edamame in a warm, sheltered site. Wait to sow until all danger of frost passes and the soil warms up to at least 60 degrees F. Consider warming the seedbed with plastic prior to sowing in areas where the soil stays cool well into spring (see page 22). Rake the bed smooth and level, and use a hoe to form furrows 3 inches deep and wide and 18 inches apart in damp soil. Inoculate the seeds with a soybean-specific rhizobial bacteria inoculant before placing them 4 inches apart in the bottom of the furrows. Cover with 1 inch of potting soil to keep the soil from crusting. Water the seeds in, and wait to irrigate again until the soil dries down to your first knuckle or the seedlings emerge in seven to ten days. For a staggered harvest, sow two crops of edamame ten days apart, or sow two varieties with different maturation times on the same day.

Growing

Constructing a hoop house over the bed just after sowing and tenting it with row cover fabric helps the emerging seedlings stay warmer and drier. It also protects plants from insect pests and hungry deer, rabbits, groundhogs, and gophers. Foliar-feed with diluted liquid

---

INOCULATING LEGUMES

Rhizobial bacteria live in most soils, but coating legume seeds with a rhizobial bacteria inoculant before sowing increases the amount of nitrogen that gets fixed in the soil. The inoculant is a dry, dark powder that contains tons of rhizobial bacteria. Check the inoculant's label and make sure it contains the right bacteria for the legume you are growing (most inoculants contain more than one strain of bacteria). To inoculate seeds, place them in a wire mesh strainer and run them under water. Place the damp seeds in a plastic or paper bag along with a few tablespoons of rhizobial bacteria. Give the bag a good shake to coat the damp seeds, then sow them. If you've presprouted peas, simply sprinkle the inoculant over the seeds before sowing. Purchase new inoculant every year.

organic fertilizer 6 weeks after sowing, and water whenever the soil dries down to the top of your first knuckle. Thin to 8 inches apart when the plants grow large enough to handle and mulch with 2 inches of straw or dry grass clippings.

Harvesting

Bushy edamame plants grow to 2½ or 3 feet tall. When most of the green, fuzzy pods begin to plump up, take a peek inside one. If the beans are nearly touching and their *hila*—the points where the seeds are attached to the pod—are still green, it is time to harvest. Most of the pods on the plant mature all at once; they begin to yellow and the beans turn starchy in the space of just two or three days. Edamame beans stay sweet longer when stored if the pods remain attached to the plant after harvest. Pinch individual pods from the plants if you plan to eat the beans immediately; otherwise, use sharp scissors to cut off the entire plant, pods and all, at the soil line.

Storing

Pull the leaves off the plants and compost them. Bunch two or three plants together and place them in a large resealable plastic bag. Zip the bag three-quarters of the way shut and store in the refrigerator crisper drawer for up to one week.

Cooking Ideas

Edamame beans make excellent finger food. To prepare, boil fresh pods for 2 minutes. Drain, then pile the hot pods into a bowl and sprinkle with salt. To eat, simply squeeze the beans out of their pods and into your mouth. To use cooked beans in recipes, pop them out of their pods. Try substituting shelled edamame for chickpeas in hummus, stir them into a succotash, or add them to vegetable soup just before serving.

Delicious Varieties

Each soybean variety needs a certain amount of darkness each day to trigger flowering. Day length is dependent on latitude (gardens in northern latitudes have longer days, and thus fewer hours of darkness, than gardens farther south). In general, gardeners in the north must grow varieties that mature in 90 days or less because they are less sensitive to day length. No matter where you garden, check with your local cooperative extension to find the best edamame varieties for your region.

'Envy'. 75 days. One of the earliest edamame varieties. Bred at the University of New Hampshire, the plant grows to 2 feet and produces bright-green pods. Open-pollinated.

'Owen'. 120 days. Compact, 2-foot-tall plants produce loads of pods. A good choice for the southern third of the United States (below the Kansas-Oklahoma border). Open-pollinated.

EDAMAME

Glycine max

PLANT FAMILY: Fabaceae (Leguminosae)

EDIBLE PARTS: Seeds

POTENTIAL PROBLEMS: Japanese beetles, slugs, cucumber beetles, bean beetles

Herbed Edamame Salad

SERVES 4

2 pounds edamame pods or 2 cups shelled edamame

4 large ears sweet corn, shucked

1 cup halved cherry tomatoes

6 scallions, white and light-green parts only, thinly sliced

¼ cup torn basil leaves

¼ cup Everyday Vinaigrette (page 225)

Salt

Freshly ground pepper

This simple summer salad comes together in minutes and is easy to customize. Add chopped sweet or hot peppers, mix in cilantro or dill instead of basil, substitute thinly sliced red onion for the scallions, or serve the salad over Bibb lettuce leaves.

. . . .

In a large pot over medium-high heat, boil 2 quarts water. Add the edamame pods and boil for 2 minutes. Drain and run under cold water until cool. Shell the edamame into a large bowl. (If using shelled edamame, cook according to package directions.)

Cut the corn kernels from the cobs directly into the bowl with the edamame. Scrape off the corn pulp and release the corn "milk" by running the back of the knife down the cob. Gently fold in the tomatoes, scallions, basil, and vinaigrette until well combined. Season with salt and pepper to taste before serving, either at room temperature or chilled.

Fava Beans

Preparing fava beans is a labor of love. They must be shucked, blanched, and peeled before being used in most recipes. This requires work, no doubt, but it comes with a reward at the end: delicious beans with a delicate, nutty flavor. Along with the beans, you can also eat the whole pods when they are young and tender, as well as the plant's fabulous greens; big, succulent, and delicious, they rival spinach for both earliness and flavor. The leaves also make a nutritious cover crop, feeding the soil with both nitrogen and organic matter when turned under.

Planting

Favas (also known as broad beans) grow between 3 and 5 feet tall and like full sun and cool soil. They are best suited to places with long, mild springs, as they prefer to flower and set pods when daytime temperatures hover in the 60s and 70s. In spring, sow the beans as soon as the soil warms to 45 degrees F and is workable. Make two successive sowings two weeks apart. In areas where wintertime temperatures do not usually dip below 20 degrees (USDA zone 9 and warmer), favas may also be overwintered for a midspring harvest. Sow a single fall crop six weeks before the first frost.

Use a hoe to make furrows 4 inches wide and deep and 1½ feet apart in damp soil. Inoculate the seeds and set them into the bottom of the furrows at 3-inch intervals. Bury the seeds with 1½ inches of potting mix (to prevent soil crusting) and firm them with the palm of your hand. Fava seeds often rot in cool, wet soil, so water the seeds in and then wait to irrigate again until the soil dries down to the top of your first knuckle or until the seedlings emerge, usually within ten to fourteen days. Gradually backfill the furrow with soil to help stabilize the rangy plants as they grow.

Growing

Protect newly planted seeds with a tent of bird netting. Remove the netting once the seedlings reach 4 inches tall and then thin out—and eat—every other seedling. Allowing the soil to dry out, especially as favas' sweet-smelling blossoms appear, results in poor *pod set* (the number of pods that develop on the plant) and poor bean yields, as do temperatures over 80 degrees. Mulch with 2 inches of straw and water whenever the soil dries down to the bottom of your second knuckle. Foliar-feed with liquid organic fertilizer when the plants grow to about 1 foot and again when they flower.

Tall and rigid, fava bean plants often lean over as the pods mature. Building a "corral" around the plants provides extra support and keeps them upright. Simply drive a 6-foot-tall bamboo pole into each corner of the fava bean plot and string twine horizontally between the poles at 12-inch intervals. After harvest, pull and compost the plants or use them as a cover crop. Cut the stalks down, chop them up with a sharp spade, and dig them into the garden's soil. Allow at least two weeks before replanting the bed.

Harvesting

Harvest fava greens by pinching back the growing tip plus one additional set of leaves when the plants reach about 18 inches tall and again when they flower. Fava bean pods

grow like rungs on a ladder up the stem of the plant. When they first emerge, the pods grow skyward and may be harvested at 3 to 4 inches. As the pods mature, their outer skin toughens and they droop down. Begin checking for maturity when you feel seed bulges through the pods and they look plump and glossy. To test for readiness, pop open a pod and pull out a bean. The bean's hilum is located where the seed attaches to the pod. Aim to harvest while the hila are green and the beans are about nickel size. If the hila turn brown or the seeds grow much larger, they become quite starchy and lose their distinct flavor and buttery texture.

Storing

Store fava greens as you would arugula (see page 87). Store fava beans in their pods in a plastic bag in the refrigerator for up to five days. Shuck the beans just prior to cooking. The tough outer skin must then be peeled off all but the very smallest beans. To make this job easier, blanch the beans for 3 minutes in boiling water and then plunge them into an ice bath. Squeeze the kelly-green beans out of their skins before adding them to recipes.

Cooking Ideas

Substitute fresh fava greens for basil in pesto recipes. Wilt thinned plants or greens in warm olive oil and spoon them onto garlic-rubbed toast, or add them to a frittata or an omelet. Prepare small young pods as you would snap beans (see page 139 for ideas). Toss whole blanched and peeled beans into pasta dishes or whole-grain salads, along with a salty cheese, roasted garlic, and wilted greens. Purée the beans with olive oil, lemon juice, fresh ricotta cheese, and sea salt; spread on crostini, and top with a sprinkle of mint and a few whole beans. Or make a salad with spring lettuces, whole fava beans, toasted Marcona almonds, Manchego cheese, and your favorite vinaigrette.

Be aware that a condition known as favism causes an allergic-type reaction in some people when they consume fava beans: eat only a small amount the first time you try them.

Delicious Varieties

Make sure to choose large-seed fava varieties. Small-seeded types, which are known as faba, field, or bell beans, produce very starchy beans and are best used as a cover crop.

'Aquadulce'. 80 days spring sown, 250 days fall sown. The tastiest fava I've grown. Yields large pods that contain seven or eight beans with a distinct nutty flavor. Heirloom.

'Broad Windsor'. 70 days spring sown, 240 days fall sown. A popular British variety with shorter, 4-foot-tall plants and pods with three or four large beans. Hardy to 12 degrees F. Excellent choice for fall plantings. Heirloom.

FAVA BEANS

Vicia faba

PLANT FAMILY: Fabaceae (Leguminosae)

EDIBLE PARTS: Leaves, immature pods, seeds

POTENTIAL PROBLEMS: Aphids, powdery mildew

Grilled Fava Beans

SERVES 4

2 pounds fava beans in their pods

Olive oil

Sea salt

Chef Matthew Dillon, who shared this recipe with me, often grills fava beans on the wood-fired grill outside his Seattle restaurant, The Corson Building. The beans take on a slightly smoky flavor when grilled and steam in their pods as they cook, which makes them easy to slip out of their tight skins. Sometimes the bean skins become quite tender and the beans can be eaten whole, no peeling required. Serve the beans on a platter, either in their pods or shucked.

. . . .

Bring a grill to medium heat. Wash the fava bean pods, place on a large tray, and drizzle olive oil over them until they are well coated. Sprinkle with salt and place directly on the grill. Cook, turning occasionally, until the pods are blistered and black in spots, 6 to 8 minutes. To check if the beans are ready, split a pod open and pop the beans out of their skins: perfectly cooked beans will be tender and buttery, not crunchy or mushy.

SNOW PEA

ENGLISH PEA

SUGAR SNAP PEA

Peas

Pea vines look delicate, but their heart-shaped leaves stand up to frost and even snow. These cool-season legumes are grown primarily for their pods and seeds, but pea shoots, the tender, subtly pea-flavored tips of the plants, deserve a place at the table too. Pea varieties fall into three distinct categories: snow, English (also known as shelling or garden peas), and sugar snap. Snow peas have thin, tender, edible pods and taste best when harvested young, just after the peas form. English peas produce a fibrous, unappetizing pod, which protects the plump, sweet seeds hiding inside. Sugar snaps offer the best of both worlds: crunchy, edible pods and sugary peas.

Planting

Folk wisdom suggests soaking peas in water overnight and sowing them outdoors around Saint Patrick's Day, but the seeds germinate more reliably when presprouted (see page 134) and sown not by a calendar date but when the soil warms up to 50 degrees F. The vines grow best in full sun and when air temperatures stay below 75 degrees. In areas where spring warms up rapidly, consider planting pea seedlings, because they mature three to four weeks before directly sown plants. Peas also grow well from seedlings in fall in most climates. Transplant them 60 days before the first hard frost or when temperatures stay consistently in the low to mid-70s.

Wait to sow peas until the soil is dry enough to work. If you don't have time to presprout the seeds, soak them in tepid water for two to four hours only and then sow them immediately. Sow inoculated seed in damp soil 1 inch deep and 1 inch apart in rows 6 to 8 inches apart. This close spacing allows you to harvest an early crop of pea shoots. Cover the seed with potting soil to prevent crusting problems. Sow two or three successive crops at two-week intervals. Water the seeds in and then wait to irrigate again until the soil dries down to the top of your first knuckle or the seedlings emerge, usually within seven to ten days. Plant seedlings 2 inches apart and at the same depth they were growing in their pot. Protect newly planted seeds with a tent of bird netting; remove the netting when the seedlings become 4 inches tall.

Growing

Peas have two basic growth habits: bush and climbing. Bush varieties grow anywhere from 6 inches to 3 feet tall, while climbing types grow to 6 feet or more. Both types benefit from support and prefer to twine their tendrils around wire mesh, twigs, or taut string. Grow them on a trellis, or push twiggy tree trimmings into the ground alongside a row of peas. Train them up and around the trellis/twigs twice a week. Water whenever the soil dries down to the base of your second knuckle; foliar-feed two weeks after the seeds germinate and again when they begin to flower.

Presprouting seeds indoors before planting them in the garden reduces the chance that they will rot in cool, wet soil because each seed will have a growing root that can take up water. Presprouted seeds usually pop up out of the soil a full week before those that are planted directly into the ground.

To presprout pea seeds, wet a double layer of paper towels. Arrange the seeds in a single layer on one half of the paper towels. Fold the other half of the paper towels over the seeds so they are encased. Slide the folded paper towels into a resealable plastic bag and zip the bag three-quarters of the way closed. Place the bag in a warm spot (I usually leave mine on the kitchen counter). Every day, slide the paper towels out of the bag and take a peek at the seeds. Be sure to keep the paper towels quite moist, rewetting as needed. As soon as you notice little roots emerging from the seeds, usually within three to four days, it is time to sow them. Handle the seeds carefully, as the

brittle roots snap off easily; sow them root side down. You can use this same technique to presprout corn seed.

Harvesting

Pea shoots may be harvested from any type of edible pea vine (ornamental sweet pea flowers, pods, and vines are not edible) and typically include the top emerging leaves, one or two bigger leaves, tendrils, and even blossoms and tiny peas. When the peas reach 4 to 6 inches tall, thin out—and eat—every other plant. Once the plants grow to 12 inches tall, clip off the tip of each vine plus one larger leaf, making the cut right above the next lowest leaf. New growth will soon emerge from the base of that leaf. Use 2- to 3-inch-long shoots in salads and 4- to 6-inch-long ones in stir-fries. I grow peas in a container on my patio exclusively for shoots; I harvest them every seven to ten days, and usually get four or five harvests from one sowing.

Harvest snow pea pods within a week after they form, when they are flat, tender, and have tiny seeds. Pick sugar snaps when the pods are plump and crisp and the peas have just a bit of space between them. Wait to harvest English peas until the pea seeds touch but the pods are still bright green. Harvest all types of peas every other day during peak production. When the vines begin to yellow, harvest the tips of each plant before pulling and composting them.

Storing

Peas begin converting sugars to starch immediately after harvest. Store peas in their pods in a plastic bag in the refrigerator crisper drawer and eat them within 2 days maximum. Wrap pea shoots in a paper towel and refrigerate them in a perforated plastic bag for up to one week.

Cooking Ideas

Heat 2 teaspoons of oil in a cast-iron skillet over medium-high heat. Add three big handfuls of snow or sugar snap peas and cook, stirring often, until the pods are browned in places, about 4 to 6 minutes. Sprinkle with coarse sea salt and toss with soy sauce and sesame oil or with butter and lemon juice. Serve immediately. Add ¼ cup shelled English peas, a handful of pea shoots, a bit of chopped chervil or cilantro, and a slivered clove of garlic to miso soup one minute before serving. Slice snow or sugar snap pods into slivers and add to coleslaw or salad. Add pea vines to a salad mix with baby lettuces and Johnny-jump-up flowers, or sauté them with garlic until just wilted and squeeze fresh lemon juice over the top.

Delicious Varieties

To avoid problems with pea enation mosaic virus, which is transmitted by aphids and stunts the plants, grow resistant varieties, including 'Oregon Sugar Pod II' and 'Green Arrow'.

'Golden India'. 60 to 70 days. A climbing snow pea with incredible two-toned purple flowers followed by pale-yellow snow peas. The pods taste best harvested at 3 inches. Open-pollinated.

'Sugar Ann'. 52 days. An extra-early sugar snap pea that produces loads of very sweet, petite pods on 2-foot-tall vines. Open-pollinated.

'Tom Thumb'. 50 to 55 days. A shelling pea that grows only 6 to 8 inches tall and produces five or six pods per plant. Developed in the late eighteenth century, this super dwarf variety is particularly cold tolerant and perfectly suited for container gardening. Heirloom.

'Wando'. 70 days. A remarkably heat- and cold-tolerant shelling pea that produces pods packed with seven or more peas. A good choice for later sowings and Southern gardeners. Grows to 30 inches tall. Open-pollinated.

PEAS

Pisum sativum

PLANT FAMILY: Fabaceae (Leguminosae)

EDIBLE PARTS: Stems, leaves, flowers, pods, seeds

POTENTIAL PROBLEMS: Aphids, cutworms, wireworms, pea enation mosaic virus, powdery and downy mildew

Pea Shoot Salad with Shaved Parmesan and Lemon Vinaigrette

SERVES 4

½ teaspoon lemon zest

2 teaspoons freshly squeezed lemon juice

1 small clove garlic, minced

½ teaspoon white balsamic or white wine vinegar

¼ cup extra-virgin olive oil

Sea salt

4 to 6 cups lightly packed pea shoots

2-ounce piece Parmesan

Freshly ground pepper

This salad was inspired by a dish I had at Franny's, a wonderful Italian restaurant in Brooklyn, New York. At Franny's they believe that "simple is best," and this salad—tender pea shoots adorned with a vibrant lemon vinaigrette and shavings of salty Parmesan—embodies their mantra perfectly.

In a medium bowl, whisk together the lemon zest and juice, garlic, and vinegar. Slowly drizzle in the olive oil, whisking until the vinaigrette is emulsified. Add salt to taste.

Place the pea shoots in a large bowl. Use a vegetable peeler to shave the Parmesan over the salad. Drizzle the vinaigrette over the pea shoots and cheese and toss to coat. Season to taste with pepper. Serve immediately.

Snap and Shell Beans

Beans fall into two general categories: snap and shell. Typically, snap beans are grown for their tender, immature pods, and shell beans, including lima, runner, and soup beans, are grown for their fresh or dry seeds. But this is not a hard-and-fast rule. I often shell and use the seeds from snap beans that lingered in the garden too long; likewise, I often harvest and cook young shell bean pods.

Planting

Beans have two growth habits: bush and pole. Bush bean varieties grow to between 1½ and 2 feet tall and produce a concentrated crop of pods, making them ideal for canning and freezing. Pole beans grow 6 to 8 feet tall. They produce smaller individual harvests, but set flowers and pods all season, often resulting in a greater total yield. Grow both bush and pole beans in full sun; wait to sow until all danger of frost has passed and soil and daytime air temperatures stay above 60 degrees F. Expect beans to germinate within one week.

Sow bush beans every two weeks in summer, stopping 10 weeks before the average first frost. Grow them as a border around raised beds and in front of taller plants. To sow, use a hoe to make a 4-inch-wide, 4-inch-deep furrow. Drop seeds into the bottom of the furrow at 2-inch intervals and cover them with ¾ inch of soil. Pole beans need support. I grow my beans up a fence trellis (see page 5 for directions) and build bamboo teepees (see page 5) because they create a tall focal point in the garden—and a fun hiding spot for kids. Sow six seeds ¾ inch deep in a ring around each pole. Make two plantings of pole beans, three weeks apart. In hot regions, plant heat-tolerant beans, such as yard-long and lima beans, in summer, because most snap and shell beans drop their flowers when temperatures persist above 85 degrees. Despite their size, beans struggle to push through crusty soil, so cover the bean seeds with a ¾-inch layer of damp potting mix instead of garden soil if your soil tends to crust as it dries.

Growing

Tent newly sown beans with bird netting. Wait to remove the netting until the seedlings are well rooted and about 4 inches tall. Thin bush beans to 4 inches apart when they grow big enough to handle. As they grow, gradually backfill the furrow with soil to support the plants. Thin out pole beans to three plants per pole.

Place a 3-inch layer of straw or dry grass clippings around the base of bush and pole bean plants; mulching prevents the bush beans' tips from rotting when they touch damp soil. It also smothers weeds and keeps the plants' roots cool and consistently moist—conditions that are especially important for optimal blossom and pod set. Foliar-feed only if the plants' foliage begins to yellow. Water whenever the soil dries down to the top of your first knuckle. Use a soaker hose to irrigate, if possible, because beans are susceptible to several fungal diseases, and keeping their foliage dry prevents disease problems.

Harvesting

Bean flowers, which range in color from white to peach to pale violet, taste faintly beanlike and make a pretty garnish. Simply pinch them off as needed. Two- to three-inch-long baby beans have extra-tender pods. Shell bean pods taste best harvested at this stage, but I usually wait and harvest snap beans until they grow 5 or 6 inches long. Mature snap bean pods feel velvety, easily snap in half, and have plump, tender pods and very small seeds. Pinch or cut—never tug—beans off the plant; harvest when the plants are dry to prevent spreading disease. Check for mature pods every other day in summer. If snap bean pods bulge with seeds, shell them and cook the beans.

Allow shell beans to fill out their pods. The beans taste best—and have a moist, meaty texture—if harvested just as the pods begin to yellow and wrinkle while they are still pliable. If you'd like to store dry beans for the winter, harvest the pods after they become dry and brittle.

Storing

Place snap or shell bean pods in a perforated plastic bag and store in the refrigerator crisper drawer for up to one week. Store fully dry beans in their pods in a warm, dry location for about a month. Then shuck the dry beans from their crackly pods and store in a lidded glass jar; use within one year.

Cooking Ideas

Garnish salads with bean flowers. Beans with fat pods, especially Romano-style and traditional snap beans like 'Kentucky Wonder', grill best; load the beans into a grilling basket or place them crosswise across the grate to prevent them from falling through. Grill the beans over medium heat, turning occasionally, until they are crisp-tender and browned in spots (about 8 to 10 minutes). To dress up plain grilled or roasted beans (see page 142 for roasting instructions), toss them with a few tablespoons of teriyaki sauce and garnish with toasted sesame seeds; top with crisp pancetta. My Grammie always prepares slender haricots verts by blanching them in boiling water for 2 minutes and then pan-frying them in butter and garlic until they are perfectly tender-crisp, about 2 minutes more. Squeeze

fresh lemon juice over the slender beans before serving. Purple beans turn green when cooked—a transformation that kids, especially, find fascinating.

To cook fresh shell beans, place 2 cups of beans in a pot with 7 cups of water, along with herbs, garlic, or onion, if you like. Bring to a boil. Cover the pot, reduce the heat to a simmer, and cook until the beans are tender: 30 to 45 minutes, depending on their size. Drain the beans and discard the other vegetables. Toss the cooked beans with butter and chopped herbs or pesto, add to pasta dishes, or use in succotash.

Delicious Varieties

Beans offer wonderful diversity—pods can be purple, yellow, green, cream, or even mottled; slim, fat, round, or flat; seeds can be red, pink, violet, white, yellow, and black. If diseases, including mosaic viruses, bacterial blight, or powdery mildew, commonly strike in your garden, look for one of the many disease-resistant bean varieties.

'Garden of Eden'. 65 days. Pole. A fabulous snap bean with large, flat, grassy-green pods that stay tender and sweet even as they age. Amazing flavor. Harvest at 6 to 8 inches. 'Romano Purpiat' is a similarly shaped bean, but with bright purple pods. Heirloom.

'Tongue of Fire'. 70 days. Bush shell bean. Produces beautiful purple-and-cream-striped, stringless pods that taste good harvested young, but the large, flavorful beans are the real treat. Heirloom.

'Vernandon Filet'. 50 to 60 days. Bush. My absolute favorite green bean. 'Vernandon' is an extraordinarily slender French haricot vert type with a robust flavor. Pick it small, 6 inches maximum. Open-pollinated.

llllllllllllllllllllllll **SNAP AND SHELL BEANS** llllllllllllllllllllllll

Phaseolus vulgaris

PLANT FAMILY: Fabaceae (Leguminosae)

EDIBLE PARTS: Flowers, pods, seeds

POTENTIAL PROBLEMS: Mexican bean beetles, wireworms, mosaic virus, downy mildew

llllllllllllllllllllllllllllllllllllllllllllllllllllllllllllllllllllllllllllllllllllllllllllllllllllllllll

Spicy Roasted Snap Beans with Raita

FOR THE RAITA:

1 cup plain Greek yogurt

¾ cup finely chopped cucumber

2 tablespoons minced cilantro or flat-leaf parsley

1 tablespoon finely snipped chives

Salt

Freshly ground pepper

FOR THE BEANS:

1 pound snap beans, washed and trimmed

1 tablespoon olive oil

¼ teaspoon ground cumin

¼ teaspoon ground coriander

½ teaspoon smoked hot paprika

Sea salt

Freshly ground pepper

Roasted green beans make a great side dish, but they are even better as finger food, especially if you serve them with this irresistible dipping sauce. Cumin, coriander, and smoked paprika add a kick to the beans, and the raita—an Indian-inspired dip with cilantro and cucumber—cools things down. Use any extra raita as a spread in pita sandwiches.

· ·

To make the raita, in a small bowl combine the yogurt, cucumber, cilantro, and chives. Season to taste with salt and pepper.

To make the beans, preheat the oven to 500 degrees F. Place the beans in a large bowl. Drizzle with the olive oil and toss to coat. Sprinkle the cumin, coriander, and paprika over the beans, season to taste with salt and pepper, and toss again.

Spread the beans in a single layer on a rimmed baking sheet. Roast, stirring occasionally, until they are tender, crispy, and browned in spots, 12 to 15 minutes. Serve the beans piled high on a platter next to bowl of raita for dipping.

CHAPTER FIVE

THE
SQUASH
FAMILY

MOST VEGETABLES ARE SHORT AND GREEN. This inescapable fact creates a distinct design challenge in the kitchen garden. Enter the big, beautiful cucurbit family. The bold leaves; yellow, trumpet-shaped flowers; and gorgeous, colorful fruit of squash, cucumbers, and melons become much-needed focal points when trained onto a trellis. Growing these plants vertically saves room for other vegetables, especially in small gardens. Trellised plants also have fewer disease problems because the air moves freely through the foliage, and bees find the flowers more easily, reducing pollination problems. Of course, when allowed to grow along the ground, cucurbits form an attractive carpet over the soil. Plant them below pole bean trellises or at the edge of a corn patch and allow the vines to scamper between the plants, shading out weeds and making efficient use of garden space.

PLANTING CUCURBITS 101

The most common advice given to growers of cucurbits is to plant them in a "hill" because the plants' fleshy roots prefer to grow in loose soil. But I find that the mound of soil gradually erodes over the season, leaving the plants' roots exposed, so I plant my cucurbits in a shallow well. Dig a 6-inch-deep, 12-inch-wide basin. Place a 2-inch layer of compost or composted manure in the bottom of the well and dig it in. Then sow three squash seeds ½ inch deep and 2 inches apart from each other in the bottom (sow cucumber and melon seeds ¼ inch deep). Cut off the two weaker plants at the soil line when the seedlings get their second set of true leaves.

Or plant a single seedling in the bottom of each well. Large cucurbit seedlings do not grow well—transplant them when their first true leaves are just beginning to emerge. If a container has more than one seedling, cut the weakest one off at the soil line before planting. Remove the remaining plant from its container and plant it at the exact same depth it was in its container. Soak the soil around the seedlings with diluted liquid organic fertilizer. Gradually backfill the wells as the plants grow.

Cucurbits have two growth habits: bush and vine. Varieties that vine grow into rangy plants that can take up 30 square feet or more of garden space if left to sprawl. Bush varieties have compact, upright growth. Both types fit into small gardens as long as you grow varieties that vine, including 'Trombetta' summer squash and 'Lil' Pump-Ke-Mon' pumpkins, up a fence trellis (see page 5) or a bamboo teepee (see page 5) to free up real estate in the garden for other vegetables. Some of the vine varieties have tendrils that twine around trellises, and others do not; either way, if you want the cucurbits to grow up, it helps to train them onto the trellis.

HAND-POLLINATING CUCURBITS

Most cucurbit varieties are *monoecious*, which means that the plant has both male and female flowers. The plants produce fruit only if the female flowers are pollinated with pollen from a male flower. Bumblebees, honeybees, and other insect pollinators usually play Cupid, transferring pollen between male and female flowers, but if that doesn't happen, the baby cucumber, squash, or melon will just wrinkle and rot away. If you notice a pollination problem on your cucurbits, you can step in and hand-pollinate the flowers.

First, an anatomy lesson: Female flowers have a baby fruit right behind the flower; male ones don't. Female flowers also have a stigma—a sticky, bun-shaped female reproductive organ—inside. Male flowers have stamens (the male reproductive organ), which look kind of like Popsicles dipped in bright yellow pollen.

Cucurbit flowers open for a single day. Aim to hand-pollinate early in the day, just after the flowers open.

1. Clip off a male flower and carefully remove its petals to expose the pollen-covered anthers.

2. Rub the pollen onto the stigma in the center of a female flower, leaving a dusting of pollen behind.

3. Use one male flower to pollinate up to three female flowers. If the squash behind the female flower begins to grow, you've done your job right! To encourage more insect pollinators, plant flowers that produce lots of nectar and pollen, including sweet alyssum, cosmos, sunflowers, bachelor's buttons, and flowering cilantro, near your cucurbits.

Cucumbers

Cucumbers make fantastic pickles, but not all cucumbers are suited to pickling. If you plan on putting up jars of sweet bread-and-butter pickles, gherkins, or tangy dills, grow one of the so-called pickling cucumber varieties because their thin skin absorbs brine readily and their crisp flesh helps the fruit stay crunchy. All other types are best suited to eating fresh, including lemon, English, Beit Alpha, slicing, and Asian (or "burpless") varieties.

Planting

Wait to sow or transplant cucumbers until after all danger of frost passes and the soil warms up to 65 degrees F (use clear plastic to warm the soil early in cooler climates; see page 22). Plant seedlings or sow three seeds ¼ inch deep in a shallow basin as described on page 145. Thin out directly sown seedlings by cutting off the two weaker plants at the soil line when they develop their second set of leaves. Place a plastic cloche over seedlings and newly sown seeds (or construct a hoop house and tent it with a row cover; see page 23) to keep the soil warm, encourage rapid growth, and protect the plants from fluctuating temperatures and cucumber beetles and other pests. Grow cucumbers in full sun, except in very warm climates, where they prefer to grow under corn, tomatoes, or in other spots that

offer dappled afternoon shade during the hottest part of summer. Space the plants 12 inches apart when growing them on a trellis or 24 inches apart if they are allowed to sprawl. For a longer harvest, plant two crops three weeks apart.

Growing

Vent the cloche if temperatures soar above 75 degrees. Remove the cloche when the cucumber's leaves touch its sides, or the row cover when the plants begin to flower. Encourage small wasps to pollinate cucumber flowers by planting cilantro around the plants and allowing it to flower. Pay special attention to the soil's moisture, especially when the plants are under cover, and water whenever it dries down to the top of your first knuckle. Tuck mulch around the plants' base when the soil temperature reaches 70 degrees. Foliar-feed when the plants begin to lengthen their vines, again when they flower, and every two weeks after that. If growing plants on a trellis, encourage their tendrils to twine around the wire or twine, and train the plants up off the ground. High concentrations of *cucurbitacins*—compounds with a bitter flavor—develop in the fruit when cucumber plants experience high temperatures (in the mid-90s or above), nutrient stress, and/or drought. Keeping the soil evenly moist and fertilizing cucumbers at just the right time ensures that you'll harvest plenty of sweet, crisp fruit.

Harvesting

Harvest pickling cukes at 2 to 3 inches for gherkins and 4 to 5 inches for larger pickles. Cut slicing, English, and Beit Alpha cucumbers from the vine at 6 to 8 inches. Some Asian slicing cucumbers (like my favorite, 'Satsuki Midori') taste good when harvested at 8 to 12 inches long. Use scissors to snip the fruit with stem off the vine. Overmature fruits begin to yellow and develop a tough skin, large seed cavities, and hard seeds. Fruits that experience drought grow contorted or curve up like the letter J. Check for mature fruit every other day during the peak production period.

Storing

Store dry cucumbers in a perforated plastic bag in the refrigerator crisper drawer for up to 10 days. If the fruit tastes bitter, peel the cuke, as the cucurbitacins accumulate in its skin and stem, not the flesh.

Cooking Ideas

Add cucumber slices to a pitcher of water, vodka, or sake; refrigerate and strain before serving. To make a refreshing *agua fresca*, purée three large (8-inch) cucumbers with 1 quart of water and the juice and zest of two limes. Strain the purée though a double layer of cheesecloth. Add simple syrup to taste and a bit of fizzy water if you like.

For quick "pickles," slice cucumbers thinly, sprinkle with salt and pepper, and immerse them in apple cider vinegar; chill overnight. Or cover sliced cucumbers and peeled, thinly sliced ginger with rice vinegar and a few drops of chile oil and sesame oil; marinate overnight in the fridge. Drain, remove the ginger, and serve sprinkled with toasted sesame seeds. When packing cukes into jars for dill pickles, add at least two sprigs of dill flowers, two hot chiles, and a few peeled garlic cloves to each jar before pouring in the brine.

Delicious Varieties

'Alibi'. 50 days. An extra-early, very dependable pickling cucumber. Produces large yields of uniform, crisp fruit. Resistant to cucumber mosaic virus, downy and powdery mildew, and scab. Hybrid. When growing pickling gherkins, choose a variety specifically bred to be harvested small, like 'De Bourbonne'.

'Mexican Sour Gherkin'. 60 to 70 days. Not a true cucumber, this tiny fruit (*Melothria scabra*) looks like a baby watermelon but tastes like a slightly sour cucumber. The powdery mildew–resistant vines grow nearly 10 feet tall and are covered with fruit; harvest when they are about 1 inch long and tender. Eat whole, slice in half and add to salads or stir-fries, or pickle. Heirloom.

'Satsuki Midori'. 65 days. My all-time very favorite vegetable. This rare Asian slicing cucumber has a wonderful flavor with delicate melon undertones and hardly any seeds. The plant climbs exceptionally well, and the fruit never develops a bitter skin. Harvest between 10 and 12 inches. Heirloom.

CUCUMBERS

Cucumis sativus

PLANT FAMILY: Cucurbitaceae

EDIBLE PARTS: Fruit

POTENTIAL PROBLEMS: Cucumber beetles, squash bugs, squash vine borers, bacterial wilt, downy mildew, powdery mildew

Cucumber Wedges with Chile and Lime

Two 8- to 10-inch-long Asian cucumbers, chilled

1 lime

Sea salt

2 teaspoons spicy, flavorful chile powder, such as Chimayo

In Mexico vendors troll the beaches selling plastic beer cups filled with fruit drenched in fresh lime juice and sprinkled with salt and hot chile powder. Melons, mangos, papayas, and cucumbers are all served this way. Refreshing on their own as a snack, these cucumbers also make a quick and simple side dish for sandwiches, burgers, and tacos.

I use the bright orange-red Chimayo chile powder when I make this recipe. This spice comes from Chimayo, New Mexico, and it has an amazing spicy-sweet flavor. I buy it from a farmer at the Santa Fe Farmers' Market who sells it out of his stall from plastic garbage cans, but it is also available online and is worth ordering.

· ·

Wash the cucumbers and slice off the ends. Halve each crosswise and then slice each half lengthwise, so you have 4 pieces. Then halve each quarter lengthwise to make wedges. Place cucumbers in a large bowl. Halve the lime and discard any seeds. Squeeze lime juice over the cucumber wedges and toss gently to coat. Dust with salt and chile powder. Serve immediately.

Melons

Melons worship the sun, soaking up its rays all summer long. When allowed to lounge in the garden until perfectly ripe, the fruits become syrupy sweet and soft enough that the dull edge of a spoon slices cleanly through their tender flesh. Watermelons, muskmelons, and honeydew are the most popular melons, but true cantaloupes, which have a smooth rind that is divided into segments, and casabas and Crenshaws offer different flavors and lovely fruit.

Planting

Melons do not tolerate frost, prefer to be planted in soil that is at least 65 degrees F, and thrive when daytime temperatures range up into the 80s and nighttime temperatures stay in the mid-60s. Plant melons in a hot spot in your garden (a sunny, sheltered bed against a wall or fence is ideal) and consider growing them on black plastic stretched over the soil. The sunshine-absorbing black plastic keeps the soil warm all season long, radiates heat, and eliminates weeds, thus encouraging the vines to grow fast and produce more fruit. Purchase a UV-resistant black plastic mulch from a nursery or mail order catalog.

Install the plastic two weeks before you plan on sowing or transplanting melons. Rake the soil smooth and level. Lay the plastic over the bed and pin it into place with U-shaped fabric pins, making sure to stretch it tightly. When you are ready to plant, cut a large X in the plastic and tuck the flaps under, exposing a 2-foot square of soil. Space plants 1½ to 2 feet apart if trellising and 3 feet apart when allowed to sprawl.

Direct-sow or transplant melon seedlings into the warm soil as described on page 145. Melon seedlings mature faster than direct-sown crops and are the best choice in cooler climates. Just be sure to transplant homegrown or purchased seedlings right after their first leaf begins to emerge and harden the seedlings off before setting them outside. If you don't want to use plastic mulch, help warm up the soil by setting a glass cloche over the spot where you plan to transplant seedlings.

Growing

Encourage fast growth early in the season by immediately placing a cloche or a hoop house tented with ventilated plastic or row cover fabric over individual seedlings or newly sown seeds (see page 21). Vent the cloche if temperatures rise above 75 degrees. Remove the cloche when the melon leaves touch its sides, and the row cover when the plants begin to flower, so that pollinators can do their job. Water whenever the soil dries down to the top of your first knuckle. Foliar-feed with liquid organic fertilizer every other week. Leave the black plastic in place all season—it lasts several years if rinsed off, air-dried, and stored indoors for the winter. If you aren't using plastic, wait to mulch with grass or straw until the vines begin to lengthen or the soil stays above 70 degrees. Melons produce the highest yields when the vines sprawl out over the black plastic, but they also grow well up trellises.

Train smaller melons (those with fruits that average 3 pounds or less) onto a wire trellis. Check on them twice a week and coax the vines upward around the trellis. Prevent the fruit from separating from its stem by fashioning a sling out of pantyhose or other stretchy material and tying it to the trellis.

Harvesting

Allowing a melon to fully ripen on the vine is critical; once harvested, the fruit's sugars begin to dwindle and melons soften up only marginally. Muskmelons (commonly, though incorrectly, called cantaloupes) have a netted skin. Watch for them to turn from dusky green to a buff color. When fully ripe, a muskmelon's stem detaches from the vine with ease, leaving a clean scar on the fruit: this stage is called "full slip." True cantaloupes are extremely popular in Europe, especially in France, but they are still quite rare in the United States. These very fragrant, sweet melons have defined, half-moon-like ribs. Their skin is typically smooth and unnetted—though some varieties have warts—and they do not slip off the vines when ripe. Watermelons also do not slip from the vine, but the skin area where they rest upon the ground turns a buttery yellow when ripe, and the curly tendrils near their green stems dry and turn dark brown. Other melons, including casaba, Crenshaw, and honeydew, lighten in color as they ripen. Press your thumb into the blossom end; it softens slightly as melons mature and smells sweet. Use scissors to cut melons that do not slip off the vine. Check for ripeness daily as the fruit begins to mature.

Storing

Do not wash melons before storage. Keep them at room temperature for three to four days. Refrigerate uncut fruit in the refrigerator crisper drawer for up to one week. Wrap cut fruit in plastic and refrigerate for up to three days.

Cooking Ideas

For melon-flavored Popsicles, purée 6 cups of peeled, seeded melon with 1 quart water and the juice of one lime. Strain through a double layer of cheesecloth and stir in simple syrup to taste. If needed, stir in some water to make a slurry before freezing in Popsicle molds. Compose a salad of 'Tom Thumb' butter lettuce, melon cubes, prosciutto, and white wine vinaigrette. Serve melon wedges with chile, lime, and salt (see Cucumber Wedges with Chile and Lime on page 151). For a fresh take on salsa, finely chop muskmelon or honeydew and stir together with diced tomatoes, minced garlic, minced serrano chile, cilantro, and lime juice; serve with grilled fish.

Delicious Varieties

One of my favorite seed companies, Baker Creek Heirloom Seeds, features a huge range of melons from all over the world and is a wonderful place to start looking for varieties. When growing melons in a cooler climate, choose a variety that matures in 80 days or less.

'Charentais'. 75 to 90 days. This heirloom French melon is known for its exceptionally sweet, orange-colored flesh and sublime flavor. A true cantaloupe, its fruit is the size of a grapefruit and is round with pale, greenish-gray skin and subtle ribs that are defined by darker green stripes.

'Hearts of Gold' muskmelon. 70 days. This classic muskmelon is incredibly sweet and dependably produces 2- to 3-pound juicy fruit. Heirloom. 'Halona', a disease-resistant hybrid variety, and 'Sweet Granite', a reliable heirloom, also produce delicious fruit.

'Moon and Stars'. 85 days. This lovely watermelon has a dark-green, almost black rind, speckled with irregular dots of bright yellow. There are two varieties, one with yellow flesh and the other with red. Heirloom. 'Cream of Saskatchewan' is an heirloom variety with whitish flesh that ripens reliably in cooler climates.

MELONS AND WATERMELONS

Cucumis melo and *Citrullus lanatus*

PLANT FAMILY: Cucurbitaceae

EDIBLE PARTS: Fruit

POTENTIAL PROBLEMS: Cucumber beetles, squash bugs, squash vine borer, bacterial wilt, powdery mildew

Mixed Melons in Lemon Verbena Syrup

SERVES 6

½ cup packed fresh lemon verbena leaves

1 cup cane sugar

1 cup cold water

8 cups melon balls scooped from a mix of honeydew, cantaloupe, and watermelon (about 8 pounds total), chilled

Lemon verbena's slightly floral flavor brings out the sweetness of melons without overpowering them. Serve this dish at brunch or as a light dessert, and use any remaining syrup to flavor iced tea.

Squeeze the lemon verbena leaves with your hands until they are bruised and very fragrant. Finely chop the bruised leaves and place in a small mixing bowl. Combine the sugar and water in a small saucepan and stir over medium heat until the sugar completely dissolves. Pour the hot syrup over the lemon verbena leaves, cover, and set aside for at least 4 hours and up to 24 hours (the syrup should turn from clear to golden brown). Strain out the leaves and chill the syrup in a covered container. The syrup may be made up to 2 days in advance.

To assemble, place the chilled melon balls in a large bowl. Add 1 tablespoon of the syrup and toss with the melon balls; repeat until all the melon balls are lightly coated—not drenched—with syrup.

Summer Squash

Summer squashes, including UFO-shaped pattypans, yellow crooknecks, and zucchini, follow the law of diminishing returns: the larger their fruits grow, the less appetizing they become. These vegetables are naturally promiscuous, so the best way to manage them is to harvest the fruits when they are quite small, no larger than the palm of your hand, and to pick—and eat—plenty of the big yellow blossoms.

Planting

Summer squashes obstinately refuse to germinate or grow when planted too early—wait to sow or transplant until after all danger of frost passes and the soil warms up to at least 60 degrees F (use plastic to warm the soil early in cooler climates; see page 22). Choose a warm, sheltered spot in full sun with well-drained soil. Direct-sow or transplant seedlings into a shallow well of soil, rather than a hill, as described on page 142. Grow climbing types on a trellis or fence, or down a rockery; space them 1½ to 2 feet apart when trellising, 3 feet apart if allowed to sprawl. Plant the upright, architectural bush varieties, such as 'Eight Ball', on either side of a pathway to mark an entrance or at the center of a raised bed; space them 3 feet apart.

Growing

Encourage fast growth by immediately placing a glass or plastic cloche over individual squash seedlings or newly sown seeds (see page 21). Or construct a hoop house over a squash row and cover it with a tent of ventilated clear plastic (see page 23). This extra layer of protection helps moderate the difference between daytime and nighttime temperatures and prevents insect pests from feeding on the small plants. Just be sure to vent the cloche if temperatures rise above 75 degrees. Remove the cloche when the squash leaves touch its sides, and the row cover when the plants begin to flower, so that pollinators can have access. It's easy to forget to water plants that are under cover, so check on them daily; summer squashes need very consistent water to produce sweet, tender fruit. Water whenever the soil dries down to the bottom of your second knuckle. Climbing summer squashes, like 'Trombetta', need a little help scrambling up a trellis: as they grow, weave their leaves in and out of the trellis. Wait to tuck a 3-inch layer of grass or straw mulch around the plants until the soil consistently stays above 70 degrees. Foliar-feed with diluted liquid organic fertilizer every three weeks.

Harvesting

Squash blossoms stay open one day and then wither. The day before they open, their frilly tips start to flare out slightly—this is your sign that they will be ready to harvest the next day. Cut blossoms, along with 1 inch of stem, as they begin to open in the morning. If

harvesting female flowers, cut right below the baby squash that is located behind the flower. Make sure to leave some male and female flowers on the plant if you also want to harvest squashes.

Harvest crookneck and zucchini varieties at 4 to 6 inches long and round varieties when they are 2 to 3 inches in diameter. To avoid scratching the tender, glossy skin of young squash on the plants' bristly foliage, place one hand over the fruit to protect it and use the other to cut the squash from the vine along with ¼ inch of stem (use a sharp knife). Check the fruit every other day and harvest if needed, as the plant's production drops severely if you allow any squash to over-mature (signs include yellowing, the mushy flower dropping off the end, and tougher skin). Harvest all fruit and blossoms before the first fall frost.

Storing

With a sharp knife, poke about 20 holes in a resealable plastic bag. Place dry squash in the bag in a single layer and store in the refrigerator crisper drawer for 7 to 10 days. Store squash blossoms in a perforated plastic bag for up to 3 days. Don't wash the flowers; just brush them off. Pinch out the flowers' stamens or stigmas and check thoroughly for any insects camping out inside.

Cooking Ideas

Arrange 15 to 20 squash blossoms on an olive oil–based pizza before baking, along with torn basil leaves and dollops of fresh ricotta and mozzarella. Tear squash blossoms into bite-size pieces and add them to a quesadilla made with a mix of Cotija and jack cheeses. Stuff squash blossoms with goat cheese or ricotta and bake at 350 degrees F until heated through. Crumble feta cheese over a platter of grilled summer squash; garnish with chopped mint and freshly cracked pepper. Add ¼ to ½ cup of grated summer squash to your favorite meat loaf recipe. Stir ¼-inch cubes of summer squash and lemon zest into a basic white risotto about five minutes before it finishes cooking. Scoop out the flesh of round or pattypan varieties like 'Benning's Green Tint' and stuff with herbs, bread crumbs, and grated cheese. Place in a dish with ¼ cup water, cover with foil, and bake at 375 degrees F until squash is tender and cheese has melted.

Delicious Varieties

'Costata Romanesco'. 52 days. This Italian variety has a delicious, nutty flavor and a firm texture. The oblong, dark- and light-green-speckled fruits have distinctive ribs. One of the best varieties for harvesting squash blossoms, as it produces prolific numbers of male flowers. Heirloom.

'Trombetta'. 58 days. The fruits of this Italian variety vaguely resemble trombones, with long, seedless necks and bulbous bases. Also known as 'Tromboncino', the vigorous vines look attractive trellised, as the fruits hang from the vine like ornaments. Heirloom.

SUMMER SQUASH

Cucurbita pepo

PLANT FAMILY: Cucurbitaceae

EDIBLE PARTS: Fruit, flowers

POTENTIAL PROBLEMS: Cucumber beetles, squash bugs, squash vine borers, bacterial wilt, powdery mildew

Shaved Summer Squash
with Pecorino Romano

1 tablespoon freshly squeezed lemon juice

2 tablespoons extra-virgin olive oil

Pinch of sea salt

Three 6- to 8-inch-long summer squash or zucchini

2-ounce piece pecorino Romano

8 to 10 basil leaves, sliced into very thin ribbons

Freshly ground pepper

This recipe looks especially pretty with shaved yellow summer squash such as 'Zephyr', pale- and dark-green zucchini such as 'Costata Romanesco', and a mix of purple and green basil, such as 'Opal' and 'Genovese'.

In a large bowl, whisk together the lemon juice, olive oil, and salt; set aside. Using a vegetable peeler or mandoline, shave the squash into paper-thin ribbons, about $\frac{1}{16}$ inch thick, to yield 3 to 4 cups. Toss the squash ribbons with the dressing and marinate at room temperature for 5 minutes.

Meanwhile, shave the pecorino Romano into thin strips with a vegetable peeler to yield about ¾ cup. Add to the squash and toss gently. Taste and adjust seasonings, adding more lemon juice if desired. Divide the mixture among 4 plates. Garnish with the basil and season with pepper. Serve immediately.

Winter Squash

Winter squashes earn their name because the fruits store well, not because they grow during cold weather. There are three main species of winter squash: *Cucurbita pepo*, home to pumpkins and acorn squash; *C. maxima*, which includes buttercup and Hubbard squashes; and *C. moschata*, known for the intense orange-fleshed butternuts. Winter squash plants also produce three delicious extra edibles: large, delicate blossoms, tender vine tips, and nutty seeds.

Planting

Grow winter squash in full sun and wait to sow or set out seedlings until all danger of frost passes and the soil warms to at least 60 degrees F. Direct-sow or transplant seedlings into a shallow well of soil, rather than a hill, as described on page 145. Space plants 1½ to 2 feet apart when trellising and 3 feet apart when allowed to sprawl. In cold climates, choose varieties that mature in under 80 days and, if the plants do not perform well, try growing them on black plastic as you would with melons (see page 153).

Growing

Encourage fast growth early in the season by immediately placing a cloche or hoop house tented with ventilated plastic over individual seedlings or newly sown seeds. Vent the cloche if temperatures hit 75 degrees, and remove it when the squash leaves touch its sides. Remove the row cover when the plants begin to flower, so that pollinators can have access. Mulch insulates the soil and moderates its temperature, so wait to apply a 3- or 4-inch layer of grass or straw until the vines begin to lengthen or the soil consistently stays above 70 degrees. Water whenever the soil dries down to the bottom of your second knuckle. Foliar-feed every three weeks with diluted liquid organic fertilizer. Plants growing on a trellis need some guidance—check on them twice a week and coax the vines upward around the trellis. As the squashes mature, make sure their stems are firmly attached to fruits and vines. Support larger fruits by fashioning a sling out of pantyhose or other stretchy material and tying it to the trellis.

Harvesting

When the vines grow to about 6 feet long, pinch off the top 3 or 4 inches of the growing tips. This encourages the fruit to mature, and you can use the edible tips in the kitchen. Harvest squash blossoms as you would with summer squash (see page 157). Test the maturity of the fruit by pressing your thumbnail firmly into the skin—if it doesn't puncture, the squash is ready for harvest. Use a sharp knife to cut the squash from the vine along with at least 2 inches of stem.

Storing

Store unwashed squashes in a warm, dry, sheltered spot for three weeks to encourage their skins to harden further. After this curing process, move them to a cool, dark spot (between 50 and 60 degrees). Check on them regularly and immediately use any that begin to soften. Wash right before cooking. Acorn, sweet dumpling, and delicata squash keep about three months. Pumpkins, Hubbard, butternut, and spaghetti squash keep four to six months.

Cooking Ideas

The seeds from all winter squash taste delicious roasted. I am especially partial to the smaller seeds of acorn and butternut squash because they get quite crispy and make a tasty addition to winter salads. Scoop the seeds from the squash, pick off any fleshy strings, and then coat them lightly with oil and a dusting of salt. If you like, sprinkle spices over the seeds: chile powder, ground cumin and coriander, and sweet or hot paprika are all good choices. Spread seeds out on a baking sheet and roast at 300 degrees F, stirring occasionally, until they turn golden brown or begin to pop, about 15 to 20 minutes. Add peeled, cubed winter squash to stew at the same time you add potatoes. Cut acorn or dumpling squash in half, scoop out the seeds, and place halves cut side down on a greased, rimmed baking sheet; add ½ inch water and roast at 375 degrees F until tender. Serve with butter and brown sugar or stuff with leftover risotto. Tender squash vine tips taste delicious added to soups; simply finely chop and add to a brothy soup 3 to 5 minutes before you are ready to serve. See squash blossom recipe ideas on page 158.

Delicious Varieties

'Cornell's Bush Delicata'. 80 days. This bush variety is a cross between delicata and acorn squash and resists powdery mildew. Its tender skin does not need to be peeled, and ½-inch slices cook in under 20 minutes when roasted at 425 degrees F. Open-pollinated.

'Honey Bear'. 85 days. A fabulous acorn-type squash with dense, sweet flesh that caramelizes when roasted. Each half of the 1-pound squash makes a perfect single-serving meal when stuffed with a whole-grain pilaf. The compact bush plant resists powdery mildew and fits in nicely in small gardens. Hybrid.

WINTER SQUASH

Cucurbita spp.

PLANT FAMILY: Cucurbitaceae

EDIBLE PARTS: Fruit, seeds, flowers, tender vine tips

POTENTIAL PROBLEMS: Cucumber beetles, squash bugs, squash vine borers, bacterial wilt, powdery mildew

Butternut Squash Tacos
with Spicy Black Beans

SERVES 4 TO 6

2 jalapeños

1 serrano chile (optional)

½ medium butternut squash, peeled, seeded, and cut into ½-inch cubes (about 5 cups)

½ cup chopped white onion

3 tablespoons extra-virgin olive oil, divided

1½ teaspoons ground cumin

1½ teaspoons ground coriander

5 teaspoons ancho chile powder, divided

1 teaspoon salt

2 garlic cloves, minced

One 15-ounce can fire-roasted, diced tomatoes

Two 15-ounce cans black beans, one can drained

½ cup chopped cilantro, divided

12 small corn tortillas

½ cup crumbled Cotija or feta cheese (about 2 ounces)

Lime wedges

Butternut squash has a tendency to go mushy when roasted, because squash cubes steam when they are crowded into a pan. I've found that scattering the squash in a thin layer across the bottom of a rimmed baking sheet helps the pieces develop crunchy, caramelized bits. Because this recipe calls for so much squash, I divide it between two pans and rotate them in the oven halfway through the roasting process.

Preheat the broiler. Place the jalapeños and serrano in a broiler pan and broil, turning a few times, until charred and blistered in spots, 3 to 4 minutes. Remove and set aside.

Change the oven setting to bake at 400 degrees F.

In a large bowl, toss the squash and onions together with 2 tablespoons of the olive oil; sprinkle with the cumin, coriander, 2 teaspoons of the ancho chile powder, and salt, and stir to coat. Divide the mixture between 2 rimmed baking sheets, spreading the squash thinly and leaving some space between pieces. Roast for 20 to 25 minutes, or until the squash and onion edges begin to caramelize. Rotate the pans and stir halfway through.

Meanwhile, peel, stem, and seed the peppers and finely chop. Heat the remaining olive oil in a large saucepan over medium-high heat. Add the garlic and cook for 1 minute; add the tomatoes. Allow the tomatoes and garlic to bubble briskly for 5 to 10 minutes, or until the tomatoes reduce to a loose sauce. Sprinkle the remaining ancho chile powder over the tomatoes, and stir in the peppers and beans. Cook over medium heat for 10 minutes, stirring carefully to keep the beans whole. When they reach your preferred consistency, remove from the heat, stir in ¼ cup of the cilantro, and adjust seasonings as needed.

Heat a cast-iron skillet over medium-high heat. Warm the tortillas one by one, about 10 seconds per side. To assemble the tacos, use a slotted spoon to transfer a few tablespoons of beans onto each warm tortilla. Place a mound of roasted squash and onions on top of the beans. Shower the tacos with Cotija, the remaining cilantro, and a squeeze of lime juice.

CHAPTER SIX

THE CABBAGE FAMILY

SOME OF THE PRETTIEST AND MOST INTERESTING vegetables belong to the cabbage (brassica) family. Two of my favorites are the Italian heirloom 'Nero di Toscana' kale and Romanesco broccoli. 'Nero di Toscana' has narrow, deeply rumpled, dark-greenish-gray leaves that mature at nearly 1 foot long. The plants grow close to 4 feet tall and take on the look of a palm tree as you harvest the leaves from the bottom up. Romanesco broccoli, which is actually a type of cauliflower, is a natural geometric phenomenon. If you examine its lime-green spires you'll see that they are fractals: a geometric pattern that repeats an infinite number of times, no matter how small the scale becomes.

Brassica foliage ranges from forest green to dusky purple to chartreuse, and the family includes the vegetables highlighted in this chapter, as well as Asian greens, arugula, radishes, mustards, broccoli rabe, turnips, and rutabagas. If allowed to bolt, many of the brassicas produce tender, delicious flower buds (which are often called "rabe") and sweet, nectar-rich, entirely delicious flowers.

All brassicas grow best in cool weather and in soil that has a steady—but not heavy—supply of nitrogen. Plant them following legumes, or scratch alfalfa meal into the soil before planting. An irritating number of insect pests find brassicas irresistible, including imported cabbageworms, cabbage loopers, cabbage maggots, aphids, and flea beetles. The easiest way to organically deal with these pests is to deny them access to your brassicas—just build a hoop house over the bed after planting and cover it with a light row cover.

Broccoli and Cauliflower

Broccoli and cauliflower heads sit like eggs in a nest of gray-green leaves. I plant these big brassicas in a straight row down the middle of a bed and then underplant them with a carpet of red and green baby greens. Extend the broccoli harvest a month or more by skipping varieties that produce a single large head in favor of sprouting ones like 'DeCicco', 'Packman', or 'Purple Sprouting', which produce loads of tender *side shoots*—small florets that emerge from the stem for several weeks after the central head has been harvested.

Planting

Broccoli heads are actually tightly closed flower buds, while cauliflower curds are the plant's crumpled, malformed (but delicious!) flower stalks. These brassicas grow best from small seedlings, ideally with only three or four true leaves. Stressed seedlings, which have woody stems, root-bound roots, or red-tinged leaves, often *button*—prematurely form a tiny, button-size head. Once a button forms, the plant and heads virtually stop growing.

Broccoli forms the best heads when daytime temperatures range between 60 and 70 degrees F; for cauliflower, the range is 55 to 65 degrees. Seedlings exposed to prolonged temperatures below 50 degrees usually button. *Ricing*, a condition in which cauliflower curds loosen and take on the appearance of rice, happens when the heads are exposed to temperatures in the 40s as they form.

These myriad temperature considerations make timing when to plant tricky, especially in spring. Rather than guessing, ask a vendor at your farmers' market for localized timing advice and variety recommendations. Improve the chances of a good spring crop by choosing a variety that adapts to variable weather and matures in less than 80 days, such as 'Fremont' cauliflower or 'Windsor' broccoli. Install a hoop house tented with a light row cover over the young plants to protect them from insect pests and moderate temperature fluctuations (see page 23). Since temperatures stay warmer under a row cover, you can transplant seedlings as soon as nighttime temperatures stay above 45 degrees and the soil is workable.

Fall-harvested plants often perform better because the seedlings grow quickly in warm soil and the air temperatures progressively cool down. Insect pest populations are also on the decline. Transplant seedlings for fall crops during the summer. Check the seed packet or seedling label for each variety's "days to maturity" and then time the planting so the heads are ready for harvest right around the time of the first frost. Plant two or three small, successive crops one week apart. In regions with mild winters, plant sprouting broccolis in late fall for an early spring harvest.

Grow broccoli and cauliflower in full sun. Scratch alfalfa meal into the soil prior to transplanting to give the young seedlings a steady supply of nitrogen (follow the label's recommended application rate). Plant the seedlings 18 to 24 inches apart. If a container contains more than one seedling, cut all but the strongest one off at the soil line before planting. Water the seedlings in with diluted liquid organic fertilizer.

Growing

Try to maintain uninterrupted growth once the seedlings are in the ground, as nutrient deficiencies and drought encourage buttoning. Foliar-feed the plants every other week for the first six weeks with diluted liquid organic fertilizer. Side-dress with a granular organic fertilizer (follow the label's recommended application rate) or spread 1 quart of compost around each plant when the heads begin to form. Foliar-feed broccoli after the first cutting to encourage side shoot development. Avoid overhead watering, which encourages black rot and fusarium wilt. Water, either with a soaker hose or by hand, whenever the soil dries down to the bottom of your second knuckle. Mulch with a 3-inch layer of straw to keep the soil cool and moist and to prevent weeds.

Sunlight discolors cauliflower curds. Self-blanching varieties, like 'Bishop', have outer leaves that fold themselves over the head as it grows, protecting it at least partially from the sun. Many heirloom and early-maturing varieties must be blanched—denied sunlight—in order to produce snowy-white heads. When the head reaches the size of an egg, gather the long outer leaves together and secure them tightly over the head with a rubber band. Check on the band daily, adding more bands as needed, to ensure that the leaves stay tightly wrapped and the head stays completely covered until the cauliflower is ready for harvest. Purple and yellow cauliflower varieties and broccoli do not require blanching. Protect broccoli and cauliflower plants from the many insects that attack them by placing a hoop house tented with a row cover over the bed and leaving it in place all season.

Harvesting

Harvest broccoli when the buds on the central head are tightly packed together and before they begin to elongate and flower (though all is not lost if they do, as the flowers are tasty and the loose buds can still be stir-fried). Harvest cauliflower while the curds are tightly packed and the heads are 4 to 6 inches in diameter. Use a sharp knife and cut about 6 inches below the bottom of the head. Cut side shoots back to the main stalk when their buds are still tightly closed. Don't discard broccoli and cauliflower leaves—they are delicious! After harvesting the heads and side shoots, cut off the leaves and then compost the stalks.

Storing

Store broccoli and cauliflower in a loosely sealed, perforated plastic bag in the refrigerator crisper drawer for five to seven days. Break the heads into smaller "trees" and then cut them into bite-size pieces if you like. Peel off the outer layer of broccoli stems with a vegetable peeler so the florets and stems cook at the same rate. The green larvae of cabbage moths and cabbage loopers often creep into broccoli and cauliflower heads. Soak the heads in cold salt water for half an hour—any worms hiding inside will float to the top—and rinse the heads thoroughly before cooking. Store broccoli and cauliflower leaves as you would Swiss chard.

Cooking Ideas

Boiling broccoli and cauliflower results in limp, waterlogged florets. Instead, load trimmed, peeled florets into a steamer basket and place in a saucepan filled with 2 inches of boiling water. Steam until the stems pierce easily with a fork, just 2 to 3 minutes. Sprinkle finely grated white cheddar, or drizzle garlic butter and fresh lemon juice, over the hot steamed heads. Make a grilled cheese sandwich with Gruyère and finely chopped steamed broccoli. To roast cauliflower, lightly coat the florets with olive oil, spread them out in a single layer on a rimmed baking sheet, and cook at 450 degrees until tender; toss with toasted slivered almonds and dried currants. Use broccoli and cauliflower leaves as a substitute for collard greens. Cut out the tough central rib before cooking.

Delicious Varieties

'DeCicco'. 48 days. This Italian broccoli variety grows well in spring and fall and produces a small central head followed by lots of side shoots. For the heaviest side shoot production, harvest the central head when it reaches 3 inches across. Open-pollinated.

'Purple Peacock'. 70. This incredible multipurpose plant is a cross between kale and broccoli. It has deeply serrated, edible leaves that look like 'Red Russian' kale. It produces tons of purple-stemmed, extra-tender broccoli florets after the small central head is harvested. Grows to 3 feet tall. Open-pollinated.

'Veronica'. 85 days. A Romanesco-type cauliflower with lime-green spires. Harvest when the heads reach 7 inches across. Prone to bolting and buttoning in spring, so plant in late summer for fall harvests or in midwinter in climates that stay above freezing. Hybrid.

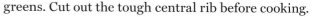

BROCCOLI AND CAULIFLOWER

Brassica oleracea var. *italica* and *Brassica oleracea* var. *botrytis*

PLANT FAMILY: Brassicaceae

EDIBLE PARTS: Flower buds and stalks

POTENTIAL PROBLEMS: Aphids, imported cabbageworms, cabbage loopers, cabbage maggots, cutworms, flea beetles, clubroot, downy mildew, fusarium wilt

Garlicky Roasted Broccoli

SERVES 2 TO 4

6 large garlic cloves, roasted

½ cup olive oil

¼ teaspoon soy sauce

1 large head broccoli, cut into small florets (about 4 cups)

¼ teaspoon red pepper flakes

Sea salt (optional)

This dish was inspired by one of my favorite vegetable dishes: the delicious blasted broccoli at Black Bottle, a wine bar in Seattle's Belltown neighborhood. Tossing the broccoli in a garlicky oil, instead of with chopped garlic, eliminates the problem of the garlic burning while the broccoli roasts at high heat. Roasted garlic is often available in well-stocked olive bars, or you can roast it yourself (see page 200 for instructions). Refrigerate the extra garlic oil and use it within three days. I like to brush it on pizza dough before assembling the pizza or use it as a dip for crusty bread.

Preheat the oven to 450 degrees F. In a blender or food processor, purée the roasted garlic with oil and soy sauce. Taste the oil; if desired, add more garlic cloves, as it should taste quite garlicky.

Place the broccoli in a large bowl and drizzle with 3 tablespoons of the garlic oil. Toss until the florets are well coated. Spread the broccoli on a rimmed baking sheet and sprinkle with red pepper flakes and salt to taste. Roast, stirring occasionally, until the broccoli is fork-tender and quite brown and crispy in spots, 15 to 18 minutes.

Brussels Sprouts

Brussels sprouts could easily have materialized from the imagination of Dr. Seuss. Their stout stalk grows 3 feet tall or more and looks like a column studded with miniature cabbages and topped with a floppy rosette of leaves. The sprouts maintain their outward appearance for a month or more after harvest, but develop their infamous strong taste if stored for only a few days off the stalk. If you have an aversion to brussels sprouts, reserve final judgment on their flavor until you've eaten them just after harvest, when they taste sweet and mild.

Planting

Brussels sprouts taste sweeter if harvested after the first light frosts. Plant them in early to midsummer (about 90 days before the first frost) for a fall harvest. Transplant small seedlings, ideally those with only three or four true leaves. Stressed seedlings that have woody stems, tightly wound root-bound roots, or red-tinged leaves do not grow well and often fail to produce sprouts. Choose a spot in full sun. Scratch alfalfa meal into the soil prior to transplanting (follow the label's recommended application rate). Space the plants 18 to 24 inches apart. Gently remove each seedling from its container, being careful to keep the root ball intact and disturb the roots as little as possible. Plant the seedling at exactly the same depth it was in its pot. If a container contains more than one seedling, cut all but the strongest one off at the soil line before planting. Water the seedlings in with diluted liquid organic fertilizer. Seedlings can be hard to find: look for them at farmers' markets, ask your favorite nursery to stock them, or start them indoors four to six weeks before you plan to plant them out.

Growing

Protect the small seedlings from pests by constructing a hoop house over the bed and tenting it with a light row cover (see page 23). Remove the cover when the plants outgrow it. Brussels sprouts need a consistent supply of nitrogen as they grow. Foliar-feed the young seedlings with diluted liquid organic fertilizer three weeks after transplanting. Then spread 1 quart of compost around each plant when the sprouts begin to form. Drought stress during the hot summer months checks the plants' growth and reduces yields, so water whenever the soil dries to the bottom of your second knuckle. Mulch with a 3-inch layer of straw to keep the soil cool and moist and prevent weeds.

As the plants grow, the sprouts begin to form in the *leaf axils*—the juncture where the leaves meet the stems. The sprouts look like tiny buttons at first, but they swell as time goes on. Cut the lowest six leaves off where they attach to the main stem when you first notice the sprouts; continue removing the lower leaves as they yellow. If you want all the sprouts to mature on a stem at once, cut the top of the plant off with pruners when the lowest sprouts are ½ inch in diameter. Otherwise, just let the plants grow.

Harvesting

Brussels sprouts mature from the bottom of the stalk up. Overly mature sprouts look puffy, and their outer leaves yellow and split open. Harvest the sprouts when they are 1 to 1½ inches in diameter, their leaves are bright green (or deep purple) and tightly furled, and the sprouts feel firm when squeezed. Break off the leaf right below the sprout and then twist the sprout off the stalk. Brussels sprouts tolerate temperatures down into the 20s but should be harvested if the ground freezes. To do so, cut the top of the stalk off with pruners and the stalk off at the soil line. If you plan to store the sprouts, keep them on their stalks.

Storing

Ideally, store sprouts on their stalks in a dry, cool (40 to 45 degrees F) spot, such as an unheated garage, for up to three weeks. If you have removed the sprouts from their stalks, place them in a lidded plastic container lined with a paper towel and store in the refrigerator crisper drawer for no more than three days.

Cooking Ideas

Cut pancetta or bacon into small pieces and fry until crisp. Remove and place halved brussels sprouts in the hot grease, cut side down. When the sprouts begin to brown, turn the heat to medium-low, add ¼ cup water or broth, and cover the pan. Cook until the sprouts pierce easily with a knife; serve with chopped candied pecans and the pancetta. Shave raw sprouts with a mandoline and add to salads and slaws, especially those with a creamy dressing. Toss halved sprouts with olive oil and roast at 450 degrees F: drizzle with herb butter (see Dill Compound Butter on page 57) before serving.

Delicious Varieties

'Falstaff'. 85 days. Gorgeous 2-foot-tall plants with purple sprouts and green leaves flushed with violet. Heirloom.

'Long Island'. 80 to 115 days. Compact plants produce up to 100 sprouts per stalk over a long period. Heirloom.

|||||||||||||||||||||||||||||| **BRUSSELS SPROUTS** ||||||||||||||||||||||||||||||

Brassica oleracea var. *gemmifera*

PLANT FAMILY: Brassicaceae

EDIBLE PARTS: Sprouts

POTENTIAL PROBLEMS: Aphids, imported cabbageworms, cabbage loopers, cabbage maggots, cutworms, flea beetles, black rot, clubroot, downy mildew, fusarium wilt

Roasted Brussels Sprouts with Capers

40 small (1-inch-diameter) brussels sprouts, yellow or shriveled outer leaves removed and stems left intact

2 tablespoons extra-virgin olive oil

2 teaspoons Dijon mustard

Sea salt

Freshly ground pepper

2 teaspoons capers, drained and rinsed

Minced parsley, for garnish

Roasting brings out the natural sweetness in brussels sprouts, and mustard complements their earthy flavor. Serve these sprouts warm with mashed potatoes and roast chicken.

. . . .

Preheat the oven to 450 degrees F. Halve the sprouts lengthwise. In a large bowl, whisk together the olive oil and mustard; season to taste with salt and pepper. Add the sprouts to the bowl and toss until they are thoroughly coated with the olive oil mixture. Arrange them in a single layer, cut side down, on a rimmed baking sheet. Roast until they are tender, outer leaves are browned, and cut sides are a very deep golden brown, 20 to 25 minutes. Shake the pan occasionally as the sprouts roast, but do not turn them over. Place the sprouts in a serving bowl, stir in the capers, and garnish with parsley.

Cabbage

My favorite cabbage, 'Chieftain Savoy', has deeply crinkled, forest-green leaves that collect droplets of dew in the morning (see photo on page 167). Savoy cabbage leaves make beautiful wrappers for cabbage rolls. But if you plan on making coleslaw, grow red and green varieties with tightly packed, crunchy leaves, such as 'Tendersweet' and 'Primero'. Pale-colored heads with tender leaves, such as 'Kaitlin', make the best sauerkraut.

Planting

Cabbage tolerates temperatures up to 80 degrees F, but grows best in the low to mid-60s. Mature plants survive down to 25 degrees, but young transplants often bolt before forming a head if they are exposed to temperatures below 45 degrees for several days. Get around these tricky temperature preferences in spring by choosing early varieties that mature in under 70 days, such as 'Gonzales', and by growing cabbage from seedlings. Directly sown crops do not compete well with weeds and often bolt when hot weather hits. Aim to transplant in late winter or spring as soon as the soil becomes workable and air temperatures consistently stay in the mid-40s. Plant two successive crops two weeks apart. Transplant seedlings 90 days before the first frost for fall crops; for a staggered harvest, plant mid- and late-season varieties at the same time.

Plant seedlings when they have two or three true leaves, as larger seedlings and those with a woody stems often bolt before forming a head. Choose a spot in full sun, and dig alfalfa meal into the soil before transplanting (follow the label's recommended application rate). Growing cabbage plants closer together encourages smaller heads, which saves space in the garden and also makes the heads more manageable to use in the kitchen. In a 3-foot wide bed, plant two *staggered rows* of cabbage—rows that are slightly offset in order to give the plants plenty of room to mature. Space the rows 12 inches apart and the seedlings 10 to 12 inches apart. Water the plants in well with diluted liquid organic fertilizer.

Growing

To protect the plants from fluctuating temperatures and prevent problems with pests, construct a hoop house tented with row cover fabric over the cabbage bed immediately after planting (see page 23). Spread 1 quart of compost around each plant six weeks after transplanting. Water whenever the soil dries down to the base of your second knuckle. Mulch with 3 inches of straw. When weeding, avoid disturbing the shallow-rooted cabbages by hand-pulling the weeds or using a stirrup hoe.

Harvesting

Squeeze the head a couple of times a week as it forms. Harvest when it feels firm, like a well-filled volleyball. Use pruners or a sharp knife to sever the cabbage from its stem just below the head. Leave the stem and its roots anchored in the soil, and keep any remaining loose leaves intact. Pour 2 cups of diluted liquid organic fertilizer around the stem and keep the soil moist. New small cabbage "sprouts" sometimes form at the junction where the leaves join the stem. Harvest the sprouts when they are 2 inches across and firm. You can also use a knife to score an X (make the cut about ¼ inch deep) in the top of the stem to encourage four lemon-sized heads to form.

Storing

Wrap cabbage heads in plastic and store in the refrigerator crisper drawer—or in a spot that is cool (around 45 degrees) and dry—for two months or more. To store cabbage in the garden for a few weeks after the head firms up, drive a sharp spade into the soil all around the plant. This breaks the roots slightly, which prevents the heads from taking up too much water and splitting.

Cooking Ideas

Stuff large savoy cabbage leaves with leftover risotto, rice pilaf, or sausage dressing, blanching them before stuffing: bring a pot of salted water to a boil; add the leaves, two at a time, and cook until they are tender, just under a minute. Transfer the leaves to a large bowl filled with ice water to stop them from cooking. Pat the leaves dry with a towel. Cut a triangular notch, 2 inches tall and 2 inches wide, in the bottom of each leaf (the leaf will now look vaguely like an arrowhead). Place a small mound of filling at the top of the notch. Fold the bottom flaps of the leaf up and over the filling and then roll the leaf up as you would a burrito, tucking in the sides as you go.

Delicious Varieties

'Early Jersey Wakefield'. 100 days. The gold standard for coleslaw, but heads grow up to 5 pounds. Heirloom. 'Alcosa' is a hybrid variety that grows much smaller, producing 3-pound heads.

'Gonzales'. 55 days. Perfect for small gardens, the tightly packed, pale-green "mini" heads grow to softball size. The pale, sweet, extra-crisp leaves make excellent coleslaw and sauerkraut. Hybrid.

||||||||||||||||||||||||||||||||||||||||||| **CABBAGE** |||||||||||||||||||||||||||||||||||||||||

Brassica oleracea var. *capitata*

PLANT FAMILY: Brassicaceae

EDIBLE PARTS: Leaves

POTENTIAL PROBLEMS: Aphids, imported cabbageworms, cabbage loopers, cabbage maggots, cutworms, flea beetles, black rot, clubroot, downy mildew, fusarium wilt

|||||||||||||||||||||||||||||||||||||||||||||||||||||||||||||||||||||||||||||||||||||||||||||||||||||

Spicy Cabbage Slaw

SERVES 6 TO 8

Zest and juice of 1 large lime

1 teaspoon apple cider vinegar

1 tablespoon sugar

½ teaspoon salt

⅓ cup grapeseed or canola oil

2 hot chiles, stemmed and seeded

1 plump garlic clove, chopped

½ cup packed cilantro leaves

2 cups thinly sliced purple cabbage (about half of a 1½-pound head)

2 cups thinly sliced green cabbage (about half of a 1½-pound head)

1 cup shredded yellow or orange carrot (about 1 large)

½ cup thinly sliced red onion

Freshly ground pepper

Sweet, spicy, and tangy, this easy slaw makes a delicious accompaniment to quesadillas and tacos. I often mix any leftover slaw with cellophane rice noodles and Thai basil for lunch the following day. Depending on the season, sliced sugar snap peas, black kale ribbons, kohlrabi matchsticks, and thinly sliced sweet peppers make excellent add-ins to this recipe.

Place the lime zest and juice, vinegar, sugar, salt, oil, chiles, garlic, and cilantro in a blender or food processor and process until well combined.

Mix the purple and green cabbage, carrots, and onions in a large bowl. Pour the dressing over the vegetables and toss to combine. Season to taste with salt and pepper. Cover and refrigerate for at least 2 hours, but preferably overnight, stirring occasionally.

Kale

Kale is kind of like basil: you really can't grow too much of it. The small leaves add a sweet crunch to salads and the mature ones can be braised, sautéed, steamed, or roasted. I prefer the texture of varieties with flat or rumpled leaves, including 'Red Russian' and 'Lacinato', but the curly varieties taste good when very finely chopped and stir-fried. Use kale's highly ornamental leaves as a design element in the garden. Plant the dramatic 'Nero di Toscana' kale (see photo on page 184) on either side of a pathway to mark the entrance to a garden. Or sow carrots around the perimeter of a raised bed and plant a curly kale like 'Redbor' in the middle for a contrast of color and texture.

Planting

Choose a spot in the garden with full sun. Scratch alfalfa meal into the soil prior to sowing or planting (follow the label's recommended application rate). Begin direct-sowing or transplanting seedlings in spring, as soon as the soil reaches about 50 degrees F and is workable. For mature plants, aim to sow a cluster of three or four seeds every 8 inches. For salad crops, follow the directions for growing baby greens on page 85; the seeds germinate within 7 to 10 days.

Transplant seedlings when they have just two or three true leaves and avoid ones with yellow or purplish leaves, as this indicates nutrient stress. Plant the seedlings at 8-inch intervals in rows 1½ feet apart. Sow or transplant three times in spring, two weeks apart; plant seedlings for fall crops 60 days before the first frost.

Growing

When the directly sown seedlings are large enough to handle, thin out the weakest two seedlings in each cluster, ultimately leaving about 8 inches of space between each plant. Do not thin out plants sown for baby greens. Mulching in spring attracts slugs, so wait to apply a 3-inch layer of straw until early summer. Irrigate whenever the soil dries down to the bottom of your second knuckle, and foliar-feed with diluted liquid organic fertilizer once a month.

Harvesting

Harvest baby kale as described on page 85. Begin harvesting larger leaves when the plant reaches about 1 foot tall. Use a sharp knife to cut the leaves off at the point where they attach to the main stem. Harvest from the bottom up. When kale bolts it produces fabulous nutty-tasting flower buds. Snip them off just before they open, along with 3 inches of stem. For edible flowers, cut the flower head off just as the blossoms begin to open.

Storing

Store both baby and mature kale leaves and flower buds in a perforated plastic bag in the refrigerator crisper drawer, as you would arugula (see page 87), for up to one week. Wash the leaves in cold water and spin them dry just before use. Place kale flowers in a jar of water and use within two days.

Cooking Ideas

Toss 3-inch-long baby kale leaves with lemon vinaigrette and aged Parmesan. Mix baby kale, lettuce, and mustard leaves together with nasturtium flowers for a pretty and spicy salad blend. Coarsely chop a big bunch of kale and toss with 1 tablespoon olive oil, 2 teaspoons soy sauce, and a dash of hot chile oil; spread out on a rimmed baking sheet and roast at 425 degrees F for 8 minutes, stirring once halfway through. The kale comes out slightly crunchy and very tasty, but it does not look especially pretty. Sauté chopped kale with garlic until soft; toss with pine nuts and golden raisins. Cook kale flower buds as you would broccoli rabe (see page 95 for ideas), and scatter kale blossoms over salads.

Delicious Varieties

'Nero di Toscana'. 25 days (baby greens), 50 days (mature). A beautiful, tall Italian kale (also known as "dino kale") with long, narrow, deeply rumpled dark-greenish-gray leaves. Heirloom.

'Red Russian'. 25 days (baby greens), 50 days (mature). This pretty kale has tender, serrated, blue-green leaves that are set off by purple stems and veins. The leaves stay tender even when mature. Harvest the leaves at 3 inches for use in salads. Open-pollinated.

||||||||||||||||||||||||||||||||||||||||||||| **KALE** |||||||||||||||||||||||||||||||||||||||||||||

Brassica oleracea var. *acephala* and *Brassica oleracea* var. *sabellica*

PLANT FAMILY: Brassicaceae

EDIBLE PARTS: Leaves, flower buds, flowers

POTENTIAL PROBLEMS: Powdery mildew, cutworms

Co-Op Kale Salad

12 dino kale leaves, tough stems removed and leaves sliced crosswise into ⅛-inch-wide ribbons

1 large carrot, julienned

1 very ripe large avocado

1 garlic clove, minced

3 tablespoons freshly squeezed lemon juice (from about 2 small lemons)

2 tablespoons olive oil

½ teaspoon ground coriander

½ teaspoon ground cumin

¼ teaspoon sweet Spanish paprika

1½ teaspoons harissa or another hot sauce, such as Sriracha

Salt

Freshly ground pepper

2 tablespoons sunflower seeds

Co-op grocery stores are one of my favorite sources of recipe inspiration. Their deli cases are always stocked with delicious but resolutely healthy seasonal salads. Kale is most often enjoyed in salads as a baby green, but larger leaves taste good raw if sliced into very thin (⅛-inch) ribbons. For this salad, use a Tuscan black kale (aka "dino kale"), such as 'Lacinato', rather than a variety with very curly leaves. Harissa, a spicy North African condiment, can be found in specialty groceries and Middle Eastern markets.

. . . .

In a large salad bowl, toss the kale and carrots. In a separate mixing bowl, mash the avocado well and add the garlic, lemon juice, olive oil, coriander, cumin, paprika, and harissa. Mix until the dressing is very smooth.

Scrape the dressing into the bowl with the vegetables and mix with your hands, massaging it into greens until everything is well combined. (This is messy, but it helps soften the kale's texture.) Season to taste with salt and pepper, and refrigerate the salad for at least 2 hours, but preferably overnight. Fold in the sunflower seeds just before serving.

CHAPTER SEVEN

ROOTS, TUBERS, AND BULBS

GROWING ROOT CROPS IS ONE PART PRACTICAL—they store well into the winter—and also one part magical. Sowing a tiny carrot seed in spring, only to unearth a long, bright-orange root a few months later, is nothing short of miraculous. Saving plenty of room for these underrated crops is worthwhile, especially if you want to cook with more food that you grow yourself. Most root crops produce tasty tops, flower buds, and even seedpods, in addition to their roots. Learning how to harvest these extra edibles and use them in the kitchen is an easy way to increase the productivity of your garden and extend the harvest season.

This chapter features not only guides to growing roots but also guides to other crops that grow underground, including potatoes and *alliums* (garlic, leeks, onions, and shallots). These vegetables are among the most economical you can grow, because roots prefer to be directly sown, and you can save and replant your own garlic, shallots, and even some onions.

Beets

Beets are grown primarily for their chubby red, white, or golden roots, but if you take a close look at their greens, you'll surely notice their uncanny resemblance to Swiss chard. That's no accident. Beets (*Beta vulgaris* var. *esculenta*) and chard (*Beta vulgaris* var. *cicla*) are actually two different varieties of the same species. Beet leaves are smaller and more succulent than their cousin's, and their flavor has a mild, spinachlike quality that pairs well with lentils and grains, especially red quinoa and barley.

Planting

Grow beets in full sun and loose, well-drained, consistently moist soil. Direct-sow them ½ inch deep and 2 inches apart, with rows 1 foot apart. Begin sowing as soon as the soil is workable and has warmed to about 50 degrees F. Water newly sown seeds in with a gentle stream of water and keep them consistently moist. Expect the seeds to germinate in 5 to 7 days. Make three successive plantings 2 weeks apart. For fall-harvested crops, start sowing again in late summer 6 to 8 weeks before the first frost. If you want beet greens for salads, follow the directions for sowing baby greens on page 85. Help the seed germinate in hot weather by placing a burlap bag over the bed a week prior to sowing and pinning it into place with U-shaped landscape fabric pins; this will shade and cool the soil. Soak the seeds in water the night before planting. Remove the burlap and sow the seed.

Growing

A single beet seed often produces a cluster of tiny beet seedlings because the knobby "seed" is actually a fruit that contains several seeds. Letting the closely packed seedlings grow without thinning them out results in a hopeless jumble of malformed roots. Ensure a crop of lovely round roots by thinning to 4 inches apart. Or dig up each clump of seedlings and replant as you would with Swiss chard (see page 115). Don't thin baby green crops.

Apply a 3-inch layer of grass clippings around beets after thinning to keep the soil cool and prevent all but the most persistent weed seeds from germinating. Beets grown in dry soil tend to get woody and tough, so water whenever the soil dries down to the bottom of your second knuckle. Foliar-feed with diluted liquid organic fertilizer once a month.

Harvesting

Harvest beets by grasping the plant firmly at the base of the leaves. Give it a good wiggle and then pull the root straight out. Begin harvesting when the shoulders of young beets pop out of the soil (about 40 days after sowing). Pull every other one and then hill soil or compost over the shoulders of the remaining roots. Harvest them a few weeks later, when they reach 2 to 3 inches in diameter. Don't wait too long to pull—large beets develop a woody core and an unpleasant starchy flavor. Beet greens have the most succulent texture

when harvested at 6 to 8 inches long. You can grow them as a cut-and-come-again crop: just grasp the tops with one hand and cut them off 2 inches above the soil line—the leaves will soon regrow. You can also harvest the roots and twist off the tops.

Storing

Brush any excess soil off the roots and then twist off—rather than cut—the beet greens, leaving an inch-long stump on the root to prevent beet juice from bleeding out. Store the unwashed roots in a perforated plastic bag in the refrigerator crisper drawer for up to a month. Store the greens as you would arugula (see page 87); use within a few days. Wash the greens and roots just prior to use.

Cooking Ideas

Roast beets as described in the recipe on page 193. Chop roasted beets and toss them with almond butter, or arrange them over salad greens with blue cheese and candied nuts. Make a grilled cheese sandwich with thinly sliced beets and goat cheese. Place well-scrubbed baby beets in a steamer basket and set in a pot with 2 inches of boiling water; cover and cook until fork-tender. Remove from the heat and toss the beets with melted butter or a simple vinaigrette. Sauté beet greens in butter until just wilted; then twirl them into a nest shape and fill it with buttered lentils or a whole-grain salad.

Delicious Varieties

'Albina Vereduna'. 60 days. This pure white root is so sweet it can be grated and eaten raw, but it tastes best lightly steamed. Beautiful when mixed with 'Golden' and 'Bull's Blood' beets in a salad. Heirloom.

'Bull's Blood'. 35 (greens), 60 days (roots). A gorgeous heirloom beet with red roots and bold, burgundy leaves that deepen in color as they age. Perfect for growing as a salad crop or for braising greens. The intensely red roots play second fiddle to the leaves but are perfectly sweet and good for steaming. Heirloom.

'Chioggia'. 55 days. This Italian heirloom is rosy pink on the outside, but a quick slice reveals—surprise!—red-and-white bull's-eye rings inside. Especially good for salads. Heirloom.

|||||||||||||||||||||||||||||||||||||||||||||| BEETS ||||||||||||||||||||||||||||||||||||||||||||||

Beta vulgaris var. *esculenta*
PLANT FAMILY: Chenopodiaceae
EDIBLE PARTS: Roots, leaves
POTENTIAL PROBLEMS: Leaf miners, downy mildew

||||||||||||||||||||||||||||||||||||||||||||||||||||||||||||||||||||||||||||||||||||||||||||||||||

Oven-Roasted Beets with Winter Citrus Vinaigrette

SERVES 4

3 large beets (about 1½ pounds total), washed and trimmed

½ cup freshly squeezed blood orange juice (from about 3 medium blood oranges)

¼ cup freshly squeezed grape-fruit juice (from about 1 medium grapefruit)

2 tablespoons freshly squeezed lemon juice (from about 1 small lemon)

1 tablespoon honey

1 tablespoon champagne vinegar or white wine vinegar

6 tablespoons extra-virgin olive oil

Salt

Freshly ground pepper

1 teaspoon blood orange zest

½ teaspoon lemon zest

1 teaspoon chopped fresh thyme, for garnish

Earthy beets and a trio of citrus juices make this a bright and flavorful wintertime salad. I like to roast the beets ahead of time and marinate them overnight in the vinaigrette because they become infused with its citrusy flavor.

. . . .

Preheat the oven to 400 degrees F. Wrap the beets individually in aluminum foil. Place them seam side up on rimmed baking sheet and roast until fork-tender, 45 to 60 minutes, depending on size of beets. Carefully open the packets, draining off any juice inside. When the beets are cool enough to handle, remove the skins and discard; chop the beets into ½-inch chunks.

Combine the blood orange, grapefruit, and lemon juices in a small saucepan. Bring to a boil, reduce the heat, and simmer gently until reduced to ¼ cup. Remove from the heat and whisk in the honey and vinegar. Add the oil in a slow, steady stream, whisking until emulsified. Season to taste with salt and pepper. Toss the beets with the blood orange and lemon zests and ¼ cup of the vinaigrette; marinate for at least 20 minutes. Garnish with the thyme before serving.

Carrots

The Dutch bred the first orange carrots in the 1600s. Until that point, domesticated varieties were most likely purple, red, yellow, and white—colors that are making a comeback today. Carrot varieties are divided into categories based on their shape. Danvers types are classic Bugs Bunny carrots: long, narrow, and pointed. Imperator carrots have fat, cone-shaped roots, Nantes are cylindrical, and Chantenay types are thick, tapered, and blunt tipped. Ball carrots work particularly well for container gardeners because their short, rotund roots require only 8 to 10 inches of soil to grow.

Planting

Sow carrots in full sun in your garden's best soil—it should be level, loose, and free of rocks, clods, and weeds. Carrots demand crumbly, well-prepared soil for three key reasons: their seeds germinate slowly, the delicate seedlings struggle to push through crusty garden soil, and they develop the total length of their taproot within the first few weeks after germination.

Follow the directions for direct-sowing small seeds (page 15); sow them at 1-inch intervals and in rows 6 to 8 inches apart. Carrots germinate inconsistently if their seeds dry out during their long germination period, which can take up to three weeks. To prevent this, lay a strip of burlap over the row immediately after sowing, as you would with parsley (see page 68). Keep the burlap moist, which in turn keeps the underlying soil moist. Check under the burlap every day, and as soon as you spot seedlings poking out of the soil, pull it off.

Begin sowing carrots in spring after the soil warms up to 50 degrees F. I plant three successive crops two weeks apart in spring and again in late summer for fall harvests. The roots taste sweetest when grown in temperatures between 50 and 70 degrees and in soil that stays below 75 degrees. Carrots are biennial plants, but they sometimes bolt in the first season if the seedlings are exposed to several days of sub-50-degree temperatures. Bolted carrots taste terrible, but their pretty, umbrella-shaped flowers provide nectar for beneficial insects and pollinators.

Growing

Thin the carrot seedlings to 3 inches apart once they grow large enough to handle. Consistent soil moisture is critical: wet, mucky soil causes unappetizing hairlike roots to form, while carrots grown in dry soil taste harsh, and alternating dry and wet conditions cause cracking. Water whenever the soil dries down to the top of your first knuckle. Weeds easily overwhelm slow-growing carrots, so mulch with 2 inches of grass clippings to keep the soil cool, moist, and weed-free.

Carrots pop up out of the soil slightly as they grow, and their shoulders turn green and bitter when exposed to light. Mound compost or mulch over their shoulders to prevent

this problem, and foliar-feed their tops with diluted liquid organic fertilizer every three weeks. In areas where carrot rust fly is a problem, construct a hoop house tented with a row cover (see page 23) over the carrot bed immediately after sowing to prevent the fly from laying eggs at the base of the newly emerging seedlings.

Harvesting

Harvest when carrots are about ¾ to 1 inch in diameter. You can pull them earlier, but fully mature, deeply colored roots have the most flavor. Encourage the carrots to release their hold on the earth by first loosening the soil around them with a garden fork. Then firmly grasp the greens near the soil line, give the carrot a jiggle, pull it straight out, and gently brush off excess soil from the roots. Layer 4 to 6 inches of straw mulch around carrots after the first light frost to insulate the soil. Continue pulling carrots into the fall, but be sure to harvest them all before the ground freezes solid. In mild climates, you can keep carrots in the garden and pull them through the winter; just be aware that these biennial plants will bolt in the spring, and this ruins the roots' flavor and texture.

Storing

Carrot greens (or "tops") decay quickly, so cut or twist them off, leaving a 1-inch-long stub. Store them as you would arugula (see page 87), and use them within two or three days. Store carrots separately in a perforated plastic bag for up to one month in the refrigerator.

Cooking Ideas

Scrub, rather than peel off, the tender skin of freshly harvested carrots. Chop off the long, stringy stems of carrot tops and finely chop the leaves. Use the chopped leaves as a substitute for parsley, stir them into soup just before serving, or substitute them for basil in pesto recipes. If you don't like how a particular carrot variety tastes right out of the garden, try cooking it before declaring a verdict on its flavor. Many carrots that taste harsh when raw sweeten up and develop a wonderful spiced flavor when steamed, roasted, or grilled. Steam carrots and mash them with a couple of tablespoons of goat cheese, chopped herbs, and vegetable broth. Toss carrots in olive oil and grill over medium heat until charred in spots and easily pierced with a fork; sprinkle with chopped chervil and sea salt before serving. Make a grilled cheese sandwich with herbed cream cheese, raw grated carrots, baby arugula, and olive bread. Pickle carrots.

Delicious Varieties

'Dragon'. 75 days. Features purple flesh with a bright-orange core and spicy flavor. Best enjoyed roasted, grilled, or steamed, though its color fades when cooked. Open-pollinated.

'Napoli'. 58 days. A Nantes-type carrot that is particularly sweet, especially when pulled after a light frost in fall. The cylindrical roots slice up into ideal carrot sticks. Hybrid. 'Scarlet Nantes' is an excellent open-pollinated option.

'Yellowstone'. 75 days. This Danvers-type carrot has a classic Bugs Bunny shape with yellow, mild-flavored flesh. Very tasty raw and maintains its yellow color when cooked. Open-pollinated.

|||||||||||||||||||||||||||||||||||| **CARROTS** ||||||||||||||||||||||||||||||||||||

Daucus carota

PLANT FAMILY: Apiaceae (Umbelliferae)

EDIBLE PARTS: Roots, leaves

POTENTIAL PROBLEMS: Carrot rust fly, wireworms

Honey-Roasted Carrots

16 carrots with leafy tops

2 teaspoons olive oil

1 tablespoon unsalted butter

1 tablespoon honey

Sea salt

Freshly ground pepper

This recipe is so simple, so fast, and so good. When roasted, the carrots become tender and sweet, and the nubs of their tops caramelize. Serve them warm alongside roasted pork loin.

. . . .

Preheat the oven to 425 degrees F. Twist the tops off the carrots, leaving a 2-inch nub; wash and scrub the roots. Place the carrots on a rimmed baking sheet and drizzle with the olive oil. Roll the carrots back and forth to coat before placing in the oven.

Melt the butter and honey together in a small saucepan and keep warm. Shake the carrots occasionally as they roast. Remove from the oven when they are browned in spots and a sharp knife easily pierces them but meets a bit of resistance at their core (15 to 20 minutes, less for very thin carrots). Drizzle the honey butter over the carrots, roll them around to coat, and place them back in the oven. Shake the baking sheet frequently and remove the carrots when their skin begins to caramelize and a knife easily slides through them, about 5 more minutes. Season to taste with salt and pepper.

garlic

Garlic tastes delicious at every stage of growth. You can harvest the leaves; pull young garlic shoots—or *aillets*, as the French call them; clip off the lovely curvaceous flower buds, known as "scapes"; and eat the bulbs both when they are young and green and when fully mature. Garlic varieties are divided into two main groups: hardneck and softneck. Hardneck types typically have large cloves that encircle a hard central stem, or "neck." These cold-tolerant varieties do not store as well as softnecks, but they do produce a delicious scape. Smaller softneck cloves form in a swirl of overlapping layers and have no defined neck. This type of garlic grows well in warmer climates and is commonly found in supermarkets because it keeps for a long period.

Planting

Garlic is grown from cloves, which develop into heads (bulbs) with multiple cloves as they mature. Choose a sunny spot with well-drained, loose soil where the garlic can remain undisturbed during its long maturity period. Plant garlic in late September or October. This timing allows the cloves to develop roots before winter—shoots may or may not appear above the soil surface.

Gently break apart the garlic bulb, being careful not to disturb the papery wrapping around each clove. Plant only large, plump cloves. Use a hoe to form 3-inch-deep furrows spaced 8 inches apart. Plant garlic with the flat end of the clove down and the pointy tip up. Space the cloves 4 inches apart: this close spacing allows you to pull garlic shoots and green garlic early. Cover the cloves loosely with 2 inches of soil and water them in well.

Growing

After planting cover the bed with a 4-inch layer of loose straw mulch to protect any green growth that emerges and prevent frost from heaving the cloves out of the ground; however, do not mulch in climates with wet, mild winters. Garlic shoots begin to grow in early spring when the soil warms and the days lengthen. As soon as you notice new growth, pull the mulch away from the plants and into the spaces between the furrows. Foliar-feed in spring once a month through April. Water whenever the soil dries down to the bottom of your first knuckle. It is important to thin the garlic, pulling out every other plant when they look like scallions; otherwise the mature bulbs will be quite small. Stop irrigating when the bottom leaves begin to yellow, usually in June or early July.

Harvesting

Garlic leaves taste similar to garlic chives. You can cut one or two off when the plants are no more than 8 inches tall; slice the leaves off with a sharp knife where they meet the main stalk. Harvest garlic shoots in spring when the plants grow 12 to 16 inches tall and are still very slender.

In late spring hardneck varieties produce beak-shaped scapes (see photo on page 1). Each scape grows straight up at first and then curls into a loop before growing tall and straight topped with a *bulbil* (little bulb). Cut the scapes off where they emerge from the topmost leaves just as they begin to curl. Removing the scapes encourages the bulbs to grow bigger. Harvest green garlic after the bulb has formed but while the cloves are still fused together and the outer wrapper is pliable—at this stage the garlic's flavor is very mild. Garlic leaves yellow from the bottom up; when harvesting mature bulbs, wait until half of the leaves have yellowed. Use a garden fork to loosen up the soil around the garlic and then pull it up, ideally when the soil is dry.

Storing

Clip the tops off immature green garlic 1 inch above the bulb. Store green garlic bulbs, scapes, shoots, and leaves in perforated plastic bags in the refrigerator crisper drawer for up to 10 days. After harvesting mature bulbs, bundle six plants together and hang them in a warm, dry, shady spot for 3 to 4 weeks, or until the papery wrappers are very dry. Unless you plan to braid the tops together, trim off the leaves 1 inch above the head. Use an old toothbrush to gently remove excess soil and trim the roots to ½ inch long. Keep the bulbs in a cool, dry spot; hardnecks keep for around six months and softnecks for as long as a year.

Cooking Ideas

Chop garlic leaves and use them in recipes that call for chives. Use garlic shoots as a substitute for baby leeks or scallions: they taste phenomenal stir-fried, steamed, or grilled. Make garlic scape pesto (see page 203 for instructions), or grill or steam the scapes as you would asparagus and drizzle with butter. Chop whole green garlic heads, sauté them in olive oil, and substitute for onions in recipes. To roast mature garlic, cut off the top quarter of the head, drizzle with olive oil, and place in a covered baking dish; roast in the oven at 425 degrees F until the cloves are soft, about 20 to 25 minutes, depending on their size. Refrigerate roasted garlic in a covered container for up to one week. Squeeze the softened cloves out of their wrappers before using in recipes.

Delicious Varieties

Garlic grows best from regionally adapted varieties. Rather than suggest my favorites, I recommend you visit a local farmers' market in the fall. Ask the vendors which varieties perform best in your area, and buy bulbs directly from the growers. Once you start growing garlic, simply set aside a few of the largest, best heads when you harvest and save them for planting in the fall.

||||||||||||||||||||||||||||||||||||||||||||||| **GARLIC** |||||||||||||||||||||||||||||||||||||||||||||||

Allium sativum

PLANT FAMILY: Alliaceae (Liliaceae)

EDIBLE PARTS: Leaves, flower buds, immature and mature heads

POTENTIAL PROBLEMS: Fusarium wilt, thrips

|||||||||||||||||||||||||||||||||||||||||||||||||||||||||||||||||||||||||||||||||||||||||||||||||||||||||||

Bucatini with Fresh English Peas and Garlic Scape Pesto

SERVES 4

8 ounces bucatini or spaghetti

Eight 10-inch-long garlic scapes

½ cup finely grated Parmesan (about 1 ounce), plus more for serving

½ cup shelled walnuts

Zest and juice of ½ large lemon

⅓ to ½ cup extra-virgin olive oil

Sea salt

1½ cups freshly shelled English peas (about 2 pounds of peas in their shells)

Freshly ground pepper

The secret to perfectly cooked peas is not to cook them at all. In this recipe the heat of the pasta and its cooking water softens the peas up just slightly, bringing out their sweet flavor, which complements the rich, garlicky pesto.

Bring a large pot of salted water to a boil. Add the bucatini and cook according to package instructions until al dente. Do not drain.

Meanwhile, place the garlic scapes in a food processor and chop into small pieces. Add the Parmesan, walnuts, and lemon zest and juice; process into a rough paste. Scrape down the sides of the bowl. With the blade running, slowly drizzle in the olive oil. Process until the oil is thoroughly incorporated and the pesto is fairly smooth, about 30 seconds. Season to taste with salt.

Place the peas in a colander. When the bucatini is ready, reserve ¼ cup cooking water. Slowly drain the pasta into the colander and let it sit atop the peas like a cap for 1 minute.

To serve, place the bucatini, peas, and about ½ cup pesto in a large bowl. Add a few tablespoons reserved cooking water (this helps distribute the pesto evenly) and toss to combine. Serve immediately. Pass extra cheese and pepper at the table.

Leeks

Leeks are easy to grow, and their handsome, upright foliage looks pretty in the garden, especially when ringed by a border of curly parsley, 'Bull's Blood' beets, or ruffled leaf lettuces. Plant an early leek variety, such as 'Roxton', that you can harvest through the summer, and a long-season, cold-tolerant variety such as 'Bleu de Solaise' for fall and winter harvests.

Planting

Leeks grow best from seedlings rather than from seeds, because the seeds germinate slowly and are easily overwhelmed by weeds. Choose a spot in full sun with well-drained soil. Scratch a granular organic fertilizer into the soil before planting (follow the label's recommended application rate). Begin transplanting seedlings in spring as soon as the soil becomes workable and warms up to about 50 degrees F. Plant shorter-season and long-season varieties at the same time, as they will mature at different rates. Use a hoe to create 6-inch-deep, 6-inch-wide furrows 1 foot apart. Plant the seedlings 2 inches apart and 2 inches deep in the bottom of the furrow. Water the seedlings in with a gentle stream from a watering can.

Growing

Gradually backfill the furrow as the leeks grow. As the summer progresses, continue to mound more soil (or straw mulch) all the way up to the point where their fan of leaves begins. Hilling up the soil around leeks blanches their stems, keeping them white, tender, and mild. Like all alliums, leeks have shallow root systems and grow best with consistently moist, but not soggy, soil. Water whenever the soil dries down to the top of your first knuckle. Foliar-feed every three weeks with diluted liquid organic fertilizer. Make sure there is at least 4 to 6 inches of straw covering the soil when the first light frost occurs.

Harvesting

Harvest leeks any time after they grow to pencil size. I often thin out every other leek at this baby stage and allow the ones that remain to grow 1 to 2 inches in diameter. To harvest, grasp a leek firmly at the base, rock it back and forth to loosen it, and then pull it straight out of the ground. If it resists pulling, loosen the soil around it with a garden fork. Leeks overwinter in mild climates; in colder areas, pull all remaining leeks before the ground freezes solid in fall or early winter. Leeks that flower develop a woody core, so pull the plants if you spot the beginnings of a flower stalk shooting up from the center. Or let one or two flower and go to seed, as the spicy flowers are edible and leeks sometimes self-sow. In the spring, transplant volunteer seedlings into furrows when they have grown to 3 or 4 inches high.

Storing

Since leeks can be harvested at so many stages, I usually just leave them in the garden and pull them as needed. If you must store leeks, trim off their roots and cut the leaves down to 3 inches above the blanched white base; store in a plastic bag in the refrigerator crisper drawer for up to three weeks.

Cooking Ideas

Bundle three whole baby leeks, using one of their leaves to tie them together, drizzle with olive oil, and then grill over medium heat until soft and charred in spots. Serve plain or drizzle a mustard vinaigrette over them. Chop large leeks into rings, sauté in olive oil, and add to frittatas and omelets. Leek greens aren't particularly appetizing once the plant matures, but they make an excellent addition to homemade vegetable stock. Pick leek flowers just after they open, pull them apart, and use the spicy blossoms as a garnish.

Delicious Varieties

'Giant Musselburgh'. 105 days. Dependably produces 2- to 3-inch-diameter leeks with blue-gray leaves. Good for fall and winter harvests. Heirloom.

'Roxton'. 85 days. This early variety grows quickly and produces leeks starting in early summer. The slender stalks are perfect for grilling. Hybrid.

||||||||||||||||||||||||||||||||||||||||||| **LEEKS** |||||||||||||||||||||||||||||||||||||||

Allium ameloprasum
PLANT FAMILY: Alliaceae (Liliaceae)
EDIBLE PARTS: Stalks, flowers
POTENTIAL PROBLEMS: Thrips

||||||||||||||||||||||||||||||||||||||||||||||||||||||||||||||||||||||||||||||||||||||||||||

Silky Braised Leeks

SERVES 2

4 large leeks

3 tablespoons butter

1 cup chicken broth

2 tablespoons white wine (optional)

½ cup packed finely grated Parmesan (about 1 ounce)

I read about preparing leeks this way in a *New York Times* article written by Anne Raver many years ago. The leeks caramelize and turn buttery soft as they cook. I like to eat them on toasted sourdough bread, but they make a good side dish for roasted chicken as well.

. . . .

Preheat the broiler and move an oven rack to the top position. Place the leeks in colander and rinse thoroughly to remove any grit. Cut off their roots and dark green tops, leaving only white and pale-green parts. Halve the leeks lengthwise.

Melt the butter in a large heatproof skillet over medium heat. When it foams, place the leeks in the pan cut side down. Cook, jiggling the pan occasionally, until the bottoms of the leeks turn golden brown, 8 to 9 minutes. Do not turn the leeks over.

Add the chicken broth and white wine to the pan. Bring to a boil over medium heat, then reduce to medium-low. Simmer briskly until the broth reduces to a few tablespoons and becomes syrupy, and the leeks shrink and become quite tender, about 25 minutes. Dust the Parmesan over the leeks and slide the pan under the broiler. Watch carefully and remove the pan as soon as the cheese melts and turns golden brown, about 2 minutes. Serve warm, making sure to scrape the dark brown sauce from the pan over the leeks.

Onions

There are three main types of onions: bulbing (*Allium cepa*), multiplier (*A. cepa* var. *aggregatum*), and bunching (*A. fistulosum*). Multiplier onions form a cluster of white, yellow, or red bulbs just under the soil line. Bulbing onions can be harvested early before they form bulbs, or later, when the bases of their overlapping leaves enlarge and form a bulb. Bunching onions form clumps of slender stalks and are considered to be true scallions because they never bulb up; however, the terms "scallion" and "green onion" are often used for any young onion without a bulb because they look and taste very similar and can be used interchangeably. Spring onions are bulbing onions with a base that is just beginning to swell—they are larger than scallions but smaller and sweeter than onions with mature bulbs.

Planting

Bulbing onions are *photoperiodic*, which means they require a certain number of daylight hours to initiate bulb formation. Long-day varieties, which grow best in the northern part of the United States, form bulbs when the days are 15 hours or longer. Short-day varieties initiate bulb formation when the days are 12 to 13 hours long, and are best suited to the southern third of the United States (below the Kansas-Oklahoma border). Day-neutral and intermediate onions bulb up in most areas. Onion varieties that are the wrong day length for your area will grow, but they will not form a bulb.

Bulbing onions may be grown from seed, sets (small whole onions), or seedlings, which are sold in containers or bare-root. You can also start seedlings indoors under lights (see page 14). I prefer seedlings because they root quickly, reliably bulb up, and can be planted close together and thinned out when they are the size of scallions and again at the spring onion stage. Directly sown plants mature slowly, and sets usually bolt before forming a bulb, so both are better suited for growing as scallions or spring onions only.

Choose a spot in full sun with well-drained soil. Plant onions in spring as soon as the soil can be worked and reaches 50 degrees F. Scratch a granular organic fertilizer into the soil before planting (follow the label's recommended application rate). Use a hoe to create 4-inch-deep, V-shaped furrows 1 foot apart. Lay the individual seedlings out on one side of the furrow, spacing them 2 inches apart and spreading their roots out. Bury the roots and the lower third of the seedlings by drawing the soil on each side of the furrow together. Adjust the seedlings' planting depth (pull them up if they are too deep or add more soil if they are too shallow) and then firm the soil around them. Water the onions in with a gentle stream from a watering can.

Plant bulbing onions from small sets (about ¾ inch in diameter) or seed as soon as the soil reaches 45 degrees. Plant the sets 1 inch apart and 1½ inches deep in rows spaced 1 foot apart. Broadcast the seeds over smooth, level soil and follow the directions for direct-sowing small seeds (see page 15). The seeds take up to three weeks to germinate.

Growing

Thin directly sown seedlings to 1 inch apart in all directions as soon as they are large enough to handle. Thin onions planted as seedlings or sets to 2 inches apart when the plants grow to the size of a fat pencil. As the plants grow taller and wider, thin out every other one to give the bulbs room to form. Hand-pull weeds frequently, because they rob water and nutrients from the shallow-rooted onions. Foliar-feed the onions three weeks after planting and again when bulbs begin to form. Water whenever the soil dries down to the top of your first knuckle; stop watering when onion tops begin to yellow. As the bulbs form, they often push themselves out of the soil; do not mound soil or mulch around the bulbs, as this prevents the outer leaves from drying into a protective papery wrapper.

Harvesting

Bulbing onions may be harvested at any time. I tend to plant them thickly and then thin out plants gradually over the season as they grow, leaving some to bulb up. If you want to store bulb onions, wait to harvest until about three-quarters of the tops yellow. Then fold the tops over right above the bulb and wait one week before pulling the onions from the ground.

Storing

Store scallions and spring onions in a perforated plastic bag lined with a damp paper towel in the refrigerator for up to two weeks. If you plan on storing bulbing onions, lay them out in a warm, dry, shaded, and well-ventilated spot until their leaves become com-

pletely dry and the outer layers of the bulb feel papery. If braiding the tops together, do so when they are dry but still pliable. Otherwise, cut the tops off, leaving a ½-inch nub above the bulb, and store the onions in a cool spot (50 to 60 degrees) in a mesh bag. The so-called storage onions like 'Australian Brown' typically have a stronger, hotter flavor and keep longer than mild sweet onions such as 'Red Candy Apple'. Storage onions last four to six months; use sweet onions within two months.

Cooking Ideas

Cut scallions into rounds and stir into crepe batter before cooking. Slice spring onions in half length-wise; marinate in olive oil with chopped herbs, grill over medium heat until tender and charred in spots, and serve with grilled meat, fish, or an omelet. Scatter caramelized onions (see page 49) and grated Gruyère cheese over puff pastry and bake until the pastry is golden. Sauté sliced onions in a mix of olive oil and butter until very tender, season them with freshly ground coriander seed, and serve over cooked lentils and rice. Save onion tops for homemade soup stock.

Delicious Varieties

'Borettana' cipollini. 90 to 100 days. A long-day bulbing onion that produces small, flattened, disklike bulbs with an exceptionally sweet, mild flavor. My very favorite onion for grilling and baking.

'Granex'. 80 days. Known for its extra large, very sweet bulbs. This short-day variety is perfect for frying or caramelizing and sugary enough to eat raw in salads. 'Walla Walla' is a comparable long-day variety that reliably bulbs up in the North.

Multiplier Onions

Plant multiplier onions from sets in fall at the same time as garlic (see page 199). Space the sets 6 inches apart and bury them so that their necks are even with the soil line; they will sprout in spring. In very cold climates plant them in spring at the same time you would onion sets. Use a fork to lift multiplier bulbs when the leaves begin to die back. Store them as you would bulbing onions; save some bulbs and replant them in fall. Egyptian walking onions form a cluster of bulbs underground and a cluster of small bulbs aboveground; replant bulbs from the top cluster and eat the underground bulbs.

Bunching Onions

Plant these perennial onions from seeds, sets, or seedlings in spring at the same time as you would bulbing onions. Harvest the slender stalks when they reach 12 inches tall. Use a garden fork to lever the clump out of the soil, harvest up to two-thirds of the onions, and then settle the clump back into the soil so the remaining onions can continue to multiply. In spring, divide the clumps to ensure a steady supply. Try 'Evergreen Hardy White' and 'Deep Purple'.

BULBING ONIONS

Allium cepa

PLANT FAMILY: Alliaceae (Liliaceae)

EDIBLE PARTS: Leaves, stalks, bulbs

POTENTIAL PROBLEMS: Thrips

Balsamic-Roasted Onions

SERVES 6

12 cipollini onions, peeled and
root ends trimmed off (about 2
pounds)

¼ cup (½ stick) butter, melted

¼ cup balsamic vinegar

3 tablespoons maple syrup

1 teaspoon minced fresh thyme

Sea salt

Freshly ground pepper

Roasting brings out the natural sweetness in little cipollini onions, and the balsamic vinegar adds tang. Serve warm with roasted chicken or at room temperature as an addition to a meze platter.

. . . .

Preheat the oven to 450 degrees F. Score an X in the top of each onion, cutting about halfway through. Spread them out in a large oiled baking pan or 2-quart baking dish. In a small bowl, combine the butter, vinegar, and maple syrup, and drizzle over the onions, turning to coat well. Arrange the onions, cut side down, on the pan. Sprinkle with the thyme and season to taste with salt and pepper. Cover the pan with aluminum foil and roast until the onions are soft, about 30 minutes. Remove the foil, turn the onions over, baste them with the vinegar sauce, and continue baking until they are very tender, lightly browned, and glazed, 15 to 25 more minutes, depending on size. Serve with any sauce left in the pan.

Potatoes

Not all potatoes are created equal. Knobby fingerling potatoes retain their firm texture when cooked, making them ideal candidates for potato salads (so long as you don't mind their skins, as their gnarled shape makes them hard to peel). Starchy baking potatoes, such as the famous russet, have thick skins and dry flesh that turns light and fluffy when baked or boiled and mashed. Boiling potatoes such as 'All Red' have thin skins and waxy flesh with a very low starch content, so they retain their shape when cooked. All-purpose potatoes such as 'Yukon Gold' have firm flesh with a moderate starch content, so they mash well but also retain their shape when boiled or grilled.

Planting

You can grow potatoes from tubers purchased at the grocery store or a farmers' market, but it is more prudent to purchase seed potatoes—small whole tubers—that are labeled as certified disease-free. If you examine the seed potatoes, you'll notice *eyes*: growing points where sprouts emerge. Tubers with sturdy green sprouts grow rapidly and produce larger yields; *chitting* or *presprouting* encourages the development of these sprouts: Two weeks prior to the planned planting date, lay the potatoes out in a warm (70 degrees F), light spot. Turn them over every few days. Plant once they develop stout, 1- to 2-inch-long sprouts.

Plan on planting potatoes in late winter or early spring as soon as the soil can be worked and warms up to about 50 degrees. Keep in mind that frost damages potato foliage, so try to time the planting so they will sprout after the last frost. Choose a sunny spot with well-drained, loose, moist soil. Use a hoe to create 6-inch-deep furrows. Plant egg-sized seed potatoes whole. Cut larger ones into pieces crosswise, making sure each section has at least two eyes. Allow the cut pieces to cure by storing them in a warm, dry spot for two days before planting. Gently press potatoes into the bottom of the furrow with the sprouts pointing upward. Space tubers 10 inches apart and rows 2 feet apart. Backfill the furrow with 3 inches of soil. Extend the potato season by planting an early variety such as 'Viking Purple', a midseason variety such as 'All Red', and a late variety, such as 'Bintje'. Either plant them all at the same time or stagger the planting of each variety over a period of three weeks.

Growing

Once buried, a seed potato sends out a network of rhizomes (stems that grow horizontally underground). Potatoes, which are technically swollen stems called tubers, form on the ends of these rhizomes. When the seed potatoes send sprouts aboveground, spread 1 inch of compost around them. When the potatoes' foliage grows to a foot tall, use a hoe to backfill the furrow and mound soil up and around the lower half of the plants, being careful not to break them. This process, known as hilling up, increases yields by giving the rhizomes more room to form and grow underground.

After the first hilling, I prefer to mound decomposing leaves around the plants, rather than soil, because it makes harvesting much easier (I collect leaves in fall and store them outdoors in a wire bin just for this purpose). The leaves remain light, fluffy, and moist, providing the perfect conditions for growing tubers. Straw may also be used, but it does not retain as much moisture as leaves. Hill leaves or straw around the bottom third of the plants every two weeks. Stop hilling once the plants begin to bloom, because they end foliage production at this point and concentrate on tuber formation and growth.

Foliar-feed only if the plants' leaves turn yellow or develop a purplish tinge. Keep the mulch or soil as damp as a well-wrung-out sponge. Stop watering when the plants begin to yellow. In areas where Colorado potato beetles are a problem, cover plants with a row cover as soon as they sprout.

Harvesting

In summer, when the potatoes begin to bloom, plunge your bare hands down into the loose soil or mulch and feel around for small new potatoes. Tug them off the plants. For larger potatoes, wait to harvest until the plants die back to the ground in summer. Pull back the mulch and sift through it, removing any potatoes you expose. Potatoes grow in clusters on the rhizomes, and the biggest tubers are usually found lower down. Use a garden fork to loosen and turn over the soil underlying the mulch, feeling around for potatoes as you go. Set aside any potatoes that you've speared and use them immediately, as they will rot quickly in storage.

Storing

Gently brush off any excess soil. Place potatoes in a dry, dark spot at room temperature (about 65 degrees) for three weeks to help their skins cure. Pack potatoes loosely and no more than two layers deep in a box with sheets of newspaper between the layers. You can keep the box in a dry, dark, cool (ideally, 40 degrees) spot for as long as a few months.

Cooking Ideas

Boil new potatoes until easily pierced through with a knife; serve them drizzled with a generous amount of melted butter and a smattering of chopped dill or snipped chives. Try stuffing baked potatoes with tuna salad, leftover curry or *tikka masala*, chili and sour cream, baked beans, cheddar and scallions, pico de gallo, or roasted tomatoes and feta. Slice boiled all-purpose potatoes, such as 'Caribe', into ½-inch rounds; brush with olive oil and grill over medium heat until browned and crisped in spots. Mash boiled potatoes with sautéed onions, garlic, jalapeños, and cheese; stuff the mixture into corn tortillas, brush with olive oil, and bake until tortillas are crispy and cheese melts. Mash potatoes with braised kale and onions and plenty of butter.

Delicious Varieties

'All Blue'. This late-season purple potato is quite starchy, making it excellent for mashing or baking. Retains its color fairly well as long as it is not overcooked.

'Yukon Gem'. This midseason all-purpose variety resists late blight. It is very similar in flavor and texture to the popular 'Yukon Gold' but has higher yields.

POTATOES

Solanum tuberosum

PLANT FAMILY: Solanaceae

EDIBLE PARTS: Tubers

POTENTIAL PROBLEMS: Late and early blight, wireworms, Colorado potato beetles

Potato Leek Soup with Chive Crème Fraîche

SERVES 6

½ cup crème fraîche or sour cream

1 tablespoon finely snipped fresh chives

2 tablespoons finely grated Parmesan

2 large leeks, white and light-green parts only, thinly sliced

3 tablespoons butter

1 plump garlic clove, thinly sliced

5 large Yukon Gold potatoes, peeled and thinly sliced (about 1½ pounds)

Rind of high-quality aged Parmesan

2 cups chicken broth or mild-flavored vegetable broth

3 cups water

1 teaspoon salt

Freshly ground pepper

Chopped parsley, for garnish (optional)

This simple, hearty winter soup has a surprising ingredient: a Parmesan rind. The hard rind softens up in the simmering liquid and lends the soup a subtle savory flavor that is hard to put a finger on if you aren't in on the secret. Swirling a bit of crème fraîche and chives into the soup just before serving is a fun play on the classic baked potato topping.

. . . .

In a small bowl, combine the crème fraîche, chives, and grated Parmesan; set aside.

Place the leeks in a colander and rinse thoroughly to remove any grit. Melt the butter in a large, heavy-bottomed pot over medium-low heat. Add the leeks, garlic, and potatoes. Cover and cook for 15 minutes, stirring occasionally. Add the Parmesan rind, broth, water, and salt and bring to a boil. Reduce the heat to low, partially cover the pot, and simmer until the potatoes begin to break apart, about 40 minutes.

Remove and discard the cheese rind. Season the soup to taste with salt and pepper. For a chunky soup, simply stir to break the potatoes apart. For a smoother texture, purée the soup using an immersion blender. To serve, ladle into bowls and top with a dollop of chive crème fraîche. Garnish with a sprinkle of parsley.

Radishes

Homegrown radishes are delightfully crunchy and retain a mild flavor as long as you keep them consistently moist and pull them young. Radish greens have a Velcro-like texture when raw but are chock-full of vitamins and delicious cooked. As summer heats up, I let my radishes go to seed and harvest the succulent, spicy pods that develop after the plant sends up its pretty, edible flowers.

Planting

Radish seeds germinate quickly, usually in under a week. Sow them thickly, ½ inch deep and 1 inch apart; this way you can thin out and eat loads of the spicy little sprouts. Broadcast the seeds over a bed, or sow them in rows 8 to 10 inches apart under slower-growing vegetables or anywhere you find a bare, sunny spot in the garden. Garden or salad radishes—the familiar round roots—mature in just under a month. Begin sowing them as soon as the soil reaches 45 degrees F. Dig alfalfa meal into the soil before sowing (follow the label's recommended application rate). Sow a small quantity each week, but take a break once temperatures hit the high 60s, as the plants bolt quickly in the heat and the roots become spicy and develop a pithy texture when grown in soil above 75 degrees. Begin sowing again in late summer for fall harvests. Winter radishes, including black and daikon types, mature in 50 to 70 days and develop a sweet, mild flavor in cold weather. Sow them in the same manner as salad radishes, but wait to do so until two and a half months before the average first fall frost. Make three successive sowings a week apart.

Growing

Thin radish seedlings to 2 inches apart in all directions as soon as their first true leaves begin to emerge. Harvest baby radishes a couple of weeks later by thinning out every other plant; thin winter radishes to 6 to 8 inches apart. Allow the remaining roots to mature. Foliar-feed two weeks after germination with diluted liquid organic fertilizer. Drought stress causes radishes to become hot and their texture to turn from crisp to spongy. The roots also fail to plump up if the soil dries out. Stay on top of irrigation, watering whenever soil dries down to the base of your first knuckle. Mound soil over the exposed shoulders of radishes to prevent slugs from feeding on them, and don't mulch, as it provides a place for the slimy creatures to hide out. Extend the harvest season of winter radishes by mulching around them with 6 inches of straw after the first frost.

Harvesting

Radish roots pop up out of the soil slightly when they mature, but you can pull them anytime. I tend to sow them thickly and then gradually thin the plants out, first eating the sprouts and then the roots at several different sizes. Just be sure to pull salad radishes before they grow larger than 1 inch in diameter and winter radishes at 2 inches: any larger and they tend to crack, taste hot, and develop a pithy texture. To harvest, simply grasp the leaves near the soil line, give the roots a jiggle, and pull them straight out (you may need to loosen the soil with a garden fork before harvesting winter radishes). Radishes produce delicate white flowers blushed with pink; snip off the slightly spicy blossoms as they open. Pinch the pods off the plant just after they form, as the longer you wait, the tougher they become. Pull winter radishes as needed; just be sure to harvest all the roots before the ground freezes solid.

Storing

Twist off the greens, leaving a ½-inch nub; store them separately in a plastic bag in the refrigerator for up to 3 days, as you would arugula (see page 87). Refrigerate salad radishes and radish pods in a perforated bag for up to 10 days; refrigerate winter radishes for 1 month or longer. Use the flowers immediately. Wash the greens, roots, and pods just before eating.

Cooking Ideas

Add salad and winter radish thinnings to salads, cheese sandwiches, or miso soup. Substitute the greens for spinach or mustard greens in cooked recipes. Toss salad or winter radishes in olive oil and sea salt and roast at 375 degrees F until tender. Layer thinly sliced radishes on a piece of generously buttered baguette. Grate winter radishes into cabbage slaw or add them to pickled kimchi recipes. Sprinkle the flowers over salads, hot soup, or baked fish. Stir-fry the pods in a hot wok with tarragon and serve as an appetizer. Pickle radish pods or winter radishes in your favorite brine.

Delicious Varieties

'Easter Egg II'. 30 days. From one seed packet you get to harvest red, magenta, purple, violet, and white globelike radishes. I also adore 'French Breakfast', a variety with blunt red cylindrical roots and white tips. Open-pollinated.

'Miyashige'. 50 days. A daikon with long white roots flushed with pale green near the top. The roots sweeten when exposed to light frosts. Produces abundant greens. Open-pollinated.

'Rat Tail'. 45 days. This variety was bred specifically to produce crisp pods that grow up to a foot long and have an exceptional pungent, spicy flavor. Harvest the pods at a pencil-sized diameter or smaller. Open-pollinated.

RADISHES

Raphanus sativus

PLANT FAMILY: Brassicaceae

EDIBLE PARTS: Roots, leaves, flowers, pods

POTENTIAL PROBLEMS: Cabbage maggots, flea beetles, downy mildew

Tartines with Gruyère and Radish Greens

2 cups grated Gruyère (about ½ pound)

3 tablespoons unsalted butter, softened

½ teaspoon Dijon mustard

¼ cup finely chopped radishes

1 tablespoon finely chopped flat-leaf parsley

1 tablespoon finely snipped chives

¼ teaspoon freshly ground pepper

Four ½-inch-thick slices good bread

2 teaspoons olive oil

4 cups packed radish greens or mixed greens, washed and roughly chopped

Tartines—open-faced sandwiches—provide the perfect platform for enjoying slightly wilted greens. This recipe calls for radish greens, but you can substitute spinach, arugula, or turnip, mustard, or beet greens. If you're short on time, simply toast a slice of bread, slather it with pesto or olive tapenade, and top it with a slice of cheese instead of making the cheesy toasts.

. . . .

Preheat the oven to 375 degrees F and place an oven rack in the top position.

In a medium bowl, use a fork to mix the Gruyère and butter. Stir in the mustard, radishes, parsley, chives, and pepper. Divide the mixture evenly among bread slices, pressing it down slightly. Place the bread on a baking sheet and toast until the cheese puffs up and is lightly browned, 12 to 15 minutes.

Meanwhile, heat the olive oil in a large skillet over medium heat. Add the radish greens, with some water still clinging to their leaves, to the skillet. Cook, stirring frequently, until just barely wilted, 1 to 2 minutes. Spread the wilted greens evenly over cheesy toasts and serve immediately.

Shallots

Shallots are so easy to grow: just nestle a bulb into the ground and wait for it to turn into more. Shallots and bulbing onions are very closely related, but shallots form a cluster of small, tapered cloves rather than one large bulb. Red-skinned shallots are the ones most commonly found in supermarkets, but the pear-shaped 'French Grey' shallot is often called the "true shallot" because it has a rich, but very mild, flavor.

Planting

Shallots may be grown from sets (individual bulbs) or from seedlings: sets mature faster and are easier to deal with. Simply plant the individual bulbs pointy end up 8 inches apart in rows spaced 1 foot apart, at a depth so the tip just barely peeks out above the soil's surface. Scratch a granular organic fertilizer into the soil before planting (follow the label's recommended application rate).

The sets may be planted in a sunny, well-drained spot in spring or fall. The easiest way to determine the best time to plant in your climate is to plant a few sets in fall and a few in spring and see which planting performs better. In fall, plant the sets about a month before the average first hard frost. This timing allows the cloves to develop roots before winter—shoots may or may not appear above the soil surface. Plant sets in spring once the soil warms up to 45 degrees F and becomes workable. Or plant seedlings in spring at the same time and in the same manner as you would with onion seedlings (see page 208), but spaced 4 inches apart.

Growing

Shallots first send up leaves, and then individual cloves develop as the plant grows. Cover the bed with bird netting until the shallots are firmly rooted to prevent birds from pulling sets or seedlings up. Thin seedlings to 8 inches apart when they grow to the size of a pencil. Like all alliums, shallots have shallow root systems; keep the soil consistently moist, but never soggy, watering whenever it dries down to the top of your first knuckle. Foliar-feed when sets and seedlings begin to grow actively and again when the bulbs begin to form. As shallots grow and multiply, they often push themselves up on top of the soil surface. Do not hill soil or mulch around them, as this prevents the papery skins from forming.

Harvesting

Judiciously harvest leaves as needed: just be aware that the more you harvest, the smaller the shallots will be. Wait to harvest the bulbs until the tops wither and dry down. Use a garden fork to loosen the soil around the plants and then pull them up. Lay the shallots out in a warm, dry, shady spot for two weeks to allow the tops to completely dry down and the papery wrappers to form.

Storing

After curing, hang the bulbs in mesh bags or store them in a crate in a single layer. Keep them in a cool, dry, dark, well-ventilated area for up to eight months.

Cooking Ideas

Sauté shallots in olive oil and spread them over a pizza. Fry sliced shallots until crispy and use them to garnish soups. Use shallots instead of garlic in vinaigrettes and as a substitute for onion in just about any recipe.

Delicious Varieties

'French Grey'. 100 days. Oblong roots with tightly wrapped gray-blue skins that protect the pale purple flesh. Very mild in flavor; perfect for people who find the flavor of onions too strong.

|||||||||||||||||||||||||||||||||||| **SHALLOTS** ||||||||||||||||||||||||||||||||||||

Allium cepa var. *ascalonicum*

PLANT FAMILY: Alliaceae

EDIBLE PARTS: Bulb, leaves, flowers

POTENTIAL PROBLEMS: Thrips

|||||||||||||||||||||||||||||||||||||||||||||||||||||||||||||||||||||||||||||||||||||||||||||||||||

Everyday Vinaigrette

¼ cup white wine vinegar

¼ teaspoon salt

½ teaspoon sugar

2 teaspoons finely chopped shallot

2 teaspoons Dijon mustard

⅓ cup chopped herbs, such as flat-leaf parsley, chives, basil, tarragon, or thyme

¾ cup extra-virgin olive oil

Freshly ground pepper

If you grow salad greens, you should make your own dressing. The process is dead simple and takes only slightly longer than fetching a bottle of store-bought vinaigrette from the fridge. I often use shallots rather than garlic in vinaigrette because they don't overpower the salad's flavor. This particular vinaigrette is a favorite because it is so easy to change up—you can use a single herb or a combination of several; you can substitute apple cider vinegar or red wine vinegar for the white wine vinegar. It will taste a little different every time you make it, but it will always taste good. Store extra vinaigrette in a small, lidded glass jar in the refrigerator, where it will keep for several weeks. The oil solidifies in the fridge, but it quickly liquefies again when brought to room temperature, or you can microwave it briefly. Give the jar a good shake to emulsify the dressing before using.

. . . .

In a medium bowl, whisk together the vinegar, salt, sugar, shallot, mustard, and herbs until well combined. Add the olive oil and whisk until thick and well emulsified. Add pepper to taste and adjust seasonings if needed. That's it!

Turnips

Turnips taste good (really, they do): the trick is to harvest them when they are the size of a half-dollar or smaller. At this stage they are sweet and crisp enough to enjoy raw and almost unbearably cute. Turnips also produce slightly bitter, mustard-flavored greens that are so flavorful they merit being grown as their very own crop.

Planting

Turnips grow the sweetest, crispest roots when they mature in cool weather (below 65 degrees F). Grow them in full sun and in loose soil that is free of rocks.

Begin direct-sowing the seed in early spring, as soon as the soil is workable and reaches 45 degrees. Make successive sowings two weeks apart. For fall crops, resume sowing six to eight weeks before the first frost. Sow the small seeds in rows, burying them just ¼ inch deep; space them 2 inches apart and the rows 1 foot apart. Keep the seedbed consistently moist until the seeds sprout, which can take up to three weeks. In fall, lay burlap over the seeds after sowing to help keep the soil moist until germination (see page 68 for details on this technique). If you enjoy just the greens, choose a variety like 'Alltop'.

Growing

Thin the seedlings to 2 inches apart when they grow large enough to handle. Water whenever the soil dries down to the top of your first knuckle. Foliar-feed three weeks after the plants germinate. Turnips send up a seed stalk when overwintered or when spring-sown crops are exposed to temperatures in the 40s for an extended period. Allow bolted plants to form their delicious edible flower buds before pulling and composting them. In climates with mild winters, place 6 to 8 inches of straw around the turnips and pull them as needed. In colder climates, pull all the turnips after the first hard freeze and store them indoors because repeated freezing and thawing ruins their texture. If root maggots or flea beetles are a problem in your garden, construct a hoop house over the bed immediately after sowing and tent it with row cover fabric (see page 23).

Harvesting

Four to six weeks after sowing, begin harvesting baby turnips by pulling out every other plant. These gumball-size roots are exceptionally crisp and sweet. Allow the remaining turnips to continue growing, but pull them before they grow larger than 2 inches in diameter—after that, their flavor becomes quite sharp. Turnip greens may be harvested before the roots mature—simply pinch off the outer leaves as needed. The greens develop a stronger taste and rougher texture as they mature. Harvest them before they grow much larger than your hand. If flower buds (also called rabe) develop, snip them off before they begin to open, along with a few inches of the tender stem. Use blossoms as a garnish.

Storing

Twist the mature greens off turnips, leaving a 1-inch-long nub. Store greens and flower buds separately in plastic bags in the refrigerator for up to 7 days, as you would arugula (see page 87). Refrigerate turnips in a plastic bag for up to one month.

Cooking Ideas

Substitute turnips for beets in any pickled beet recipe. Boil small turnips and chunks of potato and mash together with butter, salt, and ground pepper. Sliced, crisp, raw turnips make an excellent addition to salads. Toss turnips with olive oil and a bit of soy sauce and roast at 425 degrees until tender; sprinkle with toasted sesame seeds before serving. Use turnip greens in any recipe that calls for Swiss chard, spinach, or mustard greens. Cook the flower buds as you would broccoli rabe (see Cooking Ideas on page 95).

Delicious Varieties

'Golden Ball'. 45 days. These pale-yellow turnips maintain their mellow, sweet flavor and tender texture as they mature. Perfect for roasting. Open-pollinated. Also try the heirloom 'Purple Top White Globe', which has round white roots and violet blushed shoulders.

'Scarlet Queen'. 43 days. This incredibly versatile variety features crimson roots topped with gorgeous greens that have magenta stems. Harvest the greens young to add color to the salad bowl, and slice the roots open to reveal their red-and-white-streaked core. Eat the sweet, crisp roots raw or cooked. Best grown in fall in warmer climates. Hybrid. 'Red Round' is an excellent heirloom alternative.

‖‖‖‖‖‖‖‖‖‖‖‖‖‖‖‖‖‖‖‖‖‖‖‖ TURNIPS ‖‖‖‖‖‖‖‖‖‖‖‖‖‖‖‖‖‖‖‖

Brassica rapa var. *rapa*

PLANT FAMILY: Brassicaceae

EDIBLE PARTS: Roots, leaves, flower buds, flowers

POTENTIAL PROBLEMS: Cabbage maggots, downy mildew, flea beetles

Cider-Glazed Baby Turnips

SERVES 4

2 tablespoons butter

16 small (1½-inch-diameter) turnips, quartered, greens and tap roots removed

1 teaspoon chopped fresh thyme

¾ cup apple cider

Sea salt

Freshly ground pepper

Cooking baby turnips in cider until they are glazed and caramelized enhances their natural sweetness and makes them irresistible. If you have gumball-size turnips, wash them and use them in this recipe with their greens still attached.

· ·

Melt the butter in a large skillet over medium heat. Add the turnips and cook, shaking the pan occasionally, until lightly browned in spots, about 5 minutes. Sprinkle the thyme over the turnips and pour the apple cider into the pan. Bring to a boil, then reduce the heat to medium-low. Cover the pan and simmer until the turnips are tender and easily pierced with a knife, about 5 minutes.

Remove the lid, increase heat to high, and boil, stirring the turnips often, until the cider nearly evaporates and the turnips are golden brown and glazed, about 5 more minutes. Season to taste with salt and pepper.

CHAPTER EIGHT

WARM-SEASON VEGETABLES

THE VEGETABLES IN THIS CHAPTER—corn, eggplant, peppers, tomatillos, and tomatoes—are not quick crops, but they are worth the wait. Some varieties take 70, 80, or even 90 days to mature, but they are hardly passive during that time. The plants' leaves are soaking up the sun and their roots are mining deep in the soil for nutrients. As these plants grow, they take in all that summer has to offer—long daylight hours, warm sunshine, cool water—and distill it into the very best fruit.

The prospect of harvesting a tomato and eating it right out in the garden is seductive, but don't be tempted to get a head start on the season by planting early. Setting seedlings of warm-season crops into cold soil slows their growth and can stunt them permanently. The best way to ensure you have plenty of salsa on the table and corn on the cob for grilling is to choose varieties that ripen reliably in your climate and wait until the soil is warm to plant.

Corn

On a visit to Cuba I noticed that even the smallest gardens contained a corn patch interplanted with flowers. The Cuban gardeners—who use organic practices almost exclusively—harvested the ears of corn, but they grew it primarily for its copious dusty, yellow pollen, which lures beneficial insects to the garden. Both popcorn and sweet corn are fun to grow, but they cross-pollinate easily, which results in all the ears developing starchy kernels. Avoid this problem in small gardens by planting only one variety of corn, or grow varieties that mature at least 10 days apart to ensure they do not produce pollen at the same time.

Planting

Each strand of silk on an ear of corn connects to a kernel on the cob. Missing kernels and poorly developed ears are a result of poor pollination. Plant corn in blocks of short rows, rather than one long row, to encourage full pollination. With a hoe, form 4-inch-deep furrows 1 to 1½ feet apart. Make the furrows at least 4 feet long and include four or more furrows per block of corn. Sprinkle granular organic fertilizer in the bottom of each furrow (follow the label's recommended application rate) and scratch it into the soil.

Grow corn in full sun. Wait to sow until all danger of frost passes; corn germinates slowly in soil temperatures below 65 degrees F. To help ensure a good stand, lay a piece of clear ventilated plastic over the furrows and pin it into place with U-shaped landscape fabric pins. Leave the plastic in place for a week prior to planting to warm the soil. To improve germination rates, I also presprout corn seed indoors (see page 134 for instructions). As soon as the seeds develop little roots, sow them 1 inch deep and 3 inches apart in the bottom of the furrow. Water the seeds in with a gentle stream from a watering can. Then pull the plastic back over the furrows and pin it in place. Keep the plastic over the corn until the seedlings grow tall enough to touch it—just don't forget to keep the soil under the plastic consistently moist.

Growing

Corn shoots make a fun addition to salads, but they taste best young, so thin them to 12 inches apart within seven to ten days after germination. Gradually backfill the furrow as the plants grow to help support them. Irrigate whenever the soil dries down to the bottom of your second knuckle. If the plants suffer a nitrogen deficiency, especially when young, they often fail to produce worthwhile ears. To avoid stunted, yellowed plants, side-dress with 2 inches of compost when the stalks grow knee high. Foliar-feed with diluted liquid organic fertilizer every three weeks.

Hand-pollinating each ear ensures full pollination in a small plot of corn. Pay attention when your corn sends up its *tassels*—the frilly, broomlike growth above the stalk. Give the stalks a shake every day: when you notice yellow pollen beginning to fall from the tassels, it is time to hand-pollinate. Cut down a tassel and shake the pollen directly over the silk on each ear. Use one tassel to pollinate all the ears on one stalk.

Harvesting

When the ears of sweet corn feel plump and the tips of the silks begin to brown, carefully peel back the husk and pierce a kernel with the tine of a fork. If the liquid that oozes out is milky, the corn is ready to harvest. If it is clear, wait a few more days. If it is thick and pasty, the corn is past its prime. To harvest the ear, pull it out and down in a twisting motion. Corn immediately begins converting sugar to starch after harvest, so eat it as soon as possible. Let popcorn ears dry on the stalk. Wait to harvest until the husks turn from green to tan and feel crisp and papery, and the kernels feel hard. If the weather turns wet while the ears are drying, harvest them; place the ears in mesh bags and hang them up indoors in a warm spot until they dry. Corn sometimes develops a purplish-gray fungus on the ears, leaves, stalks, and tassels. This edible fungus is known as *huitlacoche* in Mexico. If you find some on your corn, consider yourself lucky: cut it off and fold it into a quesadilla.

Storing

If you must store sweet corn, do so for as short as time as possible. Ice the ears to completely cool them down, then pack them into plastic bags and store in the refrigerator crisper drawer for three days maximum. Shuck just before cooking. Remove popcorn kernels from their ears and store them in an airtight container.

Cooking Ideas

Before grilling corn on the cob, peel the husks back and soak the ears in ice water for 10 minutes. Grill the chilled corn over medium-high heat, turning occasionally, until the kernels are tender and just slightly browned in spots, 15 to 20 minutes. Serve immediately with sweet cream butter, or brush the cobs with sour cream and then sprinkle them with crumbled Cotija cheese, fresh lime juice, and chile powder. Mix ½ cup of fresh kernels into your favorite black bean salsa or cornbread recipe, or add them to risotto.

Delicious Varieties

'Bodacious'. 75 days. This yellow sweet corn grows quite tall, and its sugary sweet ears reliably mature even in climates with short summers. Hybrid.

'Calico'. 90 days. I grow this colorful popcorn and give it as gifts during the holidays. It produces ears with yellow, brown, white, purple, red, and blue kernels. Open-pollinated.

CORN

Zea mays

PLANT FAMILY: Poaceae

EDIBLE PARTS: Kernels

POTENTIAL PROBLEMS: Corn earworms and borers, cutworms, wireworms, mosaic virus

The Patrick Family's
Southern Creamed Corn

SERVES 2 TO 4

6 ears freshly picked sweet corn, shucked (about 3 cups kernels)

¾ cup whole milk (do not substitute skim or 2 percent)

1 teaspoon sugar (optional)

2 tablespoons unsalted butter

This recipe comes from the kitchen of Kenneth Patrick, a fabulous gardener who grows corn in his Virginia backyard. Kenneth says that white, yellow, or bicolor sweet corn all taste delicious in this recipe but recommends picking the corn moments before cooking for the sweetest results.

Cut the kernels off the corn cob directly into a large saucepan. Scrape off any corn pulp and release the corn "milk" by running the back of the knife down the cob. Add the whole milk—it should just barely cover the kernels.

Heat the corn over medium-low until it is tender and the milk thickens to the consistency of cream, 12 to 15 minutes, stirring frequently to prevent the milk from scorching. Remove the pan from the heat, taste, and add sugar if needed. Stir the butter into the corn and serve immediately.

Eggplant

Eggplants are pretty, productive, and easy to grow, as long as you provide them with plenty of warmth. Their gorgeous gray-green leaves, violet flowers, and colorful fruits fit in easily at the front of perennial borders, or you can plant them at the center of a container ringed with trailing annual flowers like calibrachoa (aka Million Bells) or lobelia.

Planting

Wait to plant eggplant until all danger of frost passes and the soil warms up to 65 degrees F (use plastic to warm the soil faster in cool climates; see page 22). Choose a hot, sheltered spot in the garden that gets full sun. Space plants 1½ to 2 feet apart in staggered rows 2 feet apart. In climates with mild summers or a short growing season, grow eggplants in containers that are at least 18 inches wide and deep; black 5-gallon plastic nursery pots work particularly well. They might not be the prettiest option, but the dark plastic absorbs heat and keeps the soil warm. Place the pot right up against a wall in a spot that faces south or west and gets full sun. Plant one eggplant per container. Choose stocky transplants that are about 8 inches tall and have six to eight leaves and a well-developed, but not root-bound, root system. Water the transplants in with diluted liquid organic fertilizer.

Growing

Protect eggplants from cool nighttime temperatures by placing a cloche (see page 21) over each seedling. Vent the cloche when temperatures reach 75 degrees F. Remove the cloche when the plant begins to flower or outgrows it, whichever comes first. Flea beetles chew tiny holes in eggplant leaves, stunting the plants and reducing their yields. Mustard greens are considered a "trap crop" for flea beetles, because they love the greens to the exclusion of other plants. Sow a row or place a container of the fast-growing mustards near the eggplants to tempt the beetles away—or grow eggplants under a hoop house tented with a light row cover (see page 23). Stake or cage the large Italian types to prevent them from breaking under the weigh of their heavy fruits (see page 240 for instructions on making a bamboo support). Since mulch cools the soil, wait until it reaches 70 degrees before spreading a 3-inch layer of straw around the plants. Water whenever the soil dries down to your first knuckle, and foliar-feed every three weeks with diluted liquid organic fertilizer.

Harvesting

Only overripe eggplants taste bitter. Pick them before seed formation begins, when their skin is glossy and smooth, and they feel plump and firm. In general, let Asian varieties grow 6 to 8 inches long and teardrop-shaped eggplants 5 to 8 inches, though they may be harvested earlier. Eggplants' tips often lighten slightly in color when they reach the perfect harvest stage. Always use scissors or pruners to harvest eggplant; twisting the fruit off can damage the plant.

Storing

Ideally, store eggplants at room temperature for three to five days. If they must be refrigerated, place them in a plastic bag in the crisper drawer for up to three days. Just be aware that exposing the fruit to temperatures below 50 degrees can turn the flesh brown and unappetizing. Wash just before using.

Cooking Ideas

Eggplant soaks up a ton of oil when fried, so I prefer to roast, grill, or steam it. To grill, cut teardrop-shaped eggplants into rounds and long fruits in half lengthwise; brush with olive oil and grill until tender and slightly charred. Steam 1-inch cubes of eggplant until tender, 5 to 7 minutes. Or score an eggplant down the center about ¼ inch deep with the tip of a sharp knife and place it scored side down on an oiled baking sheet. Roast at 450 degrees F until tender but not deflated (about 15 to 25 minutes, depending on the size and shape of the eggplant).

Cube cooked eggplant and toss with olive oil, salt, and chopped herbs; serve on toasted bread. Stack rounds of grilled eggplant with beefsteak tomato slices, basil, and mozzarella; drizzle with balsamic vinegar. Pierce a whole, large eggplant all over with a sharp knife and stuff 10 of the slits with peeled garlic cloves; brush the skin with oil and place directly on a grill over medium heat. Cover and cook, turning the eggplant occasionally, until it is charred all over and wilted. Remove from grill and cool, then scoop out the eggplant flesh and garlic. Use this to make baba ghanoush.

Delicious Varieties

'Fairy Tale'. 50 days. Super-pretty, small, oblong, white-and-purple-mottled fruit. Abundant yields and a compact plant, perfect for containers. Hybrid. 'Pandora Striped Rose' is a lovely open-pollinated alternative.

'Ichiban'. 61 days. A classic Asian eggplant with glossy dark-purple, almost black skin. Very early. Tender flesh that is almost never bitter. The long fruits grill beautifully. Hybrid. 'Long Purple' is a similar open-pollinated variety that performs well in cooler climates.

‖‖‖‖‖‖‖‖‖‖‖‖‖‖‖‖‖‖‖‖‖‖‖‖‖ **EGGPLANT** ‖‖‖‖‖‖‖‖‖‖‖‖‖‖‖‖‖‖‖‖‖‖‖‖‖

Solanum melongena

PLANT FAMILY: Solanaceae

EDIBLE PARTS: Fruit

POTENTIAL PROBLEMS: Flea beetles, aphids, Colorado potato beetles, verticillium wilt

Eggplant with Lemon Tahini Dressing

1 large Italian eggplant, or 3 long Asian-style eggplants, cut into ½-inch dice (about 3 cups)

2 tablespoons tahini

1 teaspoon lemon zest

2 tablespoons freshly squeezed lemon juice (from about 1 small lemon)

2 garlic cloves, minced

¼ teaspoon salt

¼ teaspoon cayenne

2 tablespoons olive oil

2 tablespoons cold water

1 tablespoon minced fresh parsley, plus more for garnish

This dish relies on the same ingredients as the Middle Eastern spread baba ghanoush, but rather than roasting and mashing the eggplant, you cut it into cubes and steam it. Steamed eggplant cooks in under 10 minutes and develops a wonderful silky-smooth texture. Serve the eggplant over cooked brown rice or quinoa, or spoon it over toasted olive bread. Extra dressing will keep for several days in the refrigerator and tastes delicious when tossed with mixed greens, sunflower seeds, and chopped vegetables.

. . . .

Place the eggplant in a steamer basket and steam until the cubes are tender and silky—not mushy—but still hold their shape, 5 to 7 minutes. Transfer to a medium bowl and set aside.

In a small bowl, whisk together the tahini, lemon zest and juice, garlic, salt, cayenne, oil, water, and parsley. Stir the dressing into the eggplant, 1 tablespoon at a time, until the eggplant is evenly coated but not drowning in dressing. Serve warm or at room temperature, garnished with the parsley.

Sweet and Hot Peppers

Peppers only taste spicy if they contain *capsaicinoids*. Habaneros and other extremely hot peppers have higher concentrations of these pungent compounds than milder peppers like ancho chiles, and sweet peppers contain no capsaicinoids at all. Sweet and hot peppers come in a huge range of shapes and colors—yellow, orange, red, and purple. I like to grow the pretty plants down the center of a bed and above a carpet of sweet alyssum, a low-growing annual flower that blooms all season and attracts beneficial insects and pollinators.

Planting

Peppers do not abide frost and prefer to sink their roots into soil warmed to at least 65 degrees F. Planting peppers too early dooms them to a life of stunted growth and few, if any, fruits (use plastic to warm the soil faster in cool climates; see page 22). Grow peppers from seedlings and plant them in full sun. The plants become quite bushy, so space them 1½ feet apart in staggered rows 1½ to 2 feet apart. Water them in with diluted liquid organic fertilizer. If you like, plant sweet alyssum seedlings or scatter seeds under the plants after you transplant them; the fast-growing flowers will quickly fill in.

Growing

Peppers benefit from being staked, even though they do not grow especially tall, because they become quite top-heavy as the fruit develops. Place a stake alongside the plant or a cage over it immediately after planting to prevent disturbing its roots (see page 240 for instructions on making a bamboo support). Growing peppers under a hoop house tented with clear vented plastic (page 23) dramatically increases productivity in climates with cool summers. Peppers are self-fertile, which means they do not require insect pollination to produce fruit, so you can keep the plastic over the plants even when they begin to flower.

Foliar-feed every three weeks with diluted liquid organic fertilizer, and mulch around the base of the plants with a 3-inch layer of straw after the soil warms to 70 degrees. In general, it's best to irrigate whenever the soil dries down to the base of your second knuckle. However, hot peppers increase their levels of capsaicinoids when exposed to drought stress, so occasionally allowing their soil to dry and then gradually remoistening it results in super-spicy peppers. Sweet peppers produce the best-tasting fruit when their soil stays consistently moist. If your peppers lose their flowers, it most likely has to do with the weather—the flowers drop off when the temperature rises above 90 degrees or drops below 60 degrees.

Harvesting

Peppers are edible at any stage in their development—green peppers are simply unripe fruits—but they develop more flavor and nutrients (and heat if they are spicy) as they ripen.

Pick the first couple of peppers off the plant right after they form to encourage it to produce more fruit, which you can then allow to ripen fully. Do not tug peppers off plants: their brittle branches break easily. Instead, use sharp scissors to snip off the fruit. Ideally, harvest when the peppers are fully colored.

Storing

Store peppers at room temperature if you plan on using them within a day or two after harvesting. If they begin to pucker or soften, or you want to store them for a longer period, place them in a plastic bag and refrigerate in the crisper drawer for up to two weeks.

Cooking Ideas

For flavorful salsa, add both finely chopped hot peppers such as 'Fish' and sweet frying peppers such as 'Jimmy Nardello'. Grill a bunch of 'Padrón' peppers—a thin-walled, mild, flavorful pepper that produces an occasional spicy fruit—drizzle with olive oil, and serve sprinkled with sea salt on a platter. Sauté 2 cups of chopped sweet peppers in olive oil and garlic; drizzle with red wine vinegar, and then pile the peppers on slices of baguette spread with soft goat cheese and sprinkled with herbs.

Delicious Varieties

'Beaver Dam'. 80 days. Not quite sweet, not quite hot, this delicious pepper has thin walls and a big cavity that is perfect for stuffing cheese or rice into. Pickles beautifully. Looks

A PRETTY PLANT SUPPORT

Placing a bamboo support around tomatoes, peppers, eggplants, and tomatillos helps keep them upright and intact as their fruits mature.

1. You'll need two U-shaped bamboo stakes for each support. Use 3-foot-tall stakes for eggplants and peppers and 5-footers for tomatoes and tomatillos. To make the support, center one U-shaped stake over a seedling and drive both legs 6 to 8 inches into the soil.

2. Take the second stake and center it crosswise over the first (the tops of the two stakes should form a plus sign when viewed from above). Drive each leg of this stake 6 to 8 inches into the soil. You should now have a bamboo support that forms a column around the plant and crisscrosses at the top. If you like, you can tie twine horizontally between the four legs to form a cage. Space the layers of twine 6 to 8 inches apart so you can still access the plant for harvesting.

similar to an ancho chile and turns from green to chartreuse to cherry red as it ripens. My absolute favorite pepper, even though it produces only four or five fruits per plant. Heirloom.

'Bulgarian Carrot'. 85 days. This pale-orange, carrot-shaped pepper packs a spicy punch but also has a fantastic fruity taste. Adds more color and depth of flavor to salsa than jalapeños, especially when roasted. Ripens quickly, even in cool climates, and produces tons of peppers. Heirloom. Another excellent spicy pepper is 'Fish', which has striped fruit and variegated foliage and makes superb hot sauce.

'Jimmy Nardello'. 80 to 90 days. Unlike so many sweet peppers, which taste sugary but lack any real flavor, this vibrant-red Italian frying pepper has a bold, fruity taste. The pepper's crisp, thin flesh caramelizes when pan-fried in hot oil, but the long, narrow fruit is sweet enough to eat raw. Heirloom.

SWEET AND HOT PEPPERS

Capsicum annuum

PLANT FAMILY: Solanaceae

EDIBLE PARTS: Fruit

POTENTIAL PROBLEMS: Aphids, leaf miners, fusarium and verticillium wilt

Roasted Jalapeños Stuffed with Goat Cheese

6 large jalapeños

8 ounces soft goat cheese, at room temperature

2 plump garlic cloves, minced

10 Peppadews or seeded pickled cherry peppers, minced

3 tablespoons brine from Peppadews or cherry peppers

Goat cheese's mild flavor tempers jalapeños' heat, and Peppadews—a sweet pickled pepper—add a sour tang to these simple appetizers. Look for Peppadews in the deli case or olive bar of any well-stocked grocery store; if you can't find them, pickled cherry peppers make a fine substitute.

Preheat the broiler and place an oven rack in the top position. Slit the jalapeños from stem end to tip and halfway around the base of the stem, making sure not to slice through the whole pepper. Carefully remove the seeds. Place the jalapeños cut side down on a broiler pan. Broil until their skins just begin to blister, about 2 minutes. Remove and set aside until they are cool enough to handle.

Meanwhile, in a small bowl, combine the goat cheese, garlic, Peppadews, and brine. Stuff 2 tablespoons of the goat cheese mixture into each jalapeño, wiping off any cheese on the outside of the peppers. Place the stuffed jalapeños back on the broiler pan, cheese side up, and broil until the cheese turns golden brown, about 6 minutes, rotating the pan every couple of minutes to ensure even cooking.

Tomatillos

Tomatillos grow into rangy, 3-foot-tall plants and produce up to 200 fruits that dangle like paper lanterns. If left to their own devices, the plants sprawl, which makes harvesting difficult. Give them a little extra support by tying them to a bamboo stake immediately after planting.

Planting

Grow tomatillos from seedlings; wait to transplant until the soil warms up to at least 65 degrees F and all danger of frost has passed (use plastic to warm the soil faster in cool climates; see page 22). Tomatillos set more fruit if they cross-pollinate with another plant, so plan on growing at least two plants. Choose a warm, sheltered spot in full sun. Pinch off the bottom set of leaves from each seedling and plant them in a trench as you would tomatoes (see page 249). Space the plants 3 feet apart in all directions. Soak the soil around each seedling with diluted liquid organic fertilizer after planting.

Growing

Tomatillos tolerate dryish soil but produce the most fruit with consistent soil moisture. Water whenever the soil dries down to the bottom of your second knuckle, and place a 3-inch layer of mulch around the plants' base after the soil warms up to 70 degrees. Foliar-feed every three weeks with diluted liquid organic fertilizer. Tie the plants to their stakes or tuck them into the confines of a bamboo support (see page 240) as they grow.

Harvesting

Harvest tomatillos when their papery wrappers begin to turn from green to a pale tan and their fruit fills the wrapper or just pops through. The green fruits taste tangy and citrusy. They remain edible as they yellow, but their flavor loses its distinctive tartness. Check the plants twice a week for mature fruits. To harvest, simply pinch them off the plant or collect ripe tomatillos after they fall to the ground.

Storing

Store tomatillos in their husks in a paper bag at room temperature for up to one week. For longer storage, remove the husks and place the bare fruit in a ventilated plastic bag in the refrigerator crisper drawer for up to two months. To freeze, simply remove the husks, wash and dry the fruit, and then pack into freezer bags, leaving no headspace.

Cooking Ideas

Always wash the sticky film off the surface of tomatillos after husking. Add a handful of chopped tomatillos to a gazpacho recipe. To make a basic salsa verde, sauté ½ cup diced white onion, 1 minced garlic clove, and 2 chopped jalapeños in a bit of olive oil until vegetables just begin to brown. Add 4 cups husked tomatillos and just enough water to cover. Cook until the tomatillos soften and pop open if pressed with a spoon. Stir in 2 tablespoons chopped cilantro and whirl in a blender until smooth. Use the salsa verde as an enchilada sauce; serve it over rice and beans; spoon it over pork chops or grilled fish; use it as a chip dip; or stir it into shredded chicken, along with mild green chiles and corn, and stuff into tortillas.

Delicious Varieties

'Pineapple'. Small ¾-inch tomatillos with a fruity pineapple flavor that taste excellent in salsa. The prolific plants grow to only 2 feet, making them a nice choice for smaller gardens. Open-pollinated.

'Toma Verde'. A classic variety with large, 2-inch, kelly-green fruit and a sweet-tart flavor. The plants grow to at least 3 feet and produce hundreds of tomatillos. Open-pollinated.

TOMATILLOS

Physalis ixocarpa

PLANT FAMILY: Solanaceae

EDIBLE PARTS: Fruit

POTENTIAL PROBLEMS: Tomatillos rarely suffer from serious pest or disease problems.

Guacamole with Charred Tomatillos and Chiles

1 jalapeño

1 serrano chile

2 large tomatillos, husked and washed

1 garlic clove, minced

1 medium tomato, seeded and chopped into small dice

¼ cup finely minced white onion

Juice of 1 small lime (about 2 tablespoons)

1 tablespoon finely minced fresh cilantro

¼ teaspoon salt

1 cup diced avocado (about 1 large avocado)

3 cups mashed avocado (about 4 large avocados)

This recipe was inspired by Gabriel's restaurant, just outside Santa Fe, New Mexico, where they make guacamole tableside. I added tomatillos to the mix because they help prevent the avocado from turning brown.

. . . .

Preheat the broiler. Place the peppers and tomatillos on a broiler pan and broil, turning a few times, until charred and soft, 3 to 4 minutes. When cool enough to handle, stem and seed the peppers and finely chop them and the tomatillos.

In a large bowl, gently fold the peppers, tomatillos, garlic, tomato, onion, lime juice, cilantro, salt, and diced avocado into the mashed avocado. Taste and adjust the seasoning, adding more salt or lime juice as needed.

Tomatoes

My strategy when choosing which of the thousands of tomato varieties to grow is this: I always plant two delicious tomatoes that reliably ripen in my cool climate, such as 'Black Cherry' and 'Jaune Flamme', and then experiment with tomatoes that sound like fun ('Cosmonaut Volkov'), look pretty ('Chocolate Stripes'), or have a reputation for amazing flavor ('Brandywine').

Planting

Plant tomato seedlings after all danger of frost passes in spring and the soil warms to at least 60 degrees F (use plastic to warm the soil faster in cool climates; see page 22). If you examine the stem of a tomato seedling, you'll notice tiny "hairs" that grow into roots when buried in soil. The common advice to "plant tomatoes deeply" really means burying as much of the stem as possible. Planting tomatoes in a trench, rather than a deep hole, allows the plants to develop a robust root system without exposing the tender roots to cold soil.

Choose a hot spot that gets full sun. Dig a trench that is as deep as the seedling's root ball is wide. Using scissors, snip off all but the top three sets of leaves on the seedling. Take the plant out of its pot and tease the roots apart. Lay the plant horizontally in the trench. As you fill the trench with soil, angle the stem of the plant so that its leaves remain above the soil line (don't worry, the crooked plants quickly straighten up as they grow). Water the seedlings in well with diluted liquid organic fertilizer. Space the plants at least 3 feet apart for optimum air circulation. In cold climates, consider placing a season-extending product, such as a cloche (see page 21), around the seedlings immediately after planting to protect them from late frosts and temperature fluctuations.

Growing

Tomatoes left to sprawl over the soil are prone to developing problems with disease and rotting fruit. Immediately after planting, place a sturdy tomato cage or bamboo support (see page 240) over each plant, or drive an 8-foot stake into the ground directly behind each plant. I pinch out about half the *suckers*—shoots that emerge where branches meet the main stems—just after they appear, to avoid wounding the plant (see photo on page 251). This practice keeps the plant's structure open and improves air circulation—which is important for preventing fungal diseases—while maintaining enough foliage for optimal photosynthesis. Keeping the soil consistently moist prevents problems with cracking and blossom-end rot; water whenever the soil dries down to the bottom of your second knuckle. Wait to mulch with a 3- or 4-inch layer of grass or straw until the soil consistently stays above 70 degrees. As soon as the plants set fruit, begin foliar-feeding with diluted liquid organic fertilizer every three weeks. Tie the plants to their stakes or tuck them into the confines of their cages (see page 240) as they grow. In summer, plant baby greens, radishes, or cilantro in the cool, moist microclimate that exists underneath tomato plants.

Harvesting

Harvest tomatoes when they are fully colored and their flesh gives slightly when gently squeezed. Check for ripe fruit daily. Pinch off smaller tomatoes; use scissors to clip off larger ones or trusses of fruit. Harvest all the fruit when frost threatens. Set aside dark-green, very firm fruit to use in your favorite green tomato recipes. Fruits that have turned light green or greenish white ripen more reliably indoors.

Storing

Always store tomatoes at room temperature; refrigerating them ruins their flavor and texture. To ripen green tomatoes indoors, wash them gently in tepid water and allow them to air-dry. Wrap each tomato in newspaper or tissue paper. Set the tomatoes in a cardboard box in a single layer. Place the box in a warm (between 60 and 70 degrees), dark spot. The warmer the temperature, the faster the fruit will ripen. When the tomatoes turn nearly uniformly red (or the color they are supposed to be when ripe), take them out of the box and set them on your kitchen counter to finish the ripening process.

Cooking Ideas

Slice 5 cups of cherry tomatoes in half and toss with olive oil, garlic slivers, and fresh or dried herbs. Spread out on a rimmed baking sheet and roast at 375 degrees F until soft; serve over fish or toss with pasta. Blend 1 cup basil leaves with 1 cup olive oil; drizzle the basil oil over sliced beefsteak tomatoes and fresh mozzarella. Slow-roast tomatoes (see page 82), then layer them in a shallow dish with cloves of roasted garlic (see page 200) and basil leaves, cover with olive oil, and allow to marinate for several hours before serving with crusty bread.

Delicious Varieties

There are thousands of tomato varieties available, and they are divided into two main categories: determinate and indeterminate. *Determinate* plants grow to a certain height and then flower and set all of their fruit at the same time, while *indeterminate* plants grow and fruit until killed by frost. Most determinate varieties are sauce or paste tomatoes. In cold climates, avoid varieties that take longer than 80 days to mature.

'Black Cherry'. 65 days. A large cherry tomato with dense flesh and a surprisingly rich, complex flavor for a tomato of its size. Produces trusses with six to eight reddish black fruits that ripen early in the season. Productive plants but not as prolific as my other favorite cherry tomatoes, 'Sun Gold' and 'Matt's Wild Cherry'. Open-pollinated and indeterminate.

'Jaune Flamme'. 70 days. Gorgeous apricot-colored fruit on trusses of four to six toma-toes. Flavor is sweet and fruity with just the right amount of tartness. My favorite variety for slow-roasting because it turns a deep orange as it cooks. Open-pollinated and indeterminate.

TOMATOES

Lycopersicon esculentum

PLANT FAMILY: Solanaceae

EDIBLE PARTS: Fruit

POTENTIAL PROBLEMS: Blossom-end rot, late and early blight, fusarium and verticillium wilt

MORE FABULOUS TOMATOES

So many good tomatoes, so little space. Here are thirteen other delicious varieties to try:

BEEFSTEAK

'Brandy Boy'

'Brandywine'

'German Pink'

'Japanese Black Trifele'

'Momotaro'

'Mr. Stripey'

CHERRY AND CURRANT

'Chadwick's Cherry'

'Green Grape'

'White Currant'

SAUCE

'Principe Borghese'

'Striped Roman'

SLICING/SALAD

'Green Zebra'

'Stupice'

Lemony Pasta with Cherry Tomatoes

SERVES 4 TO 6

Zest and juice of 1 large lemon (about 3 tablespoons juice, 1½ teaspoons zest)

⅓ cup extra-virgin olive oil

¼ teaspoon sea salt

Freshly ground black pepper

¼ cup packed purple and green basil leaves, finely chopped

¼ cup packed flat-leaf parsley, finely chopped

1 cup packed, finely grated Parmesan, plus more for serving (about 3 ounces)

4 cups halved cherry tomatoes

16 ounces short pasta, such as strozzapreti or penne

¼ teaspoon red pepper flakes

This no-cook sauce comes together in the time it takes to boil the pasta. For a colorful dish, use a mix of tomatoes, including 'Sun Gold' and 'Chadwick's Cherry', and both purple 'Red Rubin' and green 'Genovese' basil.

. . . .

In a large bowl, whisk together the lemon zest and juice, olive oil, salt, and pepper to taste. Gently fold in the basil, parsley, Parmesan, and tomatoes, and set aside.

Bring a large pot of salted water to boil. Add the pasta and cook according to package instructions until al dente. Drain the pasta in a colander and immediately place the pasta in the bowl on top of the tomato mixture. Let sit for 1 minute to soften the tomatoes, then toss until well combined. Sprinkle with the red pepper flakes and a pinch of sea salt. Serve immediately. Pass extra Parmesan at the table.

CHAPTER NINE

FRUIT

PLANTING FRUIT IN YOUR OWN GARDEN is like giving yourself a gift. For the very modest initial investment of a few plants, you can step outside in the morning and pick raspberries for breakfast, share strawberry-rhubarb pie with friends, and put away blueberry preserves for the winter. Growing fruit at home cuts out the cost and chemicals that come with most fruit purchased from the grocery store, and the plants produce for years—in some cases, decades. The fruits discussed in this chapter—blueberries, raspberries, strawberries, and rhubarb (which is technically a vegetable but is used like a fruit)—are all easy to grow and integrate well into the ornamental landscape. The chartreuse 'Golden Alexandria' strawberry lightens up shady borders, and rhubarb's giant leaves and ruby red stems look almost tropical when planted next to cannas or hardy bananas. Blueberries, with their colorful fall foliage and pretty spring flowers, are handsome enough to warrant growing as a hedge, as long as you don't mind if your neighbors—and the birds—snag a few berries.

Blueberries

Flaming-red fall foliage, clusters of pink blossoms in spring, and colorful bark make blueberries one of the most versatile and beautiful edible plants. Blueberry varieties are divided into three main categories: highbush, lowbush, and rabbiteye. Highbush blueberries produce large fruit and grow up to 8 feet tall; lowbush types form a foot-high mat and have small but intensely flavored berries; and rabbiteye shrubs grow up to 15 feet tall and produce tons of small berries.

Planting

Blueberries require extra attention to the soil before planting, but after they are established, these easy-care shrubs need attention only a few times a year and will produce fruit for decades. Have your soil tested in the fall prior to planting: blueberries thrive in acidic soil with a pH of 4.5 to 5 and grow best in areas that have naturally acidic soil, like the Pacific Northwest. If your soil pH falls between 5 and 6.5, you can modify it with elemental sulfur. Trying to grow blueberries in soil with a natural pH of 6.5 or higher becomes an exercise in frustration, as the plants often suffer from nutrient deficiencies and perform poorly even if the soil pH is modified annually.

To increase the acidity of good garden soil one pH unit (e.g., to lower the pH from 6 to 5), spread 1¼ cups (½ pound) of elemental sulfur over every 50 square feet; in clay soils, double that amount. Work the sulfur into the soil in fall and wait four months before testing the soil's pH again. Add more sulfur if needed prior to planting.

Plant blueberries in late winter or early spring as soon as the soil is workable, ideally while the plants are still dormant. Blueberries tolerate light shade but produce the most fruit when grown in full sun. Space highbush and rabbiteye plants 5 feet apart and lowbush plants 1 foot apart. Plant container-grown plants at the exact same depth they were growing in their pots.

Bare-root blueberry plants are dug from the field while dormant, and the soil is washed from their roots. They are available via mail order and at nurseries in late winter

FREEZING FRUIT

Berries and rhubarb freeze especially well for later use. Wash berries gently in a colander and shake off excess water. Cut off rhubarb leaves, wash the stems, and slice them into ½-inch pieces. Spread berries or rhubarb pieces out in a single layer on a rimmed baking sheet and place it in the freezer. Once the berries or rhubarb pieces freeze solid, pack them into plastic bags, leaving ½ inch of headspace (room at the top of the bag), and return them to the freezer.

(blueberries, onions, raspberries, strawberries, and fruit trees are also often sold this way). Plant bare-root plants at the same depth or slightly higher than they were growing in the field (the part of the plant that was underground will look darker than the part that was above). Dig a hole that is wider than the root system and slightly shallower. Make a firm mound of soil in the center of the planting hole to support the roots. Spread the roots out over the mound, check to make sure the plant is at the correct depth, and backfill the hole, gently firming the soil around the roots as you go. Water the plant in well, and then completely soak the soil around each plant with diluted liquid organic fertilizer. If the plant sinks after watering, adjust its height.

Growing

Blueberries have shallow root systems and appreciate consistently moist soil even after they establish. Weave a soaker hose between the plants or install a drip system, and water deeply whenever the soil dries down to the bottom of your second knuckle. Keep a 2- to 3-inch layer of pine needles or wood chips over the soil. Pull back the mulch in fall and scratch a balanced granular organic fertilizer into the soil (follow the label's recommended application rate), then refresh the mulch. Check the soil's pH every other year or if the plant's older leaves begin to turn yellow. If necessary, scratch sulfur into the soil to lower the pH, using the rates recommended on page 257.

Protect the berries from birds by draping bird netting over the shrubs when the berries begin to ripen. Prevent mummy berry, a common disease that causes blueberries to shrivel, by planting resistant varieties and vigilantly removing any infected fruit. If mummy berry strikes, rake away the mulch below the plants in fall and throw it away, then lightly cultivate the soil around the plants in spring.

Pruning

Highbush and rabbiteye plants stay productive for about five years following planting; after that, annual pruning encourages new, productive growth and opens up the plant, allowing sunlight to reach the berries and air to circulate through the foliage. In late winter, use loppers to trim out any dead or diseased limbs. Then cut back one-fifth of the oldest, largest branches to the ground. Finish up by thinning out twiggy or crowded growth in the plant's center. Prune lowbush blueberries by thinning out one-third of the oldest branches each year; don't just hack off one side of the shrub—keep the plant's shape by selectively removing the branches and cutting them down to the ground.

Harvesting

Wait to harvest blueberries until they are plump and slightly yielding and fall into your hand; if you have to tug the berries off the plant, they aren't quite ripe. Harvest daily during peak ripening.

Storing

Place dry blueberries in a lidded container lined with a paper towel and refrigerate for up to ten days. Wash them right before use.

Cooking Ideas

Cook 2 cups blueberries, ½ cup water, and ¾ cup sugar over medium-high heat until a thick sauce forms; pour over warm Camembert cheese, crepes, or pancakes. Whirl frozen blueberries in a blender with almond milk for a quick smoothie.

Delicious Varieties

To extend the blueberry harvest from early summer through September, plant lowbush blueberries, such as 'Brunswick' and 'Burgundy', and a mix of early-, mid-, and late-season varieties of highbush or rabbiteye blueberries, such as 'Earliblue', 'Nelson', and 'Tifblue'.

'Sunshine Blue'. This semi-evergreen highbush variety has dusky-green leaves that turn teal and burgundy in fall; fuchsia and purple blossoms in spring; and berries that are large, sweet, and abundant. Tolerates higher-pH soils, grows 3 to 4 feet tall, and performs well in warmer climates.

|||||||||||||||||||||||||||||||||||||| **BLUEBERRIES** ||||||||||||||||||||||||||||||||||||||

Vaccinium spp.

PLANT FAMILY: Ericaceae

EDIBLE PARTS: Berries

POTENTIAL PROBLEMS: Blueberry maggots, spotted wing drosophila, botrytis, mummy berry

||||||||||||||||||||||||||||||||||||||||||||||||||||||||||||||||||||||||||||||||||||||||

Yogurt Parfaits with Almond Granola and Blueberries

3 cups old-fashioned rolled oats (not instant)

1 cup slivered almonds

¼ cup sesame seeds

½ cup unsweetened shredded coconut

½ cup maple syrup

½ cup honey

½ teaspoon almond extract

2 cups plain yogurt, preferably Greek-style

2 cups blueberries

Homemade granola is infinitely adaptable. You can swap in different nuts and seeds; use honey, maple syrup, or agave nectar for sweetener; and experiment by adding spices, vanilla, and other flavorings. I keep this almond granola on hand in the summer and eat it almost every morning with whatever berries are ripe.

. . . .

Preheat the oven to 350 degrees F. In a large bowl, combine the oats, almonds, sesame seeds, and coconut. In a liquid measuring cup, combine the maple syrup, honey, and almond extract. Pour the sweetener over the dry ingredients, stirring until they are evenly coated. Spread the granola out in an even layer on a rimmed baking sheet. Bake, stirring frequently, until it is golden brown, about 25 minutes. Remove from the oven and place the pan on a wire rack. Continue stirring until the granola cools.

To assemble the parfaits, place 3 tablespoons of the granola in the bottom of each of 4 parfait glasses or bowls. Top with ¼ cup yogurt and ¼ cup blueberries; repeat with another layer of yogurt and blueberries, and top with granola. Refrigerate leftover granola; it will keep for a month or more.

Raspberries

Productive and sweet, raspberries are the easiest fruit to grow at home. These brambleberries grow on canes and are divided into two categories: summer-bearing and everbearing. Summer-bearing raspberries, such as 'Willamette', bear fruit heavily for about a month on second-year *floricanes* (canes that grew the previous summer), while everbearing varieties, such as 'Fall Gold', produce a small flush of summer raspberries on the floricanes and a big fall crop on the current year's canes (*primocanes*).

Planting

Raspberries planted in heavy, wet soil often develop root rot. Encourage healthy plants by planting them in a 1½-foot-tall, 2-foot-wide berm or a raised bed filled with loose, well-draining soil. Choose a protected spot in full sun or very light shade that you can access from all sides for easy harvesting. Always buy certified disease- and pest-free plants or bare-root stock from a nursery when starting a new raspberry planting, because transplanting divisions from existing plantings often transfers disease and pests such as the raspberry crown borer.

Plant raspberries as soon as the soil can be worked in late winter or early spring. Thoroughly weed the planting area, taking extra care to remove perennial weeds and grass, and dig in 4 inches of compost. Plant when the canes are dormant (have no leaves) or are just beginning to bud out; fully leafed out canes do not establish as well. Stagger the plants in the bed, planting them 2 feet apart in all directions. Plant container-grown plants at the exact same depth they were growing in their pots and bare-root plants at the same depth they were growing in the field (the part of the cane that was underground will look darker than the part that was above). For bare-root plants, dig a hole that is wider than the root system and slightly shallower. Make a firm mound of soil in the center of the planting hole to support the roots. Spread the roots out over the mound, check to make sure the cane is at the right depth, and then backfill the hole, firming the soil gently around the roots as you go. Water the cane in well, and then completely soak the soil around each plant with diluted liquid organic fertilizer.

Growing

Raspberries send up loads of new canes every year. If canes pop up out of bounds, just dig them up with a sharp spade. Raspberries do not compete well with weeds, especially grass. Mulch around the canes with 2 inches of wood chips or straw and pull weeds as they come up. Consider installing a metal weed barrier around the bed if growing the berries next to a

> ### MORE ABOUT RASPBERRY TRELLISES
>
> For additional raspberry trellising ideas and instructions for building a T-bar trellis—also known as a crossbar trellis—download the publication *Pruning Raspberries and Blackberries in Home Gardens* by David W. Lockwood from the University of Tennessee Agricultural Extension Service website.

lawn. Overhead watering, especially as the berries are ripening, encourages disease; instead, weave a soaker hose through the canes or install a drip system in the bed. Water whenever the soil dries down to the top of your second knuckle. Scratch a granular organic fertilizer into the soil on each side of the row just as the buds begin to swell in spring and when the plants flower (follow the label's recommended application rate).

Training

Raspberries grow best when their long canes are confined within a T-bar trellis. To make this trellis, center a 7-foot-tall post on each end of the bed (set the post at least 2 feet deep in the ground). Create the "T" crossbars by screwing a 1½-foot-long two-by-four horizontally into the top of each post and a second crossbar 3 feet off the ground (you can add a third crossbar, if you like). Screw eyehooks into the ends of each crossbar. Complete the trellis by attaching 12-gauge galvanized wire to the eyehooks and running the wires horizontally along each side of the bed. As the raspberries grow, train the canes to stay within the confines of the wire.

Pruning

Pruning raspberries ensures that plenty of light reaches the berries and reduces disease problems by improving air circulation. It also prevents the canes from growing into a massive jumble, making harvest difficult.

SUMMER-BEARING RASPBERRIES

1. Cut off at the soil line all the canes that produced berries this season just after they finish fruiting. These floricanes will be woody, rough, and grayish brown.

2. Thin out the remaining pliable green primocanes in fall. Start by cutting spindly or less-upright canes down to the ground. Aim to keep three canes per foot of row. This spacing allows good air circulation and leaves plenty of canes for fruit. In early spring prune the tips of the canes down to the top of their trellis or to about 5 feet tall.

EVERBEARING RASPBERRIES

For a small but continuous supply of berries throughout the summer, prune everbearing raspberries as you would summer-bearing ones. If you want a bigger crop, cut all the canes back to the ground in late fall and mulch with 4 to 8 inches of straw (this strategy is also recommended for gardeners in the far North, where the ground freezes for long periods). New canes will emerge in spring and will set a large, concentrated crop in late summer or fall.

Harvesting

Pick raspberries when they are dry because wet fruit deteriorates quickly after harvest. When the berries color up fully, give them a gentle tug; ripe ones will fall into your hand, leaving behind a white core. Harvest daily during peak ripening.

Storing

Raspberries are very perishable and are best used within a day or two of picking. Layer them two deep at most in a shallow tray, cover with plastic, and refrigerate.

Cooking Ideas

Freeze raspberries and add them to smoothies. Substitute raspberries for pineapple in a pineapple upside-down cake. Purée 2 cups of raspberries with ⅓ cup water, ⅓ cup simple syrup, 1 tablespoon Chambord liqueur, and 2 teaspoons freshly squeezed lemon juice; freeze in Popsicle molds. Fold very ripe raspberries into freshly whipped cream and serve with angel food cake.

Delicious Varieties

Extend the raspberry season by planting everbearing raspberries and a mix of early-, mid-, and late-season varieties of summer-bearing raspberries. Consult with berry growers at your farmers' market or a local Master Gardener to learn about varieties that perform well in your particular climate.

'Summit'. A well-adapted everbearing variety with sweet red fruit that ripens early, making it a good choice for climates with first frosts in September. 'Golden Summit' produces delicate-flavored yellow raspberries.

'Tulameen'. Summer-bearing variety developed in British Columbia with large, fantastically flavored berries from July through August. Grows in USDA zones 6 to 9.

|||||||||||||||||||||||||||||||||||||| **RASPBERRIES** ||||||||||||||||||||||||||||||||||||

Rubus idaeus

PLANT FAMILY: Rosaceae

EDIBLE PARTS: Berries

POTENTIAL PROBLEMS: Spotted wing drosophila, anthracnose, botrytis, root rot

||||||||||||||||||||||||||||||||||||||||||||||||||||||||||||||||||||||||||||||||||||||

Raspberry-Infused-Vodka Spritzers

1 quart very ripe raspberries, plus more for garnish

One 750-milliliter bottle vodka

Club soda

Limes, cut into wedges

Mint leaves (optional)

I learned to make raspberry-infused vodka from my friends John Hurd and Justine Dell'Arringa, who grow raspberries in their beautiful Seattle kitchen garden. The vodka gradually turns a gorgeous ruby red as the raspberries steep.

Place the raspberries in a tall, narrow jar. Pour in the vodka, making sure it completely covers the berries. Seal the jar and let steep for at least 1 week. Strain the vodka through a fine-mesh sieve, pressing the raspberries with the back of a spoon to extract as much flavor as possible. Store the infused vodka in a glass bottle. Compost the raspberry pulp.

For each spritzer, mix 2 ounces chilled raspberry vodka with 4 ounces club soda in a tall glass. Squeeze in the juice from 1 lime wedge. Add ice, stir, and garnish with whole raspberries and mint.

Rhubarb

I grew up in Wyoming, where rhubarb is sometimes found out on the prairie, still growing alongside pioneer homesteads that have long since been abandoned. This extremely cold-tolerant, perennial vegetable produces slender, ruby-toned leaf stalks for years with only the most minimal of care. Rhubarb gets its tart flavor from oxalic acid and is often baked with plenty of sugar and sweet fruits to mellow its sour nature, but the stalks also taste delicious when added to savory-sweet concoctions like chutney.

Planting

Grow rhubarb from crowns (roots with buds) or container-grown plants. Crowns are available at nurseries and by mail order in late winter and early spring. Choose a crown with at least two buds. Rhubarb is a perennial vegetable, so plant it in a spot in full sun where it can remain for many years. Grow it in raised beds if your garden has heavy clay soil. Plant rhubarb in early spring as soon as the soil becomes workable and its temperature reaches 45 degrees F. For crowns, dig a hole that is slightly deeper than the crown is tall. Set the crown in the hole and make sure the tips of the pink-and-green buds are just 1 inch under the soil line. Backfill soil over the crown and firm it gently. Plant container-grown plants at the exact same height they were growing in their container. Water the crowns or plants in with diluted liquid organic fertilizer.

Growing

Rhubarb requires at least 500 hours of temperatures below 49 degrees to form new buds. The stalks emerge in spring after soil and air temperatures rise into the high 40s. Rhubarb grows to 3 feet tall or more and produces large, heart-shaped leaves. The stalks range from pale pink to red to light green, depending on the variety. Rhubarb prefers consistently moist soil because drought, long days, and high heat encourage the plant to send up a seed stalk. Pull out seed stalks as soon as they form, because they reduce bud formation—and thus yields—for the following year. Water whenever the soil dries down to the base of your second knuckle. Keeping the area around rhubarb free of weeds helps prevent rhubarb curculio, a pest that also feeds on dock plants (*Rumex* spp.). Mulch around, but not right up to, the base of the plants with 3 inches of straw to prevent weeds and maintain soil moisture.

Rhubarb produces exceptional yields and tender stalks when grown in soil with high organic matter. Spread a 1-inch layer of compost around the plants in spring just as the stalks begin to emerge and again after they die back in fall. Divide mature rhubarb plants when they begin producing fewer stalks or spindly growth, usually 8 to 10 years after planting. Dig up the whole crown in late winter or early spring before new growth emerges. With a sharp knife, cut the crown into pieces with three or four buds each and replant.

Harvesting

Wait to harvest rhubarb until after the first stalks are at least 18 inches tall and the leaves reach their mature size (typically 12 inches across or more). Hold off on harvesting rhubarb the first year after planting to give the crowns a chance to establish and form additional buds. In the second year, harvest no more than four stalks per plant. In the third year, harvest for a period of four weeks and remove only half the total stalks. After that, harvest stalks for eight to ten weeks, making sure to leave at least eight stalks per plant after each harvest. To harvest, grasp the stalks at their base and then pull and twist upward. Never cut rhubarb stalks off, because the partial stalk left behind can introduce disease into the crown as it decays. After harvest, remove and compost the large leaves because they contain toxic levels of oxalic acid.

Storing

Store rhubarb stalks in a plastic bag in the refrigerator crisper drawer for up to one month. Rhubarb also freezes well (see page 257).

Cooking Ideas

Green rhubarb varieties tend to have juicy stalks and a tastier sweet-tart flavor than red ones. Use half green and half red stalks in recipes to take advantage of the color and flavor of both types. Place 2 cups of rhubarb in a pan with ½ cup water, simmer until the rhubarb breaks apart, and add sugar to taste and a dash of vanilla extract. Spoon this compote over yogurt or into oatmeal. My friend David Perry makes rhubarb juice and freezes it. To extract the juice, place 6 to 8 cups of diced rhubarb in a large pot and cover with water. Bring to a boil and cook until the rhubarb begins to break apart. Strain the juice through a fine-mesh sieve, pressing the rhubarb pulp with the back of a spoon to extract as much flavor as possible. Sweeten the tart, calcium-rich juice with simple syrup. Drink it plain, mix it with strawberry or orange juice, or use it to make cocktails.

Delicious Varieties

'Valentine'. The wide, juicy stalks retain their ruby red color when cooked. The flavor maintains a perfect balance between sweet and tart.

'Victoria'. This variety has slender, tender, pale-green stalks blushed with pink at their base. Its mild, sweet flavor works particularly well in pie. Heirloom.

IIIIIIIIIIIIIIIIIIIIIIIIIIIIIIIIIIIII **RHUBARB** IIIIIIIIIIIIIIIIIIIIIIIIIIIIII

Rheum rhabarbarum

PLANT FAMILY: Polygonaceae

EDIBLE PARTS: Stalks

POTENTIAL PROBLEMS: Rhubarb curculio

IIIIIIIIIIIIIIIIIIIIIIIIIIIIIIIIIIIIIIIIIIIIIIIIIIIIIIIIIIIIIIIIIIIIIIIIIIIIIIIIIIIIIIIIII

Rhubarb Chutney

MAKES ABOUT 3 CUPS

4 cups chopped rhubarb, fresh or frozen

1 cup finely chopped white onion

1 garlic clove, minced

1¼ cups light brown sugar

1 cup cider vinegar

½ cup golden raisins

½ cup chopped, pitted Medjool dates (6 to 8 dates)

3 tablespoons peeled, finely chopped fresh ginger

1 teaspoon salt

1½ teaspoons curry powder

½ teaspoon dry mustard

Pinch of nutmeg

This sweet-and-sour chutney tastes especially good with sharp white cheddar in a grilled cheese sandwich. You can also serve it warm as an accompaniment to roast pork loin or at room temperature with cheese and crackers. Store it in a lidded glass container in the refrigerator for up to two weeks.

. . . .

Combine all the ingredients in a heavy-bottomed pot. Bring to a boil over medium-high heat and then reduce heat to medium-low. Simmer, stirring frequently, until the rhubarb softens and breaks apart and the chutney thickens to a jamlike consistency, 25 to 30 minutes. Remove from the heat and let cool.

Strawberries

There are five main types of strawberries: June-bearing, everbearing, day-neutral, alpine, and musk. June-bearing varieties produce one big crop in early summer, which comes in handy if you want to make a batch of jam or freeze berries for winter. Everbearing and day-neutral varieties grow best in cooler regions. They produce a small crop from spring through fall as long as temperatures stay below 85 degrees F. They are often grown as annuals, both in the ground and in containers, because their production diminishes as the plants age. Alpine strawberries tolerate light shade and produce small berries for a long period during the summer. Heirloom Italian musk strawberries yield small, intensely flavored berries in early summer and form a dense ground cover after two or three years.

Planting

Strawberries grow best in raised beds or berms because they appreciate well-drained soil. Avoid planting them in an area that was recently lawn because this can lead to problems with white grubs, which feed on strawberry and grass roots. For perennial plantings, transplant container-grown or bare-root strawberries as soon as the soil is workable in early spring. When planting bare-root strawberries, dig a hole that is deep enough for the roots to extend vertically. Build a mound in the center of the hole, spread the strawberry's roots out over the mound, and make sure the plant's crown is just barely above the soil line. Backfill the hole and double check that the uppermost roots are covered with a thin layer of soil; otherwise they will dry out. Space the plants 16 to 18 inches apart in rows 3 feet apart if growing them as perennials.

When growing strawberries as annuals, plant them at the same time as perennial plantings, or in late summer for a crop the following year. Space the plants 8 to 10 inches apart in rows 1 foot apart, staggering the plants in the rows. Grow alpine strawberries as a perennial accent plant at the front of lightly shaded ornamental borders, and musk strawberries as a ground cover in sun or dappled shade. Space both types 1 to 1½ feet apart.

Growing

All strawberries, with the exception of alpine types, produce *runners*—horizontal, leafless stems that root and develop a daughter plant when they come into contact with soil. Remove all runners when growing strawberries as annuals. In perennial crops, keep about six runners per plant and cut off all the others as they emerge. Use a hairpin to secure the runners to the soil. Position them in an evenly spaced circle about 10 inches from the mother plant. As the daughter plants grow, the rows will fill in and be 18 to 20 inches wide and 16 inches apart.

At the end of summer, dig up annual plantings and plant new strawberries in a different location. Encourage June-bearing varieties to produce more buds for the following season by renovating the plants one week after they stop bearing fruit: grasp the strawberry foliage in one hand and, using scissors, cut the leaves off 1 inch above the crown. Compost the cut foliage if it is disease-free; otherwise, dispose of it in your yard waste bin. Expect one mother plant and its daughters to yield a quart of berries. Replace perennial plants every four years and plant in a new location.

In late fall spread 2 inches of compost around the plants and cover them with a 2-inch layer of loose straw mulch (don't use grass clippings, as they tend to mat and smother the plants over the winter). When the strawberries begin to grow in spring, pull the mulch back and place it between the rows to keep down weeds. Remove any plants growing outside the designated row area. When berries begin to form, snuggle some straw up under the plants to keep the fruit clean.

The best way to prevent red stele—a common disease that causes the plants to wilt and die—is to grow strawberries in well-draining soil and plant resistant varieties. Keep the strawberry's foliage dry and reduce disease problems by watering with soaker hoses or a drip system whenever the soil dries down to the bottom of your second knuckle. Foliar-feed everbearing and day-neutral strawberries with diluted liquid organic fertilizer every two weeks until early fall. Foliar-feed June-bearing and musk varieties once in late spring and then every four weeks after the harvest ends. Foliar-feed alpine varieties once in spring and once in midsummer.

Harvesting

Strawberries won't ripen further after they've been picked, so be sure to wait until they're completely red. When harvesting, leave their green "caps" on: using your thumb and forefinger, pinch the berries off with 1 inch of stem.

Storing

Strawberries store best when layered no more than two deep in a shallow tray and covered with plastic; refrigerate for up to five days or leave them at room temperature for a day or two. Wash the berries right before use.

Cooking Ideas

Drop a few whole alpine or musk strawberries into a glass of prosecco. Stir mascarpone cheese, whipped cream, vanilla, and a bit of powdered sugar together; dip strawberries into brown sugar and then into the cream before popping them into your mouth. Add strawberries to mixed lettuces, along with toasted hazelnuts and feta or goat cheese. Place 4 cups of sliced strawberries in a bowl and sprinkle with sugar (stir in 1 tablespoon of high-quality balsamic vinegar, if you like); allow the fruit to macerate for three hours and then purée it. Pour this sauce over ice cream, yogurt, crepes, cheese blintzes, or cheesecake.

Delicious Varieties

The following strawberry varieties adapt well to a broad range of growing conditions, but also consult with berry growers at your farmers' market or with a local Master Gardener to learn about strawberry varieties that perform well in your particular climate.

'Mignonette'. This French alpine strawberry has very sweet, inch-long berries and is exceptionally productive once established. Grows well in part shade, especially in hotter climates. Hardy in USDA zones 3 to 9.

'Profumata'. An Italian heirloom, this musk strawberry produces loads of berries with a fruity, pineapple-like flavor. Bolster yields by planting one 'Russian Male' plant, a variety with lots of male flowers, for every six 'Profumata' plants. Hardy in USDA zones 5 to 10.

'Sequoia'. This June-bearing strawberry tastes phenomenal, produces heavily, and adapts to different conditions. Very disease-resistant.

'Tri-Star'. A popular day-neutral variety because it grows well in many climates and produces a big crop of large berries that freeze well. Resists red stele and verticillium wilt.

STRAWBERRIES

Fragaria spp.

PLANT FAMILY: Rosaceae

EDIBLE PARTS: Berries

POTENTIAL PROBLEMS: Aphids, slugs, snails, spotted wing drosophila, anthracnose, botrytis, red stele, verticillium wilt

Strawberry-Basil Ice Cream

5 cups sliced strawberries
(about 1½ pounds)

2 tablespoons finely chopped
purple basil

¾ cup plus 2 tablespoons sugar

3 cups half-and-half

¾ cup packed green basil
leaves, chopped

I make this pretty pink-and-purple-flecked ice cream Philadelphia style, which means the base contains just half-and-half and sugar, with no eggs. Be sure to stir the strawberries and purple basil together first so their flavors have a chance to meld while the base is prepared and chilled.

. . . .

In a medium bowl, combine the strawberries, purple basil, and the 2 tablespoons sugar; set aside to macerate.

Put the remaining sugar and half-and-half in a saucepan over medium heat. Cook, stirring occasionally, until the sugar dissolves. Remove the pan from the heat, stir in the green basil, cover, and refrigerate until chilled, 3 to 4 hours.

Place the macerated strawberries in a blender or food processor and purée. Strain the chilled half-and-half mixture; discard the green basil leaves. Stir the purée into the half-and-half mixture until well combined and freeze in an ice cream maker according to manufacturer's instructions. Transfer the soft ice cream to a quart-size plastic container and freeze until the ice cream firms to your desired consistency.

Resources

The only real way to understand a particular plant or variety is to grow it (though killing plants actually provides useful information too!). But books are full of information that can help you design better gardens, build healthier soil, and deal with problems when they come up. The following resources are ones I turn to time and again.

Regional Resources

The resource I pull off my bookshelf most often is a booklet called *The Maritime Northwest Garden Guide*, by Seattle Tilth. It provides a month-by-month planting calendar and invaluable information on varieties that grow well in my climate. This will no doubt prove useless to gardeners outside the Pacific Northwest, but I encourage you to seek out gardening references and advice specific to your area for help in determining when and what to plant in your garden.

USDA PLANT HARDINESS ZONE MAP

www.usna.usda.gov/Hardzone/ushzmap.html

FIRST AND LAST FROST DATE SEARCHABLE MAP

www.wcc.nrcs.usda.gov/climate/climate-map.html

LOCAL COOPERATIVE EXTENSION SEARCHABLE MAP

www.csrees.usda.gov/Extension/index.html

Garden Design

DESIGNING THE NEW KITCHEN GARDEN: AN AMERICAN POTAGER HANDBOOK

by Jennifer R. Bartley

This inspiring guide places contemporary kitchen garden design in a historical context and provides lots of ideas and strategies for designing interesting, productive, and beautiful edible gardens.

ANN LOVEJOY'S ORGANIC GARDEN DESIGN SCHOOL

by Ann Lovejoy

While this book does not focus on kitchen gardens, its sound design principles and its useful organic gardening advice translate well to designing edible gardens.

Heirlooms and Seed Saving

HEIRLOOM VEGETABLE GARDENING: A MASTER GARDENER'S GUIDE TO PLANTING, SEED SAVING, AND CULTURAL HISTORY
by William Woys Weaver

A fascinating book for anyone interested in the history of American kitchen gardens and the preservation of heirloom seeds. Weaver includes lively profiles of more than 280 heirloom vegetable varieties, information on saving seeds, and a compelling argument for why we should continue to grow and eat heirlooms. Note that this book is out of print but used copies can sometimes be found online, or it can be purchased on CD-ROM.

SEED TO SEED: SEED SAVING AND GROWING TECHNIQUES FOR VEGETABLE GARDENERS
by Suzanne Ashworth

The definitive guide to saving seeds from the vegetables you grow and planting them year after year.

Pests and Diseases

GOOD BUG, BAD BUG: WHO'S WHO, WHAT THEY DO, AND HOW TO MANAGE THEM ORGANICALLY
by Jessica Walliser

This flipbook-style book makes it easy to find and identify common beneficial insects and pests and offers practical, organic solutions for dealing with problems.

GROW COOK EAT PROBLEM SOLVER
by Willi Galloway

A quick guide to the pests and diseases mentioned as problems in this book. Each entry contains a description of the pest or disease, the symptoms present on affected plants, and an organic solution. You can download a PDF of this problem solver from my website (www.digginfood.com).

THE ORGANIC GARDENER'S HANDBOOK OF NATURAL PEST AND DISEASE CONTROL
edited by Fern Marshall Bradley, Barbara W. Ellis, and Deborah L. Martin

This reference is organized by plant and contains detailed descriptions of problems, common causes, and organic solutions. An indispensable resource for figuring out what is afflicting your plants.

VEGETABLE MD ONLINE

http://vegetablemdonline.ppath.cornell.edu/cropindex.htm

Compiled by the Department of Plant Pathology at Cornell University, this excellent online resource contains comprehensive disease fact sheets listed by crop. Not all of the advice is organic, but they offer several strategies for non-toxic control in each guide.

Season Extension

GARDEN TOOLS BY LEE VALLEY

www.leevalley.com

This mail-order company carries a wide variety of season-extending tools, including plastic ventilating cloches, bird netting, shade cloth, floating row covers, and row cover clamps and clips.

GRO-THERM VENTILATED PLASTIC

www.territorialseed.com

I use a ventilated/perforated plastic to protect warm-season crops and extend the season. My favorite product is Gro-Therm, a 1-mil transparent plastic film perforated with 300 holes per square yard for ventilation. It comes in 6 foot by 20 foot and 6 foot by 50 foot rolls, and it lasts for several years if stored indoors over the winter.

Seeds and Planting

One of the great pleasures of kitchen gardening is growing extraordinary varieties that are not readily available at grocery stores or even farmers' markets. I encourage you to find favorite varieties of vegetables, herbs, and fruit but to also experiment with at least one new variety or vegetable every year. These are the companies I rely upon when ordering seeds:

ABUNDANT LIFE SEEDS

www.abundantlifeseeds.com

This catalog has a well-curated collection of certified-organic, open-pollinated seeds.

BAKER CREEK HEIRLOOM SEEDS

www.rareseeds.com

I look forward to receiving Baker Creek's heirloom seed catalog every spring. The catalog offers the largest selection of heirloom seeds in the United States, including varieties that the company's owner, Jere Gettle, has collected on trips abroad. Baker Creek has a particularly phenomenal collection of tomatoes, eggplant, melons, and winter squash.

BOTANICAL INTERESTS

www.botanicalinterests.com

This family-owned company carries a large selection of certified-organic seeds in interesting varieties, and the packets feature beautiful botanical illustrations.

EVERGREEN SEEDS

www.evergreenseeds.com

Evergreen carries a huge selection of Asian vegetable varieties, including hard-to-find crops like edible chrysanthemums.

FEDCO SEEDS

www.fedcoseeds.com

Maine-based Fedco places a supplier code next to each variety, indicating which seeds were grown by small farmers and which were grown and distributed by large companies that also produce genetically modified products. Having this information allows you to make informed choices. This is an especially great resource for people who want to avoid buying varieties owned by multinational conglomerates, such as Monsanto.

HUDSON VALLEY SEED LIBRARY

www.seedlibrary.org

This nonprofit seed library offers a wonderful collection of open-pollinated and heirloom varieties. Its "art pack" seeds come in frame-worthy packages designed by New York artists; a network of 15 small farmers in the Hudson Valley grows the seeds in its "library packs."

IRISH EYES GARDEN SEEDS

www.irisheyesgardenseeds.com

A wonderful resource for seed potatoes, Irish Eyes carries a wide range of potato types, grouped helpfully according to maturity times (early, mid-, or late season). It also notes what cooking treatments the varieties are best suited for.

JOHN SCHEEPERS KITCHEN GARDEN SEEDS

www.kitchengardenseeds.com

Scheepers consistently offers a delightful range of delicious, unusual vegetable varieties from around the world. Its beautiful illustrated catalog is full of recipe ideas and cooking tips.

KITAZAWA SEED COMPANY

www.kitazawaseed.com

Founded in 1917, Kitazawa specializes in offering unusual Asian vegetable seeds. If you want to dip your toe into the wide and delicious world of Asian vegetables, order one of their Chef Specialty Gardens, which contains a range of their most popular varieties.

RENEE'S GARDEN

www.reneesgarden.com

My salad garden wouldn't be complete without Renee Shepherd's exceptional mesclun mixes, which always have the perfect blend of different greens. Try the blends of colorful lettuces, spicy greens, stir-fry greens, and Asian greens. Her seed packets are also chock-full of helpful information.

SEED SAVERS EXCHANGE

www.seedsavers.org

This nonprofit, member-supported organization is dedicated to the preservation of heirloom seed varieties. It offers vegetable, herb, and flower seeds; a limited number of live plants; seed potatoes; and garlic.

SEEDS FROM ITALY

www.growitalian.com

This wonderful company distributes seeds from the Italian company Franchi Sementi. Its superb list of essential Italian vegetables includes beans, squash, tomatoes, and artichokes.

TERRITORIAL SEED COMPANY

www.territorialseed.com

Based in Cottage Grove, Oregon, Territorial offers a wide range of vegetable seeds—as well as live seedlings, potatoes, and allium sets—adapted to the Pacific Northwest. It also carries an array of season-extending and other gardening products.

WILD GARDEN SEED

www.wildgardenseed.com

The Morton family grows all of the seeds they sell in their catalog and on their website, and they carry only organic, open-pollinated, and untreated seeds. They have a fabulous selection of unusual varieties, but most important, the Mortons are committed to breeding new open-pollinated varieties that thrive in organic conditions, including the fabulous 'Purple Peacock' broccoli.

Soil

TEAMING WITH MICROBES: THE ORGANIC GARDENER'S GUIDE TO THE SOIL FOOD WEB

by Jeff Lowenfels and Wayne Lewis

This essential guide to the life in soil and how to foster it belongs on every gardener's bookshelf. It is packed with accessible and practical information on composting, mulching, and caring for your soil. I find the soil maintenance calendar to be especially helpful.

Glossary

ANNUAL: See page 17 for definition.

BARE-ROOT: Plants that are dug from the field while dormant, and the soil is washed from their roots. Onions, raspberries, and strawberries are often sold this way.

BENEFICIAL INSECT: An insect that pollinates plants or preys on insect pests. Ladybugs, which feed on aphids, are an example of a beneficial insect.

BIENNIAL: See page 68 for definition.

BLANCH: In gardening, the technique of denying a growing plant light to prevent it from turning green, as with leeks or cauliflower. Blanching reduces bitterness and increases tenderness. In cooking, the process of dipping vegetables briefly into boiling water and then quickly chilling them; this can loosen skins, bring out color, or stop enzyme activity. Most vegetables must be blanched before freezing.

BOLT: To send up a tall stalk that produces flowers and seeds. Premature bolting is often caused by too much heat, dry soil, or crowded growing conditions.

BRASSICAS: See page 13 for definition.

CLOCHE: See page 21 for definition.

COTYLEDONS: See page 15 for definition.

COVER CROPS: Also known as "green manure." Plants grown in vegetable gardens to suppress weeds, reduce erosion, and add nutrients and organic matter to the soil. They are typically grown for a period of time, mowed, and then dug into the soil, where they decompose. Crimson clover, annual rye, buckwheat, vetch, and fava beans are common cover crops.

CROWN: The spot on a plant where stems emerge from the roots, typically right at or just below the soil line.

CUCURBITS: See page 13 for definition.

CULTIVAR: See page 29 for definition.

CUT-AND-COME-AGAIN: See page 85 for definition.

DETERMINATE: A term describing a plant that grows to a certain height and then produces most of its fruit all at once. Bush beans are a determinate plant.

DIRECT-SOW: See page 14 for definition.

FAMILY: See page 29 for definition.

FIRST FROST DATE: See page 12 for definition.

FOLIAR FEEDING: See page 27 for definition.

FURROW: See page 14 for definition.

GENUS: See page 29 for definition.

HARDENING OFF: See page 14 for definition.

HARDINESS: See page 11 for definition.

HEIRLOOM: See page 29 for definition.

HILLING UP: Mounding soil up around the stem or base of a plant, particularly potatoes or leeks.

HOOP HOUSE: See page 21 for definition.

HYBRID: See page 29 for definition.

INDETERMINATE: A term describing a plant that grows and produces flowers and fruit throughout the growing season. Pole beans are an example of an indeterminate plant.

INOCULATE: See page 121 for definition.

LAST FROST DATE: See page 12 for definition.

LEGUME: See page 120 for definition.

MULCH: Any material used to cover the surface of the soil. Depending on its composition, it can help reduce weeds, retain moisture levels, raise or lower soil temperature, or add nutrients. Straw, grass clippings, compost, gravel, plastic, and wood chips are common mulches.

OPEN-POLLINATED: See page 29 for definition.

ORGANIC MATTER: Any formerly living material that is decomposing.

PERENNIAL: See page 11 for definition.

POLLINATOR: See page 29 for definition.

RHIZOME: A modified stem that grows underground horizontally. Mint is a common edible plant with rhizomes.

ROOT-BOUND: A term describing a container-grown plant that has outgrown its pot, resulting in roots that coil around each other tightly, constricting the plant's ability to take up moisture. Avoid planting root-bound plants whenever possible, as this condition often stunts growth.

ROW COVER: See page 21 for definition.

SELF-SOW: See page 17 for definition.

SPECIES: See page 29 for definition.

THINNING: See page 15 for definition.

TRUE LEAVES: See page 15 for definition.

UNDERSOWING: Sowing smaller crops under taller crops.

VARIETY: See page 29 for definition.

Index

Note: Page numbers in italic refer to photographs.

A

acidic soil, 26, 30, 31, 257
acorn squash, 163, 164
aillets (garlic shoots), 199
alkaline soil, 257
Allium ameloprasum, 206
Allium cepa, 208, 210
Allium cepa var. *aggregatum*, 208
Allium cepa var. *ascalonicum*, 224
Allium fistulosum, 208
Allium sativum, 201
Allium schoenoprasum, 43, 47
Allium tuberosum, 43, 47
alpine strawberries, 271, 272, 273
amendments. *See* soil preparation
Anethum graveolens, 56
annuals, 17
Anthriscus cerefolium, 43
arugula
    Arugula Salad with Blue Cheese, Dates, and Hot Bacon Dressing, *88*, 89
    cooking ideas, 87
    growing, harvesting, storing, *83*, 86–87
    varieties, 86, 87
Asian cucumbers, 147, 148, 149
Asian greens
    cooking ideas, 92
    Crispy Pot Stickers with Garlicky Asian Greens, 93
    growing, harvesting, storing, *90*, 91–92
    resources, 281
    varieties, 91, 92
Asian vegetables, resources for, 280, 281
axils, leaf, 174

B

baby greens 101, 85, *85*
Bacon Dressing, and Arugula Salad with Blue Cheese and Dates, Hot, *88*, 89
ball carrots, 195
Balsamic-Roasted Onions, 211
bamboo
    column or cage supports, 240
    "corrals" for fava beans, 127

hoop houses, 23, *23*
    teepees, 5, *5*
bare soil, 31–32
bare-root plants, 257–58
Basella rubra, 111
basil
    cooking ideas, 38
    Everyday Vinaigrette, 225
    growing, harvesting, storing, *36*, 37–38, *38*
    Herbed Edamame Salad, *124*, 125
    Lemony Pasta with Cherry Tomatoes, *253*, 254
    Nona's Pesto, *40*, 41
    Shaved Summer Squash with Pecorino Romano, *160*, 161
    Strawberry-Basil Ice Cream, *274*, 275
    varieties, 37, 38, 39
Batavian lettuce, 99
beans. *See* edamame; fava beans; snap and shell beans
beefsteak tomatoes, 251, 252
beer traps, 30
bees. *See* pollinators
beets
    cooking ideas, 191
    growing, harvesting, storing, 189–91, *190*
    Oven-Roasted Beets with Winter Citrus Vinaigrette, *192*, 193
    varieties, 191
Beit Alpha cucumbers, 147, 148
bell jars, *20*, 21
beneficial insects, 17, 28, 29–30, 145, 278, 283
berries. *See* blueberries; raspberries; strawberries
Beta vulgaris var. *cicla*, 117, 189
Beta vulgaris var. *esculenta*, 189, 190
Bibb lettuce. *See* butterhead lettuce
biennials, 68
binder clips, 21, 23, *23*
bird netting, 28
bitterness, 24, 148
black plastic ground covers, 22, 153
black radishes, 218
black shade cloths, 21, 23
blanching, 283
blueberries
    cooking ideas, 259
    growing, harvesting, storing, 257–59, *258*

varieties, 257, 259
    Yogurt Parfaits with Almond Granola and Blueberries, 260
bok choy, 91–92, 93
bolting, 283
borderless garden beds, 4
Boston lettuce. *See* butterhead lettuce
botanic classification system, 29
bow rakes, 6
Braised Leeks, Silky, 207
Brassica juncea, 104
Brassica oleracea var. *acephala*, 185
Brassica oleracea var. *botrytis*, 172
Brassica oleracea var. *capitata*, 180
Brassica oleracea var. *gemmifera*, 175
Brassica oleracea var. *italica*, 172
Brassica oleracea var. *sabellica*, 185
Brassica rapa, 95
Brassica rapa var. *rapa*, 227
Brassica spp., 92
brassicas (cabbage family), 13, 16–17, 30, 85, 167–86
broad beans. *See* fava beans
broadcasting seeds, 15
broccoli
    cooking ideas, 172
    Garlicky Roasted Broccoli, 173
    growing, harvesting, storing, 169–71, *170*
    varieties, 169, 172
broccoli rabe (or "raab")
    cooking ideas, 95
    growing, harvesting, storing, 94–95
    Lemony Broccoli Rabe, *96*, 97
    varieties, 95
bronze fennel, 58–59
"browns," in compost, 9, 11
brussels sprouts
    cooking ideas, 175
    growing, harvesting, storing, 174–75
    Roasted Brussels Sprouts with Capers, *176*, 177
    varieties, 175
Bucatini with Fresh English Peas and Garlic Scape Pesto, *202*, 203
bulbils (little bulbs), *1*, 200

bulbing onions, 208, 209, 210, 211
bulbs, roots, and tubers, 187–228
bunching onions, 208, 210
burlap bags, 3, 9
"burpless" cucumbers, 147
bush basil. *See* little-leaf basil
bush beans, 138–39, 141
bush cucurbits, 145
bush peas, 133
Butter, Dill Compound, 57
buttercup squash, 163
butterhead lettuce, 99, 100, 101
butternut squash, 163, 164, *165*, 166
buttoning, 169
buying garden tools, 5–6, 31
buying seeds/seedlings, 14, 279–81
buying topsoil, 4
bypass pruners, 6

C

cabbage
    cooking ideas, 180
    growing, harvesting, storing, *178*, 179–80
    Spicy Cabbage Slaw, *181*, 182
    varieties, 179, 180
    See also Asian greens
cabbage family (brassicas), 13, 16–17, 30, 85, 167–86
Caesar Salad, Perfect, 102
cage supports, 240
cantaloupes, 153, 154, 155, 156
canvas tarps, 6
capsaicinoids, 239
Capsicum annuum, 241
Caramelized Onions and Gorgonzola Chive Sauce, Steak Sandwiches with, *48*, 49
carbon, 9
carrots
    cooking ideas, 196–97
    Co-Op Kale Salad, 186
    growing, harvesting, storing, *194*, 195–96, *196*
    Honey-Roasted Carrots, 198
    Spicy Cabbage Slaw, *181*, 182
    varieties, 195, 197
casaba melons, 153, 154
cauliflower
    cooking ideas, 172
    growing, harvesting, storing, 169–71, *172*
    varieties, 169, 171, 172
Chantenay carrots, 195
cheese
    Arugula Salad with Blue Cheese, Dates, and Hot Bacon Dressing, *88*, 89
    Cheesy Eggs with Chervil, 44

Fennel, Potato, and Apple Gratin, 60
Feta Marinated in Olive Oil with Mediterranean Herbs, *66*, 67
Lemony Pasta with Cherry Tomatoes, *253*, 254
Mustard Green Turnovers, 105
Nona's Pesto, *40*, 41
Pea Shoot Salad with Shaved Parmesan and Lemon Vinaigrette, *136*, 137
Perfect Caesar Salad, 102
Roasted Jalapeños Stuffed with Goat Cheese, *242*, 243
Shaved Summer Squash with Pecorino Romano, *160*, 161
Steak Sandwiches with Gorgonzola Chive Sauce and Caramelized Onions, *48*, 49
Swiss Chard Quesadillas, 118
Tartines with Gruyère and Radish Greens, *221*, 222
chemical pesticides, 29–30
cherry tomatoes
    cooking ideas, 251
    Herbed Edamame Salad, *124*, 125
    Lemony Pasta with Cherry Tomatoes, *253*, 254
    varieties, 249, 251, 252
chervil
    Cheesy Eggs with Chervil, 44
    cooking ideas, 43
    growing, harvesting, storing, 42–43
    varieties, 43
Chicken, Green Coriander–Marinated, 53
chiles. *See* peppers, sweet and hot
Chinese cabbage, 91–92
Chioggia radicchios, 107, 108
chitting tubers, 213
chives
    cooking ideas, 47
    Dill Compound Butter, 57
    Everyday Vinaigrette, 225
    growing, harvesting, storing, 45–47, *46*
    Potato Leek Soup with Chive Crème Fraîche, *216*, 217
    Spicy Roasted Snap Beans with Raita, 142
    Steak Sandwiches with Gorgonzola Chive Sauce and Caramelized Onions, *48*, 49
    Tartines with Gruyère and Radish Greens, *221*, 222
Chutney, Rhubarb, 269

Cichorium intybus, 108
Cider-Glazed Baby Turnips, 228
cilantro/coriander
    Butternut Squash Tacos with Spicy Black Beans, *165*, 166
    cooking ideas, 51
    Co-Op Kale Salad, 186
    Green Coriander–Marinated Chicken, 53
    growing, harvesting, storing, 50–51, *50*
    Guacamole with Charred Tomatillos and Chiles, *247*, 248
    Spicy Cabbage Slaw, *181*, 182
    Spicy Roasted Snap Beans with Raita, 142
    Swiss Chard Quesadillas, 118
    varieties, 52
circle hoes, 6
Citrullus lanatus, 155
clamps for row covers, 22, 23
clay soils, 7–8, 24
climate. *See* seasons; temperature
climbing cucurbits, 145
climbing peas, 133
climbing structures. *See* vertical garden structures
clips, 21, 23, *23*
cloches, *20*, 21
clubroot, 30
coffee bags. *See* burlap bags
cold composting, 11
coleslaw
    cabbage varieties for, 179, 180
    Spicy Cabbage Slaw, *181*, 182
compost
    basic soil care plan, 8–9
    getting rid of the lawn, 3
    making, 9, *9*, 11
    top dressing, definition of, 27
condiments
    Dill Compound Butter, 57
    Everyday Vinaigrette, 225
    Garlic Scape Pesto, Bucatini with Fresh English Peas and, *202*, 203
    Gorgonzola Chive Sauce and Caramelized Onions, Steak Sandwiches with, *48*, 49
    Guacamole with Charred Tomatillos and Chiles, *247*, 248
    Lemon Tahini Dressing, Eggplant with, 238
    Nona's Pesto, *40*, 41
    Rhubarb Chutney, 269
    Sage-Infused Vinegar, 78
container gardening, 5, 72, 284
Co-Op Kale Salad, 186
coriander. *See* cilantro/coriander

Coriandrum sativum, 52
corn
    cooking ideas, 232
    growing, harvesting, storing, 231–32, *231*
    Herbed Edamame Salad, *124*, 125
    Patrick Family's Southern Creamed Corn, The, 234
    varieties, 231, 232, 233
cotyledons, 15
cover crops, 127, 283
covering garden plants
    cloches, *20*, 21
    hoop houses, 21–22, 23, *23*, 28
    insulating the soil, 25–26
    plastic ground covers, 22, *22*, 153, 279
    See also seasons; temperature
Crème Fraîche, Chive, with Potato Leek Soup, *216*, 217
Crenshaw melons, 153, 154
crisphead lettuce, 99
crookneck squash, 157, 158
crop rotation, 30
crossbar trellises, 261, 262
crowns, 266, 267, 283
cucumbers
    cooking ideas, 148
    Cucumber Wedges with Chile and Lime, *150*, 151
    growing, harvesting, storing, 147–48, *147*
    Spicy Roasted Snap Beans with Raita, 142
    trellises, 5, 147, 148
    varieties, 147, 148–49
Cucumis melo, 155
Cucumis sativus, 149
Cucurbita pepo, 159, 163
Cucurbita spp., 163, 164
cucurbitacins, 148
cucurbits (squash family), 143–66
    hand-pollinating, 145–46
    planting 101, 13, 145
    trellises, 5, 145
cultivars, 29
cultivators, 6
curly-leaf parsley, 68, 69
currant tomatoes, 252
cut-and-come again crops, 85

D

daikon radishes, 218, 220
dandelions, edible, 32
Danvers carrots, 195, 197
Daucus carota, 197
day-neutral strawberries, 271, 272, 273
days to maturity, 13, 16, 18–19

delicata squash, 164
design. *See* planning the garden
determinates, 251, 283
dill
    cooking ideas, 56
    Dill Compound Butter, 57
    growing, harvesting, storing, *54*, 55–56
    varieties, 55, 56
dill weed, 55
Diplotaxis muralis, 86, 87
Diplotaxis tenuifolia, 86, 87
direct-sowing
    baby greens 101, 85
    broadcasting, definition of, 15
    definition of, 14
    inoculating legumes, 121
    large seeds, 14–15
    recommended crops for, 15, 16, 17
    small seeds, 15
    thinning seedlings, 15–16, *16*, 30
    watering, 12, 15, *24*, 25
diseases, 27, 30–31, 278–79
dressings. *See* condiments
drip irrigation, 25
dry fertilizers, 27
drying herbs, 35

E

earthworms, 9, *9*
easy-to-start seeds, 15
edamame
    cooking ideas, 122
    growing, harvesting, storing, 121–22
    Herbed Edamame Salad, *124*, 125
    varieties, 122–23
edible flowers, 85, *85*
edible weeds, 32
eggplants
    cooking ideas, 237
    Eggplant with Lemon Tahini Dressing, 238
    growing, harvesting, storing, 235–37, *236*
    varieties, *236*, 237
Eggs with Chervil, Cheesy, 44
English cucumbers, 147, 148
English peas, *132*, 133, 134, 135, *202*, 203
equipment, 5–6, 31
Eruca sativa, 86, 87
everbearing strawberries, 271, 272
evergreen raspberries, 261, 262–63
Everyday Vinaigrette, 225

F

fall beds, 18, 19
family, 29
fast crops, 18
fava beans
    cooking ideas, 128
    Grilled Fava Beans, *130*, 131
    growing, harvesting, storing, *126*, 127–28, *128*
    varieties, 129
fence trellises, 5
fennel
    cooking ideas, 59
    Fennel, Potato, and Apple Gratin, 60
    growing, harvesting, storing, 58–59
    varieties, 58, 59
fertilizers, 14, 26–27
Feta Marinated in Olive Oil with Mediterranean Herbs, *66*, 67
flat-leaf (or smooth) spinach, 110, 111, 112
flat-leaf parsley. *See* parsley
Florence fennel, 58–59
floricanes, 261, 262
flowers, edible, 85, *85*
flowers, intermixing in the garden, 17, 28
flowers, pollinating by hand, 145–46
Foeniculum vulgare var. *azoricum*, 58, 59
Foeniculum vulgare var. *vulgare* 'Rubrum,' 58, 59
foliar feeding, 27
footpaths in garden, 4, 32
forks, garden, 6
Fragaria spp., 273
frames. *See* hoop houses
freestanding trellises, 5
freezing fruit, 257
freezing herbs, 35
"frost blankets," 21
frost dates, 12, 13, 277
fruit, 255–75
"full slip" ripeness, 154
fungi, 30–31, 232
furrows, 14–15, 25

G

garden arugula, 86–87
garden beds. *See* planning the garden; planting the garden
garden clips, 21, 23, *23*
garden forks, 6
garden peas. *See* English peas
garden radishes. *See* salad radishes
garden sage, 75, 77

garden structures. *See* hoop houses; vertical garden structures

garden tools, 5–6, 31

garlic
  Bucatini with Fresh English Peas and Garlic Scape Pesto, *202*, 203
  Butternut Squash Tacos with Spicy Black Beans, *165*, 166
  cooking ideas, 200
  Co-Op Kale Salad, 186
  Crispy Pot Stickers with Garlicky Asian Greens, 93
  Eggplant with Lemon Tahini Dressing, 238
  Garlicky Roasted Broccoli, 173
  Green Coriander–Marinated Chicken, 53
  growing, harvesting, storing, 199–200, *199*
  Guacamole with Charred Tomatillos and Chiles, *247*, 248
  Lemony Broccoli Rabe, *96*, *97*
  Mustard Green Turnovers, 105
  Nona's Pesto, *40*, 41
  Pea Shoot Salad with Shaved Parmesan and Lemon Vinaigrette, *136*, 137
  Perfect Caesar Salad, 102
  Rhubarb Chutney, 269
  Roasted Jalapeños Stuffed with Goat Cheese, *242*, 243
  Rosemary-Rubbed Leg of Lamb, 74
  Tangy Grilled Radicchio, 109
  varieties, 199, 201

garlic chives, 45, 47

garlic scapes
  Bucatini with Fresh English Peas and Garlic Scape Pesto, *202*, 203
  cooking ideas, 200
  growing, harvesting, storing, *1*, 199, 200

garlic shoots (*aillets*), 199

genus, 29

germination, 12, 15

Glycine max, 123

Gorgonzola Chive Sauce and Caramelized Onions, Steak Sandwiches with, *48*, 49

Granola, Almond, and Blueberries with Yogurt Parfaits, 260

granular organic fertilizers, 27

grass clippings, 3, 9, 25–26, 32

grass lawn, getting rid of, 3–4

Gratin, Fennel, Potato, and Apple, 60

green manure. *See* cover crops

green onions, 208

greens, 83–118, 281

"greens," in compost, 9, 11

Grilled Fava Beans, *130*, 131

Grilled Radicchio, Tangy, 109

ground covers, plastic, 22, *22*, 153, 279

growing season. *See* seasons

Gruyère and Radish Greens, Tartines with, *221*, 222

Guacamole with Charred Tomatillos and Chiles, *247*, 248

H

Hamburg parsley, 69

hand watering, *24*, 25

handheld circle hoes, 6

hand-pollinating, 145–46

hardening off, 14

hardiness zones, 11, 277

harvesting
  baby greens 101, 85
  bolting, definition of, 283
  determinates versus indeterminates, 251
  first and last frost dates, 12, 13, 277
  floricanes versus primocanes, 261
  hila, definition of, 122
  keeping plant foliage dry, 30
  maturity rates, 13, 16, 18–19
  pod set, definition of, 127
  rhizomes, definition of, 213, 284
  season-extending devices, *20*, 21–23, *22*, *23*, 279
  side shoots, definition of, 169
  staggered harvests, 17
  succession planting, 18–19

heating up the soil, 22, *22*

"heavy" soils, 7–8

heirlooms, 29, 278, 279, 280, 281

herbal tisanes, 63

Herbed Edamame Salad, *124*, 125

herbs, 33–82

highbush blueberries, 257, 258–59

hila, 122

hilling up, 213–14, 283

hoes, 6, 31

honeydew melons, 153, 154, 156

Honey-Roasted Carrots, 198

hoop houses, 21–22, 23, *23*, 28

hoses, soaker, 25

hot composting, 9, 11

hot peppers. *See* peppers, sweet and hot

Hubbard squash, 163, 164

huitlacoche, 232

humus, 7

hybrids, 29

I

Ice Cream, Strawberry-Basil, *274*, 275

iceberg lettuce, 99, 100–1

Imperator carrots, 195

indeterminates, 251, 283

Infused Vinegar, Sage-, 78

Infused-Vodka Spritzers, Raspberry-, *264*, 265

inground garden beds, 4

inoculating legumes, 121

insecticidal soap, 30

insects
  beneficial, 17, 28, 29–30, 145, 278, 283
  pests, 21, 22, 23, 27, 28–30, 278

iron deficiency, 26

iron phosphate–based slug baits, 30

irrigation systems, 25
  See also watering

Italian parsley, 68, 69

J

Jalapeños Stuffed with Goat Cheese, Roasted, *242*, 243

June-bearing strawberries, 271–72, 273

K

K (potassium), 26

kale
  cooking ideas, 185
  Co-Op Kale Salad, 186
  growing, harvesting, storing, 183–85, *184*, *185*
  varieties, 183, 185

Korean cabbage, 91–92

L

Lactuca sativa, 101

Lamb, Rosemary-Rubbed Leg of, 74

lambsquarters, edible, 32

Latin names, 29

lawn, getting rid of, 3–4

layering, 79–80

leaf axils, 174

leaf lettuce, 99, 100

leaves, composting/mulching with, 8–9

leaves, seedling, 15

leeks
    cooking ideas, 206
    growing, harvesting, storing, *204*, 205–6, *205*
    Potato Leek Soup with Chive Crème Fraîche, *216*, 217
    Silky Braised Leeks, 207
    varieties, 205, 206
legumes, 119–42
lemon cucumbers, 147
Lemon Tahini Dressing, Eggplant with, 238
lemon thyme, 79, 80
Lemon Verbena Syrup, Mixed Melons in, 156
Lemon Verbena–Mint Tisane, 63
Lemon Vinaigrette, and Pea Shoot Salad with Shaved Parmesan, *136*, 137
Lemony Broccoli Rabe, *96*, *97*
Lemony Pasta with Cherry Tomatoes, *253*, 254
lettuce
    cooking ideas, 100
    growing, harvesting, storing, *98*, 99–100, *100*
    Perfect Caesar Salad, 102
    varieties, 99, 100–1
light requirements, 3, 5
lima beans. *See* snap and shell beans
liquid fertilizers, 14, 27
little-leaf basils, 37, 38, 39
loamy soils, 7, 8, 24
long-season crops, 19
lowbush blueberries, 257, 259
Lycopersicon esculentum, 252

M

macronutrients, 26
Malabar spinach, 111
Marinated Chicken, Green Coriander–, 53
marjoram
    cooking ideas, 65
    Feta Marinated in Olive Oil with Mediterranean Herbs, *66*, 67
    growing, harvesting, storing, 64–65
    varieties, 65
maturity rates, 13, 16, 18–19
melons
    cooking ideas, 154
    growing, harvesting, storing, *152*, 153–54
    Mixed Melons in Lemon Verbena Syrup, 156
    trellises, 5, 153–54
    varieties, 153, 154–55
Melothria scabra, 148–49
Mentha spp., 61, 62

mesclun mixes, 85, 281
microorganisms, 7, 8, 121
midseason crops, 18
mint
    cooking ideas, 62
    growing, harvesting, storing, 61–62
    Lemon Verbena–Mint Tisane, 63
    Thérèse Jarjura's Tabbouleh, *70*, 71
    varieties, 61, 62
misome, 91–92
monoecious, 145
mulching
    avoiding diseases, 31
    basic soil care plan, 8–9
    definition of, 284
    getting rid of the lawn, 3–4
    plastic ground covers, 22, *22*, 153, 279
    smart watering practices, 25–26
    weeds, 31, 32
multiplier onions, 208, 210
musk strawberries, 271, 272, 273
muskmelons, 153, 154, 155
mustard greens
    cooking ideas, 104
    growing, harvesting, storing, 103–4
    Mustard Green Turnovers, 105
    varieties, 104

N

N (nitrogen), 7, 8, 9, 26, 27, 121
Nantes carrots, 195, 197
needle-nose scissors, 6
New Zealand spinach, 111
nitrogen (N), 7, 8, 9, 26, 27, 121
Nona's Pesto, *40*, 41
NPK numbers, 26
nutrients. *See* soil nutrients

O

Ocimum basilicum, 39
onions
    Balsamic-Roasted Onions, 211
    Butternut Squash Tacos with Spicy Black Beans, *165*, 166
    cooking ideas, 209–10
    growing, harvesting, storing, 208–9, *209*, 210
    Guacamole with Charred Tomatillos and Chiles, *247*, 248
    Mustard Green Turnovers, 105

Rhubarb Chutney, 269
    Spicy Cabbage Slaw, *181*, 182
    Spinach Risotto, *113*, 114
    Steak Sandwiches with Gorgonzola Chive Sauce and Caramelized Onions, *48*, 49
    Swiss Chard Quesadillas, 118
    varieties, 208, 209, 210
open-pollinated seeds, 29
orange mint, 62
oregano
    cooking ideas, 65
    Feta Marinated in Olive Oil with Mediterranean Herbs, *66*, 67
    growing, harvesting, storing, 64–65
    varieties, 65
organic fertilizers, 14, 26–27
organic gardening resources, 277, 278, 279, 280, 281
organic matter
    building good soil, 7, 8–9, 11
    definition of, 284
    getting rid of the lawn, 3–4
organic pesticides, 30, 278
Origanum spp., 64–65

P

P (phosphorus), 26
Pacific Northwest resources, 277, 281
parsley
    cooking ideas, 69
    Dill Compound Butter, 57
    Eggplant with Lemon Tahini Dressing, 238
    Everyday Vinaigrette, 225
    growing, harvesting, storing, 68–69
    Lemony Pasta with Cherry Tomatoes, *253*, 254
    Potato Leek Soup with Chive Crème Fraîche, *216*, 217
    Spicy Roasted Snap Beans with Raita, 142
    Tartines with Gruyère and Radish Greens, *221*, 222
    Thérèse Jarjura's Tabbouleh, *70*, 71
    varieties, 68, 69
parsley root, 69
pasta
    Bucatini with Fresh English Peas and Garlic Scape Pesto, *202*, 203
    Lemony Pasta with Cherry Tomatoes, *253*, 254
pathways in garden, 4, 32
Patrick Family's Southern Creamed Corn, The, 234

pattypan squash, 157, 158
pea gravel, 4
peas
    Bucatini with Fresh English
        Peas and Garlic Scape
        Pesto, *202*, 203
    cooking ideas, 135
    growing, harvesting, storing,
        132, 133–35, *134*
    Pea Shoot Salad with Shaved
        Parmesan and Lemon
        Vinaigrette, *136*, 137
    trellises, 5, 133
    varieties, *132*, 133, 134, 135
Pecorino Romano, Shaved
    Summer Squash with, *160*, 161
peppermint, 62
peppers, sweet and hot
    Butternut Squash Tacos with
        Spicy Black Beans, *165*,
        166
    capsaicinoids, definition of,
        239
    cooking ideas, 240
    Crispy Pot Stickers with
        Garlicky Asian Greens,
        93
    growing, harvesting, storing,
        239–40
    Guacamole with Charred
        Tomatillos and Chiles,
        247, 248
    Roasted Jalapeños Stuffed
        with Goat Cheese, *242*,
        243
    varieties, 239, 240–41
perennials, 11, 28
pesticides, 29–30, 278
Pesto, Garlic Scape, and Bucatini
    with Fresh English Peas, *202*,
    203
Pesto, Nona's, *40*, 41
pests, 21, 22, 23, 27, 28–30, 278
Petroselinum crispum, 69
pH, testing for, 8
Phaseolus vulgaris, 141
phosphorus (P), 26
photoperiodic onions, 208
photosynthesis, 3
Physalis ixocarpa, 246
pickling cucumbers, 147, 148–49
pineapple sage, 75
Pisum sativum, 135
planning the garden, 3–6
    choosing a site, 3
    creating beds and pathways,
        3–4, 32
    garden tools, 5–6, 31
    maturity rates, 13, 16, 18–19
    pests and diseases, 30
    resources, 277
    See also harvesting; planting
        the garden; vertical
        garden structures

planting the garden, 11–19
    annuals, definition of, 17
    baby greens 101, 85, *85*
    bare soil, eliminating, 31–32
    bare-root plants, 257–58
    biennials, definition of, 68
    brassicas, definition of, 13
    cover crops, definition of, 383
    cucurbits 101, 13, 145
    cut-and-come again crops, 85
    easy-to-start seeds, 15
    first and last frost dates, 12,
        13, 277
    furrows, definition of, 14–15
    hilling up, definition of, 213
    legumes, definition of, 120
    maturity rates, 13, 16, 18–19
    perennials, definition of, 11
    presprouting seeds, 134, *134*
    presprouting tubers, 213
    resources, 277–81
    saving seeds, 16, 278
    soil wells versus hills, 145
    staggered rows, definition
        of, 179
    starting seeds indoors, 14, 17,
        134, *134*
    succession planting, 18–19
    thinning seedlings, 15–16,
        16, 30
    trenches, definition of, 249
    when to plant, 11–13, 277
    See also propagating;
        seedlings; sowing seeds
plastic covering on hoop houses,
    21, 22, 23, *23*
plastic ground covers, 22, *22*,
    153, 279
play chips, 4
pod set, 127
pole beans, 138–39, 141
pollinating by hand, 145–46
pollinators, 17, 29–30, 85, 145
popcorn, 231, 232, 233
pore spaces, 7–8, 12
Pot Stickers with Garlicky Asian
    Greens, Crispy, 93
potassium (K), 26
potatoes
    cooking ideas, 214–15
    Fennel, Potato, and Apple
        Gratin, 60
    growing, harvesting, storing,
        212, 213–14, *214*
    Potato Leek Soup with Chive
        Crème Fraîche, *216*, 217
    resources, 280
    varieties, 213, 214, 215
potted plants, 5, 72, 284
preserving herbs, 35
preserving leftover seeds, 16, 278
presprouting seeds, 134, *134*
presprouting tubers, 213
primocanes, 261, 262

propagating
    crowns, definition of, 266
    hand-pollinating, 145–46
    herbs, 38, 79–80
    layering, 79–80
    pollinators, 17, 29–30, 85, 145
    rhizomes, definition of, 213,
        284
    runners, definition of, 271
    self-sowing crops, 17
protecting plants. *See* covering
    garden plants; diseases; pests;
    temperature
pruners, bypass, 6
pruning blueberries, 258–59
pruning raspberries, 262–63
pumpkins, 163, 164
purchasing garden tools, 5–6, 31
purchasing seeds/seedlings, 14,
    279–81
purchasing topsoil, 4
purslane, edible, 32

Q

Quesadillas, Swiss Chard, 118

R

rabbiteye blueberries, 257,
    258–59
radicchio
    cooking ideas, 108
    growing, harvesting, storing,
        106, 107–8
    Tangy Grilled Radicchio, 109
    varieties, 107, 108
radishes
    cooking ideas, 219
    growing, harvesting, storing,
        218–19, *219*
    Tartines with Gruyère and
        Radish Greens, *221*, 222
    varieties, 219–20
raised beds, 4
Raita, Spicy Roasted Snap Beans
    with, 142
rakes, bow, 6
Raphanus sativus, 220
rapini. *See* broccoli rabe (or
    "raab")
raspberries
    cooking ideas, 263
    growing, harvesting, storing,
        261–63, *262*
    Raspberry-Infused-Vodka
        Spritzers, *264*, 265
    trellises, 261, 262
    varieties, 261, 263
resources, 277–81
Rheum rhabarbarum, 268
rhizobial bacteria, 121
rhizomes, 213, 284

rhubarb
cooking ideas, 267
freezing, 257
growing, harvesting, storing, 266–67, *267*
Rhubarb Chutney, 269
varieties, 268
ricing, 169
Risotto, Spinach, *113*, 114
Roasted Beets with Winter Citrus Vinaigrette, Oven-, *192*, 193
Roasted Broccoli, Garlicky, 173
Roasted Brussels Sprouts with Capers, *176*, 177
Roasted Carrots, Honey-, 198
Roasted Jalapeños Stuffed with Goat Cheese, *242*, 243
Roasted Onions, Balsamic-, 211
Roasted Snap Beans with Raita, Spicy, 142
Roasted Tomatoes with Thyme, Slow-, *81*, 82
romaine lettuce, 99, 100, 102
root systems, 13, 14, 24–25
root-bound, 284
roots, tubers, and bulbs, 187–228
rosemary
cooking ideas, 73
growing, harvesting, storing, 72–73, *73*
Rosemary-Rubbed Leg of Lamb, 74
varieties, 73
Rosmarinus officinalis, 73
rotating crops, 30
row cover clamps, 22, 23
row covers, 21, 23, 28
Rubus idaeus, 263
Rumex spp., 266
runner beans. *See* snap and shell beans
runners, 271

S

sage
cooking ideas, 77
growing, harvesting, storing, 75–77, *75*, *76*
Sage-Infused Vinegar, 78
varieties, 75, 77
salad radishes, 218–19
salad tomatoes, 252
salads
Arugula Salad with Blue Cheese, Dates, and Hot Bacon Dressing, *88*, 89
baby greens 101, 85
Co-Op Kale Salad, 186
Everyday Vinaigrette, 225
Herbed Edamame Salad, *124*, 125

Oven-Roasted Beets with Winter Citrus Vinaigrette, *192*, 193
Pea Shoot Salad with Shaved Parmesan and Lemon Vinaigrette, *136*, 137
Perfect Caesar Salad, 102
Salvia elegans, 75
Salvia officinalis, 75, 77
sandwiches
Rhubarb Chutney, 269
Sandwiches with Gorgonzola Chive Sauce and Caramelized Onions, Steak, *48*, 49
Tartines with Gruyère and Radish Greens, *221*, 222
sandy soils, 7, 8, 24
sauce tomatoes, 251, 252
sauces. *See* condiments
sauerkraut, cabbage varieties for, 179, 180
savoy cabbage, 179
savoy spinach, 110, 111, 112
scallions
growing, harvesting, storing, 208, 209
Herbed Edamame Salad, *124*, 125
Thérèse Jarjura's Tabbouleh, *70*, 71
scapes. *See* garlic scapes
scientific names, 29
scissors, needle-nose, 6
seasons
basic soil care plan, 8–9
first and last frost dates, 12, 13, 277
planning the garden, 3–4
season-extending devices, *20*, 21–23, *22*, *23*, 279
soil temperature, 12
succession planting, 18–19
See also temperature
seed resources, 278, 279–81
seed saving, 16, 278
seed sowing. *See* sowing seeds
seedlings
baby greens 101, 85
cotyledons versus true leaves, 15
crops to plant as, 16–17
cucurbits 101, 13, 145
hardening off, definition of, 14
inoculating legumes, 121
planting 101, 13–14, *13*
root-bound, definition of, 284
separating before planting, 13, 17, 37, 85, 115
soil wells versus hills, 145
soil workability test, 12
spacing, 14, 15, 17, 30, 31, 179

staggered rows, definition of, 179
starting indoors, 14, 17, 134, *134*
thinning, 15–16, *16*, 30
trenches, definition of, 249
watering, 12, 13–14, 15, 24, *24*, 25–26
seeds, open-pollinated versus hybrid, 29
self-sowing crops, 17
semisavoy spinach, 110, 112
shade cloths, 21, 23
shallots
cooking ideas, 224
Dill Compound Butter, 57
Everyday Vinaigrette, 225
growing, harvesting, storing, 223–24
varieties, 223, 224
sheet mulching, 3–4
shell beans. *See* snap and shell beans
shelling peas. *See* English peas
shovels, 6
side shoots, 169, 171, 172
silt soils, 7–8
slicing cucumbers, 147, 148, 149
slicing tomatoes, 252
slugs, 30
smooth (or flat-leaf) spinach, 110, 111, 112
snails, 30
snap and shell beans
cooking ideas, 139, 141
growing, harvesting, storing, 138–39, *138*, *139*, *140*
Spicy Roasted Snap Beans with Raita, 142
trellises, 5, 138
varieties, 138, 139, *140*, 141
snow peas, *132*, 133, 134, 135
soaker hoses, 25
soap, insecticidal, 30
soil, purchasing, 4
soil crusting, 15
soil moisture test, 24
soil nutrients
building good soil, 7, 8–9, 11
deficiency, symptoms of, 26, 31
fertilizers, 14, 26–27
inoculating legumes, 121
macronutrients, definition of, 26
making compost, 9, *9*, 11
resources, 281
sulfur, 257
testing, 8
top dressing, definition of, 27
soil preparation, 7–11
basic care plan, 8–9
basic composition of soil, 7–8
diseases, 30, 31

eliminating bare soil, 31–32
getting rid of the lawn, 3–4
humus, definition of, 7
insulating the soil, 25–26
loam, definition of, 7
raised beds, 4
resources, 281
testing pH and nutrients, 8
tilth, definition of, 7
See also mulching; organic
    matter; soil nutrients
soil structure, 7–8, 12, 24
soil temperature
    insulating the soil, 25–26
    season-extending devices,
        20, 21–23, *22, 23,* 279
    when to plant, 12, 277
soil testing for pH and nutrient
    levels, 8
soil texture, 7, 8
soil wells versus hills, 145
soil workability test, 12
Solanum melogena, 237
Solanum tuberosum, 215
Soup, Potato Leek, with Chive
    Crème Fraîche, *216,* 217
soup beans. *See* snap and shell
    beans
sowing seeds
    baby greens 101, 85
    broadcasting, definition of, 15
    cucurbits 101, 145
    direct-sowing large seeds,
        14–15
    direct-sowing small seeds, 15
    furrows, definition of, 14–15
    inoculating legumes, 121
    open-pollinated versus
        hybrid seeds, 29
    recommended crops for,
        16–17
    seed resources, 278, 279–81
    seed saving, 16, 278
    self-sowing, 17
    thinning seedlings, 15–16,
        16, 30
    watering, 12, 15, *24,* 25
    when to plant, 11–13, 277
spades, square blade, 6
spaghetti squash, 164
spearmint, 61, 62, *70,* 71
species, 29
spicy dishes
    Butternut Squash Tacos with
        Spicy Black Beans, *165,*
        166
    Co-Op Kale Salad, 186
    Cucumber Wedges with Chile
        and Lime, *150,* 151
    Green Coriander–Marinated
        Chicken, 53
    Spicy Cabbage Slaw, *181,* 182

Spicy Roasted Snap Beans
    with Raita, 142
    See also peppers, sweet and
        hot
Spinacea oleracea, 112
spinach
    cooking ideas, 111
    growing, harvesting, storing,
        110–11, *110*
    Spinach Risotto, *113,* 114
    varieties, 110, 111, 112
spring beds, 18, 19
spring onions, 208, 209
Spritzers, Raspberry-Infused-
    Vodka, *264,* 265
square blade spades, 6
squash family (cucurbits), 143–66
    hand-pollinating, 145–46
    planting 101, 13, 145
    trellises, 5, 145
staggered harvests, 17
staggered rows, 179
stakes. *See* bamboo
Steak Sandwiches with
    Gorgonzola Chive Sauce and
    Caramelized Onions, *48,* 49
stirrup hoes, 6, 31
storage onions, 209
storing herbs, 35
storing seeds, 16, 278
straw and grass clippings, 3, 9,
    25–26, 32
strawberries
    cooking ideas, 272
    growing, harvesting, storing,
        270, 271–72, *273*
    Strawberry-Basil Ice Cream,
        274, 275
    varieties, 271, 272, 273
succession planting, 18–19
suckers, 249, *251*
sugar snap peas, *132,* 133, 134,
    135
sulfur, 257
summer beds, 18, 19
summer spinach, 111
summer squash
    cooking ideas, 158
    growing, harvesting, storing,
        157–58, *158*
    Shaved Summer Squash with
        Pecorino Romano, *160,*
        161
    trellises, 5, 157
    varieties, 157, 158, 159
summer-bearing raspberries,
    261, 262, 263
sunlight requirements, 3, 5
supports. *See* vertical garden
    structures
sweet dumpling squash, 164
sweet onions, 209, 210
sweet peppers. *See* peppers,
    sweet and hot

Swiss chard
    cooking ideas, 117
    growing, harvesting, storing,
        115–17, *116*
    Swiss Chard Quesadillas, 118
    varieties, 117

T

Tabbouleh, Thérèse Jarjura's,
    70, 71
Tacos, Butternut Squash, with
    Spicy Black Beans, *165,* 166
Tahini Dressing with Eggplant,
    Lemon, 238
tarps, canvas, 6
Tartines with Gruyère and
    Radish Greens, *221,* 222
tassels, 232
tatsoi, 91–92
T-bar trellises, 261, 262
teas, herbal, 63
teepees, 5, *5*
temperature
    bolting, definition of, 283
    buttoning, definition of, 169
    first and last frost dates, 12,
        13, 277
    hardiness zones, 11, 277
    heating up the soil, 22, *22*
    insulating the soil, 25–26
    ricing, definition of, 169
    season-extending devices,
        20, 21–23, *22, 23,* 279
    when to plant, 11–13, 277
tent frames. *See* hoop houses
testing soil pH and nutrients, 8
Tetragonia tetragonioides, 111
Thérèse Jarjura's Tabbouleh,
    70, 71
thinning seedlings, 15–16, *16,* 30
thyme
    Balsamic-Roasted Onions,
        211
    Cider-Glazed Baby Turnips,
        228
    cooking ideas, 80
    Everyday Vinaigrette, 225
    Fennel, Potato, and Apple
        Gratin, 60
    growing, harvesting, storing,
        79–80
    Slow-Roasted Tomatoes with
        Thyme, *81,* 82
    varieties, 79, 80
Thymus spp., 79, 80
tilth, 7–8
tip burn, 107
Tisane, Lemon Verbena–Mint,
    63
tomatillos
    cooking ideas, 246
    growing, harvesting, storing,
        244, 245

Guacamole with Charred Tomatillos and Chiles, *247*, 248
varieties, 246
tomatoes
Butternut Squash Tacos with Spicy Black Beans, *165*, 166
cooking ideas, 251
growing, harvesting, storing, 249–51, *250*, *251*
Guacamole with Charred Tomatillos and Chiles, *247*, 248
Herbed Edamame Salad, *124*, 125
Lemony Pasta with Cherry Tomatoes, *253*, 254
Mustard Green Turnovers, 105
Slow-Roasted Tomatoes with Thyme, *81*, 82
Thérèse Jarjura's Tabbouleh, *70*, 71
varieties, 249, 251–52
tools, garden, 5–6, 31
top dressing, 27
topsoil, purchasing, 4
transplant shock, 13
trellises, 4–5, 261, 262
trenches, 249
Treviso radicchios, 107, 108
trowels, 6
true leaves, 15, 17
tubers, roots, and bulbs, 187–228
turnips
Cider-Glazed Baby Turnips, 228
cooking ideas, 227
growing, harvesting, storing, 226–27, *227*
varieties, 226, 227
Turnovers, Mustard Green, 105

U

undersowing, 31–32
USDA plant hardiness zone map, 11, 277

V

Vaccinium spp., 259
varieties, 29
vertical garden structures
column or cage supports, 240
"corrals" for fava beans, 127
teepees, 5, *5*
trellises, 4–5, 261, 262
Vicia faba, 129
Vinaigrette, Everyday, 225
Vinaigrette, Lemon, and Pea Shoot Salad with Shaved Parmesan, *136*, 137
Vinaigrette with Oven-Roasted Beets, Winter Citrus, *192*, 193
Vinegar, Sage-Infused, 78
vines. *See* vertical garden structures; *entries under climbing*
Vodka Spritzers, Raspberry-Infused-, *264*, 265
"volunteers," 17

W

walkways in garden, 4, 32
warming up the soil, 22, *22*
warm-season vegetables, 229–54
watering
avoiding diseases, 30, 31
building good soil, 7–8
direct-sowing, 12, 15, *24*, 25
planning the garden, 3
planting seedlings 101, 13–14
pod set, definition of, 127

smart practices, 24–26, *24*, 30, 31
soil moisture test, 24
soil workability test, 12
tip burn, definition of, 107
watermelons, 153, 154, 155, 156
weather. *See* seasons; temperature
weeds, 22, 31–32
wild arugula, 86
winter radishes, 218, 219, 220
winter squash
Butternut Squash Tacos with Spicy Black Beans, *165*, 166
cooking ideas, 164
growing, harvesting, storing, *162*, 163–64
trellises, 5, 163
varieties, 163, 164
wire trellises, 4–5, 261, 262
wood chips, 4
worms, 9, *9*

Y

yard-long beans. *See* snap and shell beans
Yogurt Parfaits with Almond Granola and Blueberries, 260

Z

Zea mays, 233
zones, 11, 277
zucchini, 157, 158, 161

About the Author

WILLI GALLOWAY is an award-winning radio commentator and writer. Willi began her career at *Organic Gardening* magazine, where she worked her way up from editorial intern to West Coast Editor. She moved to Seattle in 2003 and became an active participant in the urban agriculture movement, earning her Master Gardener certification in 2004 and serving for six years on the board of directors of Seattle Tilth—a nationally recognized nonprofit that teaches people to cultivate a healthy urban environment and community by growing organic food. This work introduced her to hundreds of other urban gardeners, and like many of them, she has grown food in untraditional places, including on the roof of an apartment building, at the Interbay P-Patch (an acclaimed community garden right in the middle of Seattle), and in the sunny front yard of her home.

Willi writes about kitchen gardening and seasonal cooking on her popular blog, DigginFood.com, and pens the weekly column "The Gardener" on Apartment Therapy's Re-Nest blog. Each Tuesday morning, she offers vegetable gardening advice on Seattle's popular NPR call-in show, *Greendays*. She also teaches a joint gardening and cooking class with James Beard Award–nominated chef Matthew Dillon at the Corson Building in Seattle, and hosts an online garden-to-table cooking show, *Grow. Cook. Eat.*, with her husband, Jon. Their garden has been featured in *Sunset* magazine. Willi currently lives and gardens in Portland, Oregon, with her four chickens, Inky, Clyde, Bumble, and Boo Boo, and her lab, Domino.